HUGH JOHNSON

on Wine

HUGH
JOHNSON
on
Wine

GOOD BITS FROM
55 YEARS OF SCRIBBLING

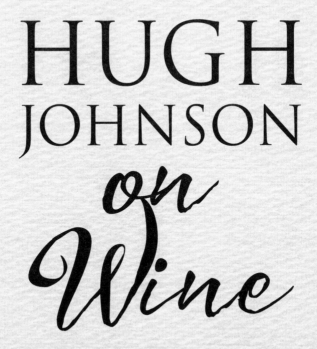

MITCHELL BEAZLEY

CONTENTS

'TIS THE CASK, NOT THE COFFER,
THAT HOLDS THE TRUE WEALTH

– *The Vintners' Song*

An Hachette UK Company
www.hachette.co.uk

First published in Great Britain in 2016 by Mitchell Beazley,
a division of Octopus Publishing Group Ltd,
Carmelite House, 50 Victoria Embankment, London EC4Y 0DZ
www.octopusbooks.co.uk
www.octopusbooksusa.com

Distributed in the US by
Hachette Book Group,
1290 Avenue of the Americas, 4th and 5th Floors, New York, NY 10020
Distributed in Canada by
Canadian Manda Group,
664 Annette Street, Toronto, Ontario, Canada M6S 2C8

ISBN 978 1 78472 262 3

A CIP catalogue record for this book is available from the British Library.
Printed and bound by CPI Group (UK) Ltd, Croydon, CR0 4YY

10 9 8 7 6 5 4 3 2 1

Group Publishing Director Denise Bates
Editor Diane Pengelly
Illustrations Paul Hogarth
Art Director Yasia Williams-Leedham
Design John Round Design
Production Manager Caroline Alberti

PAUL HOGARTH OBE RA (1917–2001) was one of the leading illustrators
and topographical artists of his day. He illustrated the fourth edition of
my *World Atlas of Wine* and the first edition of my *Wine Companion*.

INTRODUCTION

'Always scribble, scribble, scribble, eh, Mr Gibbon?' (This was the king's brother, the Duke of Gloucester, to the author of *The History of the Decline and Fall of the Roman Empire*.) 'Another damn'd thick square book, eh?' He summed up the writer's life pretty well: scribble, scribble is about the size of it.

But it's not always books. There is a mass of other scribbling to do: articles, reviews, introductions .... There is not often time to pause, reread, reflect or realise how many traces you have left in the sands of time. Legible traces, that is.

It was when we moved house after four settled decades that I discovered the evidence, in tea chests full of paper and piles of old magazines. An hour or two of desultory reading awoke buried memories. I realised that I have been chronicling the world of wine in a personal way for over half a century. Some of what I found is valid, some quaint, all (to me) nostalgic. Sometimes I am inconsistent, often I repeat myself but, taken with parts of my annual summings-up on the first pages of my *Pocket Wine Book* (we publish the 40th edition this year), it amounts to one man's wine history.

All commentators agree (and rightly) that wine has developed more in the past fifty years than in the previous five hundred. Although 'improved' is probably a more relevant word than 'developed'. Good wines have flooded into our lives from places, countries, even continents that were innocent of any wine before. What was, when I set out, very much a niche subject has blossomed into something of wide (I daren't quite say general) interest.

I started my career as a features writer with a strong bent towards travel. In a sense, I still see my wine writing as a specialised branch of travel writing – which in turn is a tiny subset of geography. Geography is closely allied to history (indeed I'm not sure why they are treated as separate subjects). I soon realised that to understand wine you have to have at least an inkling of both, and to appreciate it, an aesthetic sense tuned to what wine can offer. That comes with devoted practice.

I'm not so strong on the science side. Nor did it seem to matter when I set out. In due course its relevance became more and more plain. Technology took over from tradition in winemaking, as in most other activities, in the last decades of the 20th century. I tried to catch up by co-writing *The Art and Science of Wine* with the omniscient James Halliday (thank you, James), while I strayed off further and further into the realm of history. Studying history gave me the experience of making a TV series – a process so time-devouring that, fun though it was, once was enough.

Most of this collection consists of articles written for magazines, and most of the magazines are aimed squarely at initiates. Any writer has to imagine his readers: who are they? What do they know – and want to know? If there is a trick in reaching readers, it is gauging their level of interest. If you can tell a story, or make an exegesis read as a story, so much the better. If you can make them laugh or cry, of course, you are in business. It doesn't happen often.

I have not wholly excluded my books, however. The point of reproducing articles is that they are transient: published and, usually, forgotten. Most of this is a rescue bid for ephemera, but it isn't complete without snippets from the dozen or so books that occupied most of my time and which are, perhaps, a shade less ephemeral. At least they are available on library shelves. Like any author, I have favourite passages (sometimes, I fear, the bits stern-faced editors blue-pencil on sight). Some are scattered through this book to give it some sense of progression through its six decades. Within those decades I have tried to put things in the right order – though I'm bad at dating things. Some of the attributions are, let's say, speculative.

My first book, *Wine*, published in 1966, proved to me that I had a future in indulging myself. Then I had another magazine stint, editing the features, fashion and society hybrid *Queen* – and learning something about editing and design in the process. Then I was given the chance of a lifetime, the invitation to map the wine world (something that had never been done before) in *The World Atlas of Wine*. Something about its (rather magazine-like) blend of graphics and text, with deliberate emphasis on sound bites (or captions as we called them), clearly worked.

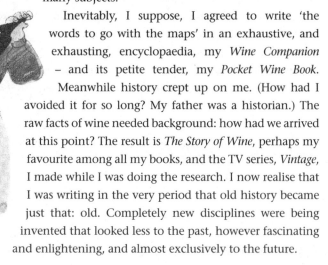

It sold so many copies that other publishers followed suit, on many subjects.

Inevitably, I suppose, I agreed to write 'the words to go with the maps' in an exhaustive, and exhausting, encyclopaedia, my *Wine Companion* – and its petite tender, my *Pocket Wine Book*. Meanwhile history crept up on me. (How had I avoided it for so long? My father was a historian.) The raw facts of wine needed background: how had we arrived at this point? The result is *The Story of Wine*, perhaps my favourite among all my books, and the TV series, *Vintage*, I made while I was doing the research. I now realise that I was writing in the very period that old history became just that: old. Completely new disciplines were being invented that looked less to the past, however fascinating and enlightening, and almost exclusively to the future.

The other thing that crept up, and wouldn't leave me alone, was my interest in plants other than the vine; especially trees. I was compelled to write a tree encyclopaedia, then a book with the insanely ambitious title *The Principles of Gardening*. Gardening had me by the fingers, green or not, and still does. I add entries two or three times a week to *Tradescant's* (or *Trad's*) *Diary*, which I started forty years ago. Wines, plants ... they are pleasures you can indulge anywhere. Always scribble, scribble, scribble ....

Wine farmers (or 'growers' as they are usually called) have been my first resort for inspiration and information. It is an unforgiving business, as I have discovered when I have tried it, and they have to be dedicated and driven – if occasionally self-deluding – souls. Wine boffins and professionals of all sorts (just how professional they get is proved by the Institute of Masters of Wine) provide endless material. Daily interaction with friends and family, other writers, wine merchants, restaurant staff and fellow drinkers provides plenty to think and write about.

My papers relating to wine, grandly dubbed an archive, are now with the Shields Library of UC Davis, the University of California Department of Agriculture and the finest wine library in the world. Many of my garden writings are in the archives of the Garden Museum in London. The articles that make up most of this book appeared in *Vogue*, *House & Garden*, *The Sunday Times*, *Man About Town*, *Gourmet*, *The New York Times*, *Cuisine*, *Wine Times* (the magazine of *The Sunday Times* Wine Club), *Decanter* and *The World of Fine Wine*. If I have not been able to trace and acknowledge everything, I take full responsibility and will make any necessary amends.

It is companions, colleagues, collaborators who make a scribbler's life worth living. It needs stimulus, feedback, criticism and encouragement. I am as lucky as anyone can be with the friendly faces around me: publisher, editors, designers, proofreaders, publicists ... the whole gang. This book has happened because Diane Pengelly, my ideal editor for five of my previous books, bullied and cajoled me into starting work – and then did most of it herself. Thank you, Diane, and all of you.

Hugh Johnson, 2016

The 1960s

OLD MONEY

This, in December 1960, was my first wine article ever. My advisors included the epicure André Simon and the tycoon Nubar Gulbenkian: choices were correspondingly lavish.

Talking turkey recently to a number of people who know their minds about wine, I was struck by the confusion that surrounds this inescapable bird. Whether you like it or not, the chances are you will be eating it again this Christmas. Whether you enjoy it or not depends very largely on what you drink with it.

A lot of people insist on Champagne, supposing that a revel is no revel without it. (The notion that you can't have fun without bubbles in your wine was successfully sold to the public in one of the first attempts at large-scale PR in the 1890s.) If you are of this persuasion, go to it. But there is another school of thought that believes Champagne and turkey were not intended by nature for each other. Unless you have a strong preference for white wines with all food – and there is no earthly reason why you shouldn't – you will probably find that red is more suited to the rich meat of the turkey. This, at any rate, is the conclusion of a synod of experts in the art of marrying wine and food.

The right wine is always a matter of the mood and the moment. To know what you like and choose what you feel like is the secret of enjoying your wine, especially at Christmas.

Nuits-Saint-Georges 1945 is difficult to get now, but the 1949 is excellent and the 1955 at its best. Hatch, Mansfield & Co, at 5 Pall Mall East, have both. ('49: 21s; '55, 16s.)

Prices were in shillings (s) and pence (d), so the Château Margaux cost £1.20 in today's money.

Château Cheval Blanc 1955: The Victoria Wine Company has this at about 28s.

Château Corbin 1955: Justerini & Brooks, Bond Street, 12s 6d.

Château Margaux 1950: Dolamore & Co, 24s.

Château Lafite 1949: Dolamore & Co, 39s.

Clos de Vougeot 1928 is virtually unobtainable now. Pommard 1929, which Hatch, Mansfield have at 27s 6d, would take its place.

Vogue, 1960

IN HONOURABLE COMPANY

Any lover of ritual is a potential punch-drinker, if not punch-drunk. It is the ceremony of it – the bowl, the circle of heads, the incantation, the splashes, the ladle, the glass, the toasts, the euphoria – that puts punch in a class far above gin-and-French (save the mark!) Martinis, or Cobblers, or Collinses, or Swizzles or Slings, or anything else perpetrated either in a glass darkly, or furtively in a jug.

The bowl is the essence of punch. It gives the party a focus, the drinkers a rallying point, the conversation a centre. There is no such thing as lack of a punchbowl. You have a bucket, a salad bowl, a tin helmet, a hollow log, a Lalique vase? Go for it. An old Eskimo woman called Parkinson used to use a dip in an ice floe, and Trader Vic⊙ tells of a party in Tahiti where they used a canoe. They pulled it up the beach, filled it with rum and pineapple juice, stirred it with a paddle, decorated it with a cherry, and the party went on for three days. But recipes come later. You see there is no bowl problem.

Punj in Sanskrit means five. Five ingredients. Spirit, water, lemon, sugar and spice. Spirit for strength, water for weakness, lemons for sourness, sugar for sweetness. Spice (for hotness, I suppose) is balanced by ice (cool).

Sanskrit because the drink was found by thirsty John Company⊙ men in India, their wine having all perished one way or another en route. Claret would not keep in the torrid zone anyway, even if it survived the journey, and Madeira fetched such a fantastic price – if you had the strength of mind to bring it back again from the Indies – that it paid to drink the local stuff.

Some of the best recipes for punch are buried in family vaults with the last of the line. Diligent research, though, and experiment in my own retorts, have brought to light the formulae that follow. Before we go, the rules of the game:

1. The best ingredients make the best punch: don't rely on the fiery kick of your no-star brandy turning to honeyed warmth in the pot.
2. Ice means a small iceberg, not a hailstorm of little cubes.
3. For cold punch, make all the ingredients cold beforehand; for hot, make it hot. Tepid anything is horrible, but tepid punch is worse.
4. Make it in full view. This is where the ritual comes in. Is there any sight so restorative as gallons and gallons of drink with the lid off?
5. How many gallons? Allow plenty and worry about what you are going to do with it when you see how much is left ....

Giles Congreve, *About Town*⊙, 1961

Vic's 'Polynesian' restaurant in the basement of the London Hilton was all the rage

(the nickname of The Honourable East India Co)

Giles Congreve was a nom de verre I used for a while. About Town *was a cheerful men's lifestyle magazine.* At first Man About Town, *it dropped the* Man – and *could well have dropped the* Town

AQUA VITAE

Put it this way. A bottle of wine is 90 per cent water. Water is bulky stuff: heavy and not in the least morale-raising. Not, with freight costs what they are, worth toting around on an international scale.

Distil wine, though – take out the volatile essence of the thing by boiling it – and you leave the water behind. You get ten times the taste, smell and strength per unit volume: in fact a drop of the old how's-your-father.

The genial drinker, sad to say, who proceeds on this principle will stub his toe on a bit of chemistry long before he is marched away by the excise men. The nuisance value of science is clearly demonstrated by the fact that if you fill your kettle with Haut-Brion and switch on, carefully collecting the aromatic vapours as they arise, far from finding yourself with a tenth of a kettle of quintessence of Haut-Brion, you will have on the one hand some dark red paint, and on the other a liquid which would be spat out by a dying mercenary.

The practice of distilling is not quite as simple as the principle. Nor does the drinking begin as the precious spirit drips from the condenser. It takes time, patience, good oak barrels, and maybe just a touch of vanilla before the essence is fit to drink. Hence, alas, the price of brandy.

Brandy is the best spirit, but wine is not the only thing you can distil. Anything that contains starch or sugar can be fermented and distilled to make a spirit of sorts (and, as you will find in a quick whip round of some of the less-frequented Asiatic hostelries, is). Rice, cactus juice, flowers, petrol (not recommended for amateurs), boot-polish (obscure, and losing popularity after a series of disastrous vintages) are all sources of heart's ease – and stomach's disease – in different countries.

At the moment a wave of flavoured vodkas is upon us. At Crockford's© in these past few weeks, believe it or not, members have been heard calling repeatedly for 'Polish drink' (the English phonetic equivalent of Jarzebiak, a vodka flavoured with rowanberries).

The Balkans, Russia, Poland and Scandinavia have a variety of aqua vitae of a very different provenance. They distil grain or potatoes – it doesn't matter which – to a very high degree of rectification. They even filter the spirit through charcoal to get rid of any flavour. They then add a flavour of aniseed or herbs and bring it down to what they consider drinkable strength with water. I may say I am at odds with the Poles over this: 140° proof (the strength of their 'Plain Spirit' – absolute alcohol is 175° proof) seems to me to be bragging.

In the East, Major Bloodnok© country, arak, arrack, arack or arrak is the word for any number of brews of no gastronomic distinction whatever. The ones I have tasted seemed to me to demand too high a price, both before and after, for any pleasant sensations they may

a London gaming club; not, alas, mine

Major Denis Bloodnok, military idiot and former plumber's mate (Retd), a fictional character from the 1950s BBC Radio comedy The Goon Show. *He was played by Peter Sellers*

have induced. It may be the distillate, the distiller or the still, or it may just be my prejudiced palate, but my advice if you value your health is to stick to methylated spirits.

From this vast array of light disguises for alcohol it is hard to discriminate and select. Nor is there much point in spluttering through bottle after bottle in search of an elixir. There isn't one. I can think of three ardent waters however that have characters well worth meeting and, to me, memorable.

One is a very old Kirsch, which OW Loeb and Co have in their cellars in Robert Street, Adelphi. Age has brought out the cherry flavour and smoothed the spirit into something very fine. Another is Calvados, Normandy's apple brandy, which leads the fruit-brandy field from Slivovitz. The traditional use of Calvados is to make *un trou normand*⊕ through a full stomach during a rich meal. It works like an auger. This makes it sound like a medicine, though; in fact, its digestive properties are mentioned only as an excuse for another glass.

literally, a Norman hole: served as a middle course in a large meal to restore appetite

The third is a new arrival in Europe: Mexican tequila. Cactus whisky. Two sorts of cactus are tapped in Mexico, and the juice fermented and distilled. Mescal, peons' plonk, is considered unsuitable for export because the mescaline in it gives you such sweet dreams. Tequila is alcohol innocent of additives, but the perfect base for a sour. For this sublime drink you need fresh limes, tequila, sugar and ice. A strong man's alternative involves orange juice and chillies. Heady stuff.

Giles Congreve, *About Town*, 1962

A GREAT YEAR FOR BORDEAUX

However often wine men tell you it is folly to judge a vintage until a good six months after the picking, it is hard to resist the mood of excitement in Bordeaux now.

I am staying at Loudenne, the Gilbey family's⊕ château in the Médoc. The house must have seen hundreds of vintage house parties since it was built, in the days when all Bordeaux, and not just bits of it, was English. Not many of them can have been as sure as we are of a really splendid wine when it is ready to drink in – who knows? – five, ten, twenty years' time.

I married a Gilbey cousin. I even courted her at Loudenne during this very vintage

Loudenne is not a great classified growth. Its best wine, unusual for the Médoc, is white and dry like a Graves. The château is more distinguished for its beauty – a long, low, rose-pink building standing among vines and meadows on the gentle slope down to the River

Gironde – and its hospitality. Great wine is not grown here, but the château's long barns are the take-off point for all the clarets Gilbey's and their associated firms buy for the English market. Their own harbour on the river, where white yachts have often been seen among the freighters and barges, used to give them a head start on wine shipped from Bordeaux, forty miles farther up the river. Now, sad to say, truck transport is cheaper.

It is terribly important that 1964 should be a good vintage in France. The endless downpour of last summer made this scene a very different one this time last year. Sodden bunches of grapes, rotting on the dripping vines, gave very little wine worth the name. This year the weather has been so good that it has even made up for some of the lost ripening time of the new green vine-wood. The quantity will not be exceptional, but growers I have spoken to confidently expect a wine with tremendous colour, body, staying-power and general deliciousness.

In the end it rained almost non-stop.

Prices, unfortunately, will be (to use a vino/stockbroking term) as firm as ever. Nothing has happened to ease the pressure that demand is putting on supply. Nor, it seems, will it for some time.

Gradually, though, we can expect the growers in outlying districts, away from the famous names, to get the hang of the improved methods of winemaking that are being developed in the richer cellars every year. Already districts on the unfashionable side of the Gironde are getting well placed on English lists and even bottling some of their own wine: a great mark of distinction for what used to be sold as red bordeaux and no nonsense. The news here, in short, is that everybody's wine is going to be good, and the best very expensive. There is everything to gain by watching out for the lesser growths (Loudenne, come to think of it, included) so long as they have a famous shipper's name somewhere about their person.

Gilbey's alas became part of International Distillers & Vintners, and eventually of the absurdly named Diageo.

The Sunday Times, 1964

WINE FOR PICNICS

Picnics can stick in your memory when three-star restaurants have all merged into one great ruinous excess. I have flashbacks of childhood picnics in the hills of Scotland, sandy sandwiches on beaches, mugs of soup in the cockpits of yachts, wine and peaches among the boulders of a dried-up creek in Sicily, apples and cheese by the Necanicum River in Oregon – even a can of consommé by the roadside in Mexico with a flat tyre and night falling. All these meals – little-planned or not planned at all, as some of them were – had the great element of a picnic – the open air – and they are unforgettable. The joys of picnicking are not the joys of the exquisite, the rarefied, of rich sauces and great growths of wine, but the simple pleasure of refreshment. Bread, cheese and beer is a prefect meal under a hayrick at harvest time, if the bread be warm and crusty, the cheese creamy and strong and the beer as cold as a stone. So, perfect picnic wines are not wines to hold up to the light, to nose and ponder over. It is hardly ever necessary to pay more than $3 a bottle for outdoor wine, with the exception of Champagne.

The virtues of Champagne are too obvious to mention. Its disadvantages are the care you must take not to shake it up so that it behaves like a geyser when you open it, and the cooling problem. Warm Champagne is a terrible thing. But for lunch in sunlight or dinner in moonlight, on terrace, backyard, quarterdeck or coral reef, cold dry sparkling Champagne is the essence of fresh-air celebrations.

For hot-weather beach picnics when fingers are salty and toes sandy, at a barbecue or just with a hamper of cold meat and sandwiches, tomatoes, cheese and fruit, rosé wines are ideal. They stand up better than any wine to the rough-and-tumble of getting the party to the beach. They don't even mind (I say this with baited breath in the presence of experts who won't hear of it) a lump of ice in the glass. In fact, slight dilution of a heady wine (rosés can be deceptively strong in effect) is a good idea under a hot sun. The French, who are so downright practical, and hence capable of gestures of the utmost disrespect to wine, often mix a rosé or red with iced lemonade on picnics. The younger the child, the higher the proportion of lemonade, but even the youngest has his drink tinged with red.

Sparkling rosés are good as well. Burgundy's *Oeil de Perdrix* (do partridges really have pink eyes?) pretty well sums up the joys of summer and eating out of doors. As with Champagne, of course, you must take care not to shake the bottle. The Portuguese half-sparkling Mateus Rosé, which has enough bubbles to find it a lively feeling on your tongue but not enough ever to fizz and foam, overcomes that difficulty.⊛

Many of my best picnics have been roadside ones far from home, bought piecemeal along the way and eaten in a borrowed field. For this kind of impromptu meal, in a strange place among strange people, there is really only one wine to drink: the wine of the country.

Ten years later Mateus was the world's most popular wine. Boom was followed by bust. Time for a revival?

(American) *House & Garden*, 1964

BURGUNDY AND BLACK FROST

(then chairman of the National Theatre)

'Burgundy', said Viscount Chandos© prophetically last year, 'is appropriate to black frosts and the smell of wood fires.' It is the wine that belongs to game and great barons and saddles of roast meat – winter food. It has had such a long run of appropriateness so far this year that it is a wonder there is any left.

For genuine burgundy is never in ample supply. With Chablis to the north and Beaujolais to the south it shares the doubtful honour of being the most imitated wine in the world.© A great deal of it is, in the technical language of the trade, 'stretched'. When you consider that Bordeaux has twelve times the area of vineyards, producing almost fifteen times the amount of wine (for burgundy's grape, the Pinot, is by no means prolific) and that bordeaux is scarce enough to reach unearthly prices, the question is bound to arise: where does all the burgundy come from?©

Today it's the rarest that are faked.

Certainly a great deal of wine from the Midi, where everything withers except the grape, finds its way north to Burgundy. It can fulfil a useful purpose there, building up wines of dull, thin years (or growths) into something like the robust creatures we expect of Burgundy. Corbières, for example, in Languedoc, produces a full, balanced wine with a splendid colour that comes in very handy in off years. But nobody is anxious to discuss what must, for the most part, be a matter for conjecture.

Contrast the naivety of our knowledge of burgundy in those days to today's almost obsessive intensity.

Most wine lists in this country usually put their burgundies under the names of their communes, which have become almost, as it were, generic terms. Thus one expects Gevrey-Chambertin to be a heavy©, full-bodied wine – even for burgundy. Volnay, on the other hand, or Beaune, having been endowed by nature with a more slender frame and delicate sweetness, should conform to (at least) these characteristics.

heavy? Not these days

Roughly speaking, the red wines of Burgundy are heaviest from the north, lightening towards the south (where the whites come from). And, as the Burgundians say, it's the vineyard that matters. A wine, therefore, that comes from a single vineyard will tell you so. Under the commune name – for example, Beaune – will appear another name. It might be one of the outstanding growths, as well known as Les Grèves, or one of the good ones, such as Les Theurons.

It is hard to remember these not-particularly-memorable names, but harder still to find them. Single-vineyard burgundies are scarce, their prices are high and the average off-licence simply does not stock them.

Outside this specialised field the most important thing about a burgundy is its shipper, some of whom have made reputations for reliability. Many of them are also owners of some of the vineyards whose wine they sell. Their names appear on the labels of their wines. It is a pity they do not appear more often on wine lists, too. Ordering burgundy without knowing who was responsible for it – as one sometimes has to in restaurants – can feel rather like buying a pig in a poke.

John Congreve⊕, *The Sunday Times* 1964

EIGHTEEN HOURS IN JEREZ

There are vintage festivals and vintage festivals. There are Bacchic bean feasts with all the befuddled fumbling of wreathed maidens that Titian did so well, and there are mere damp village fêtes with a straggle of schoolchildren – more up Lowry's street.

Jerez's (say that after half a bottle) *feria* for the new sherry vintage is the first of the year, and by far the best. It starts on a Tuesday in September, gathers momentum steadily until the weekend, and the dying strains are the following Monday.

The daily programme – or what of it I can remember – goes something like this. Reveille (pianissimo) at 11.30am; coffee and sweet buns and honey on the patio by the fountain (or alternatively a quick dip from a deserted beach just in front of your hotel room); to the municipal park for the dressage at the military stud farm; kept spellbound by the *caballeros* and their birds using the long sandy walks for inspired showing-off.

To one of the twenty palatial sherry bodegas to see the cask I was allowed to sign last year, slap its flank and help to hollow it a bit; invited for an early lunch (half-past three) before the bullfight, in a Casa Pupoid⊕ white house on a green hill of vines, heavy now with amber clusters.

To the bullfight; almost faint with heat, rage, fear, noise and the smell – never again; asked at 7 for refreshment in a bodega garden; sherry and tea and blessed shade; back to the hotel for a bath and sleep.

Called at 9.30pm to dress for dinner; curiously peckish on leaving hotel, so dive into little bar opposite, famous for tapas; wash down four or five giant prawns to the accompaniment of brilliantly subversive conversation from more or less permanent residents; going to be late for 10pm invitation – rush; am first guest at 10.30; host arrives at 10.45; sherry and tapas until nearly 11.30; then the long cool dinner of a summer night.

Condé Nast, my employers from 1960 to 1964, didn't like their employees writing for organs that didn't belong to them. They paid me, to start with, £12 a week, which barely paid my rent, and certainly not my aspirational expenses. For freelance work I lurked as Giles Congreve, and for The Sunday Times, for a reason I don't remember, as his brother John.

Casa Pupo was the Chelsea shop that introduced simple Spanish taste to London

One o'clock, off to the gardens, invited to a private *casetta*, a little Rex Whistlerish pavilion among a score of such elegant structures, all belonging to the great sherry dynasties, under the trees; thread way through funfair to reach it (six shots with air rifle for a flamenco dolly: the sights must have been fixed); a scene of marvellous grace inside: long dresses, candles and balloons – and Champagne at last. Leant over the rail for an hour to watch the desultory outbreaks of flamenco in the crowd under the lamplit trees, and listen to the fistfuls of music, clicking of castanets and the clattering of hooves.

the carthusian monastery or charterhouse; a great gothic building – wonderful under a full moon

One party leaves at four to see the Cartuja© by moonlight; another leaves with a party going swimming; by five I am asking the night porter for a magnum of Vichy Catalan water to take to bed.

The Sunday Times, 1960s

WINE
INTRODUCTION

I retired from what my future parents-in-law accepted as proper employment in 1964 to write a book. Judy and I married in 1965 and Wine *was published the next year. A fruitful honeymoon. I wrote the first paragraph early one winter morning waking from a dream. It was my Kubla Khan moment – sadly, my only one.*

Think, for a moment, of an almost paper-white glass of liquid, just shot with greeny-gold, just tart on your tongue, full of wild-flower scents and spring-water freshness. And think of a burnt-umber fluid, as smooth as syrup in the glass, as fat as butter to smell and sea-deep with strange flavours. Both are wine.

Wine is grape juice. Every drop of liquid filling so many bottles has been drawn out of the ground by the roots of a vine. All these different drinks have at one time been sap in a stick. It is the first of many strange and some – despite modern research – mysterious circumstances that go to make wine not only the most delicious, but also the most fascinating, drink in the world.

It would not be so fascinating if there were not so many different kinds. Although there are people who do not care for it, and who think it more than a nuisance that a wine list has so many names on it, the whole reason that wine is worth study is its variety.

From crushed grapes come an infinite number of scents and flavours, to some extent predictable, to some extent controllable – to some extent neither. The kind of vines, where they are planted, how they are pruned, when they are picked, how they are pressed and how long they are aged all bear on the eventual taste. And behind each of these factors there is a tradition or argument or set of reasons why it should be done this way rather than that, and a wonderful variety of ideas about the ideal in view.

Wine is the pleasantest subject in the world to discuss. All its associations are with occasions when people are at their best: with relaxation, contentment, leisurely meals and the free flow of ideas.

The scope of wine is neverending. To me its fascination is that so many other subjects lie within its boundaries. Without geography and topography it is incomprehensible; without history it is colourless; without taste it is meaningless; without travel it remains unreal. It embraces botany, chemistry, agriculture, carpentry, economics – and any number of sciences whose names I do not even know. It leads you up paths of knowledge and byways of expertise you would never glimpse without it. Best of all, it brings you into friendly contact with some of the most skilful and devoted craftsmen, the most generous and entertaining hosts you will find anywhere.

Wine, Hugh Johnson, Mitchell Beazley, 1966

IS FUN CITY WORTH THE FARE?

O ut and back, Heathrow to Kennedy, on a twenty-one-day excursion ticket. It costs £107.3s. You arrive, five hours later in the day than your hosts admit, in a fuming bedlam. Ten minutes of it is enough to convince you that you have never seen a city before.

New York is the city of cities, just as certainly as Fujiyama is the mountain of mountains, or the Salisbury the pub of pubs. And as mountain air is bracing, and West Country air relaxing, so New York air (what little there is of it) is the hormone treatment for worldliness.

I can walk down one of the grimy avenues – a roaring traffic-slum between buildings like portraits of Dorian Grey, showing the cupidity of their owners in every wink and pock of their outrageous façades – and feel ten feet high.

Mayor Lindsay christened New York 'Fun City'. The Air Pollution Control Association retaliated with a poster of a man in a gas mask, captioned 'Fun City Survival Kit'. Public transport carries advertisements with lambs skipping around above the legend 'Be Kind, Be Gentle', while the driver of the bus lets fly with his horn at an old woman and a little child crossing the street. Best of all is the other inspired motto on the sides of Fifth Avenue buses: 'Decry Complacency'. The city knows its faults, and revels in them.

The way I feel about New York, I would go there just to stride about on its free stilts as other people would go to the seaside to be supine. There is urgency and beauty in every breath of it, from the shower-bath humidity that drenches it in summer to the lovely murderous moment in winter when a taxi, its tyres humming through the night down the avenue, bursts through one of the pale spectres of steam from a subway grating and rushes on.

In 1967 the then-new Editor of The Sunday Times, Harold Evans, made me Travel Editor.

So strong a flavour of its own has this extraordinary city that it makes up for all its lack of grace and subtlety. It is like going to a brilliantly acted and persuasive play whose plot appals you and whose conclusions you reject: it is the best entertainment in the world.

Much of what makes New York so worth visiting is included in the price of the ticket. It costs nothing to look. Nowhere else on earth is there so much (some beautiful, more ugly, but all fascinating) to look at. There is beauty in the mountainous buildings of Manhattan, seen from a distance over the water, either from the nickel-a-ride Staten Island Ferry (known, and rightly, as the biggest travel bargain in the world), or from Brooklyn Heights against the tangerine sky of evening.

And there is beauty of a different kind over on Riverside Drive, in that heart-rendingly nostalgic (even to an Englishman) *Saturday Evening Post* cover scene: the boys in their ballpark under the golden planes by the thruway, when the light fades and the twinkling lamps come up on the George Washington Bridge; a king-size nocturne leading to New Jersey, Virginia, Louisiana, and beyond.

The sense of scale, of being on the edge of the great continent, is irresistible. You will hear a New Yorker talk about 'the coast' and realise that he is talking about the Pacific shore, two and a half thousand miles away. Ten miles out of Manhattan there are road signs announcing that the area is 'thickly settled' – implying that the rest is still all jackals and Indians; and to all intents and purposes, so empty is the enormous land, it is.

The Fifth Avenue shops, the Park Avenue apartments, the Broadway sky signs, the red-carpeted platform where the 20th Century Limited, as audaciously romantic as its name, slides to a halt, seventeen hours out of Chicago; all of them are of a piece, of New York: larger than life.

The Sunday Times, 1967

SUNNY AUSTRIA-ON-SEA

My first bright little coinage to describe Portugal was Austria-on-Sea. It was the spick-and-spanness of it all after the crumbling slums of Spain, the blue-and-white tiles, the whiter-than-white wash and, perhaps most of all, the little men in grey uniforms, whom I took at first to be soldiers or police, along every road. Road-menders, as it turned out – but uniformed road-menders seemed to me more like the Tyrol than Iberia.

Real Spain-lovers rarely take wholeheartedly to Portugal. It seems to them to betray the throbbing integrity of the peninsula. The

Portuguese are not proud enough or dirty or rich or poor enough. Their food is not strong and heavy enough. Their bulls are not killed.

What cools the blood of the Portuguese, and even seems to make itself heard in the sibilants of their strange language, is the Atlantic Ocean. You cannot get much farther than a hundred miles from it in Portugal – and when you get that far you are in country that is getting very like Spain.⊖

Nevertheless Portugal is far from being one long sea coast. Naturally it was on the coast that tourism started: first the sandy shore near Lisbon became a refuge for exiled royalty; then the beaches north of Oporto began to build hotels; then, most recently, the Algarve in the south came out in bungalows. But inland Portugal also benefits from the sea in having a wonderfully fruitful, temperate climate. To me the Minho, north of the River Douro up to the Spanish border, and the hills south of the Douro, which seem to have no particular name but roll in crests and dingles of dark pine and slivery gum tree to the Dão wine country, are some of the loveliest places on earth.

All this beauty was ravaged in the 1960s when many Portuguese returned from self-imposed exile under the Fascist government. They brought money and modern taste – or no taste at all.

It is hard to believe that farmland can have so much of the quality of a garden – above all in scale, for the fields are tiny and irregular, the peeling eucalyptus massive and mature, the lanes deep and narrow, the streams overgrown and the granite-and-white buildings heaped with vines and flowering climbers. With its chapels, cloistered farmyards, a hundred varieties of ox-wain and harness, the shade of vine-trellises, the colours of camellia, rhododendron and azalea, the bearded fruitfulness of corn, the Minho is like a subtropical pre-Industrial-Revolution Devon.

At a *pensão* in the Minho I have had the feeling of being in France before World War I, in a place where local culture is rich and intact. Where local cooking, besides, is of total purity: great earthen pots of lampreys in dark sauce, a steaming nightmare of octopus, a great kettle of clams, roast pork on a board, raw beef, a basin of small lettuce leaves over which mild onion is grated for the salad. There is *Serra da Estrela*, ewe's milk cheese, the oranges that are the Portuguese passion, and clusters of tangerines hardly bigger than walnuts, unbelievably sweet, still on their twigs and framed in leaves.

The wine, which in all the Minho is *vinho verde*, slightly sharp and prickly new wine, either palest yellow or dark purple, is brought in blue-and-white pitchers to the table.

Only half an hour's drive inland, though, the peace of country Portugal is perfect. The land has a cultivated face, with baroque village churches and country houses, elephant-grey stone filled in with white, of great beauty. Distances are short, making the Minho ideal for meditative, pottering sort of touring: there are no long straight roads to be eaten up – the distance to the next ancient little town is enough.

The Sunday Times, 1967

ALL AT SEA IN A MAJESTIC STORM

. . . There was time for a British Rail breakfast (their strong point) and lunch (one of their weak ones) before Newcastle, and then a bit of shunting and we were down by the river. The ship calmly served us tea and dry spicy cakes while tugs pulled her into the stream; the pilot took to his cutter; an unexpected Norman keep frowned over the mouth of the river; the wind freshened and the ship gently started to roll.

Dinner was excellent. Most of the passengers appeared, and took new heart from the salmon trout mayonnaise and the roast chicken. The bar after dinner was full of stories of rough crossings of the past. We put our noses outside and noted that the wind was rising, and the sea swelling, and went to bed content.

I had been asleep about half an hour when the stool took off and crashed into the cabin door©. I swung my legs out and trod on the carpet, to find my feet flying away from me. I sat down hard; the stool came back and got me. I crawled back into my bunk; a great lurch and I was floating in the air three inches above it. No hope of sleep; I reconciled myself to spending the night hanging on.

the Fred Olsen Line crossed the North Sea in all weathers

The view through the porthole, as soon as it was light, was spectacularly beautiful. The sky was blue, and the wild sea under it shimmered in the light. From the crest of the waves racing away from the ship's side a plume of spray flew furiously. For a second the glass would be underwater; then for a moment in a cloud of spray; then another wave, far above, would race off, its crest jostling and disintegrating in the screaming wind.

From the boat deck, the sight of the storm was majestic. An intermittent hail of spray flew up the ship's side, hitting the bottoms of the lifeboats like gunshot. The wind howled and wailed. Waves that seemed far higher than the ship as she lay in a trough bore down upon us and lifted us like a dinghy.

In the dining room there was chaos. The air was full of hearty Norwegian breakfast. A cylinder of cheese rolled to and fro across the deck while plates and cups of coffee exploded like shells against the walls. The stewardesses performed fantastic feats of balance for the benefit of the four passengers in the room, only to see their labours wasted in the next consignment of airborne provisions.

The morning sped by. We were told that the wind had reached force ten, that an oil rig was disintegrating somewhere not far off, and that men were being swept off trawlers on all sides. All too soon the wind began to drop, and we began to wonder whether the chef would attempt the famous *koldtbord*, the Norwegian smorgasbord, one of the chief attractions of the voyage. If anything could be better than the air full of coffee and cheese it would be the air full of gravlax and eggs with dill and pickled herrings and cold pork.

By the evening the ship, well under the lee of Norway, was moving at full speed and smoothly again. The long run up the undramatic Oslofjord lasted well into the morning of the next day. Oslo, at the end, was an infinitely more interesting and charming city than I had expected. But it was out in the North Sea, with the tough little ship, built for just such crossings, alone in the frenzied wind and water, that the real excitement lay for me. Our island, half the year, is surrounded by the elements at their most dramatic and beautiful. It was an experience I shall never forget to go out to see them, and to meditate on the poor folk who have to, and have had to since the Vikings set sail for the West, face them without the promise of a *koldtbord* and a warm bunk.

The Sunday Times, 1968

The 1970s

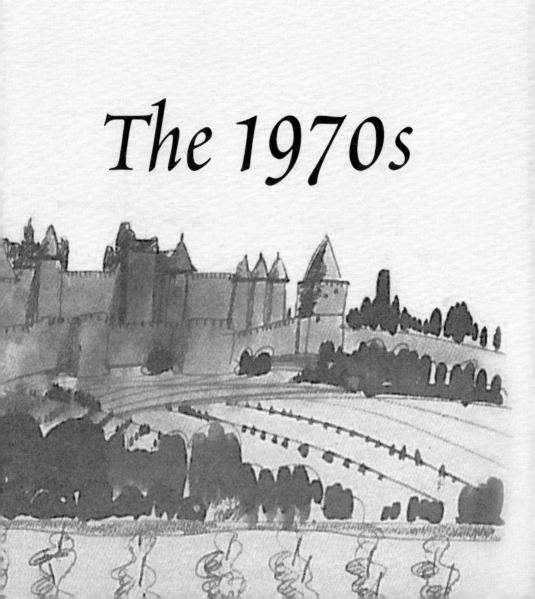

THE WORLD ATLAS OF WINE
INTRODUCTION

Introductions are always the last things to be written, so this is spring 1971.

Maps, to me, since first I started on the happily absorbing study of wine, have been the vital, logical ally. Even the roughest sketch-map has always helped me, as a framework for organising memories and impressions. With a map, distinctions and relationships become clear. Things fall into place.

This is how this atlas came into being. Bit by bit it dawned on me that maps on a large enough scale are more than aids to navigation, they are pictures of the ground and what goes on on it; that it was possible, as it were, to take a reader up into a high mountain and show him all the vineyards of the earth.

The relation between maps and wine could not be more intimate. Wine is, after all, the unique agricultural product whose price depends entirely on where it comes from. The better the wine, the more exactly it locates its origin – down, eventually, to one diminutive field in a simple village lying under what Stendhal© described as 'an ugly dried-up little hill': Romanée-Conti.

author of Le Rouge et le Noir, *1830*

We have only to see how eerily accurate classifications of quality can remain for over a century to realise that it is the exact spot of earth that is the governing factor. Men change; techniques and fashions change; owners, machines, even the climate changes. What does not change is the soil, the elevation, and the exposure. The trial and error of centuries has established where they are best – yet strange to say they have never been comprehensively mapped.

Here are a few of the Atlas's opening sentences, crafted to entice you, reader ...

FRANCE When the last raindrop has been counted, and no geological stone is left unturned, there will still remain the imponderable question of national character that makes France the undisputed mistress of the vine; the producer of infinitely more and more varied great wines than all the rest of the world ....

BURGUNDY The very name of Burgundy has a ring of richness about it. Let Paris be France's head, Champagne her soul; there is no doubt about what Burgundy is: her stomach. It is a land of long meals, well supplied with the best materials. It is the most famous of the ancient duchies of France. But long before it was either, even before Christianity came to France, it was famous for its wine.

A Burgundian understandably feels a certain reverence towards the commonplace-looking ridge of the Côte d'Or, as towards an unknown god. One is bound to wonder at the fact, witnessed by the tongues and palates of generation after generation, that a few small parcels of land on this hill give superlative wine, each with its own positive personality, and that others do not. Surely one can discover the facts that distinguish one parcel from another – giving to some grapes more sugar, thicker skins, a pulp more rich in minerals?

One can. And one cannot. There are millions of facts to collect and collate. Soil and subsoil have been analysed time and again. Temperature and humidity and wind direction have been recorded; must examined under the microscope ... yet the central mystery remains. One can put down only certain physical facts, and place beside them the reputations of the great wines. No one can prove how they are connected.

BORDEAUX If the name of Burgundy suggests richness and plenty, Bordeaux has more than a hint of elegance about it. In place of the plump prelate who seems to symbolise Burgundy, Bordeaux calls to mind a distinguished figure in a frock coat. Picture him tasting pale red wine from a crystal glass. He has one thumb tucked into his waistcoat, while through the open door beyond him there is a glimpse of a turreted house, insubstantial in the pearly seaside light. He enters his moderate enthusiasms in a leather pocket book, observing the progress of beauty across his palate like moves in a game of chess. Aspects of Bordeaux appeal to the aesthete, as Burgundy appeals to the sensualist. One is the nature of the wine: at its best indescribably delicate in nuance and complexity. Another is the sheer intellectual challenge of so many estates in so many regions and sub-regions that no one has mastered them all.

CHABLIS No wine sends one rummaging more desperately for descriptive phrases. There is something there one can so nearly put a finger on. It is hard but not harsh, reminds one of stones and minerals, but at the same time of green hay; actually, when it is young, it looks green, which many wines are supposed to. Grand Cru Chablis tastes important, strong, almost immortal. And indeed it does last a remarkably long time; a strange and delicious sort of sour taste enters into it at ten years or so, and its golden-green eye flashes meaningfully.

ITALY The Greeks called Italy *Oenotria* – Land of Wine. The map reminds us that there is little of Italy that is not more or less wine country. Her annual production is now easily the biggest in the world.⊝ Yet what is at the same time amiable and maddening about her is her age-old insouciance about it all. With a few important

No longer: it is a battle with France. And China is number seven.

exceptions, Italian wine has always been, with its delights and disappointments, enough to drive any tidy-minded wine merchant to drink.

SHERRY COUNTRY Finesse – meaning fine-ness in its most literal sense, a combination of strength and delicacy – is not one of the qualities you normally find in scorched-earth wines. Where the sun fairly grills the ground, and the grapes ripen as warm as fruit in a pie, wine sometimes develops wonderful thews and sinews, power and depth. But finesse ...?

This is sherry's great distinction. It is a question of chalk, of the breed of the Palomino grape, of huge investment and long-inherited skill. Not every bottle of sherry, by a very long way, has this quality. But a real Fino, the rarely shipped unstrengthened produce of the bare white chalk dunes of Macharnudo or Sanlúcar de Barrameda, is an expression of wine and wood as vivid and beautiful as any in the world.

There are little bars in Jerez where the tapas, the morsels of food without which no Jerezano puts glass to mouth, constitute a banquet. From olives and cheese to prawns, to raw ham, to peppery little sausages, to lobster claws, to miniature steaks streaked with amber onions, the path of temptation is broad and long.

Sadly, Jerez today is a shadow. Eheu fugaces ...

Your little *copita*, a glass no more imposing than an opening tulip, fills and empties with a paler wine, a cooler wine, a more druggingly delicious wine than you have ever tasted. It seems at the same time dry as dust and just teasingly sweet, so that you have to sip again to trace the suggestion of grapes.

THE ALTO DOURO Of all the places where men have planted vineyards, the upper Douro is the most improbable. To begin with there was not even soil: only 60-degree slopes of slate and granite, flaking and unstable, baked in a 100-degree sun. It was a land of utter desolation. The vine, however, is the one useful plant that is not quite deterred by these conditions. What was needed was the engineering feat of putting soil on the Douro slopes and keeping it there.

TOKAY Yellow-painted four-in-hand gigs overtake grey old wagons of barrels on the road into Tokay. The cobbles are covered in mud and straw. A mist steams up from the Bodrog river, wreathing the coppery vines on the hill. From the door of the *Halászcsárda*© comes a great smell of pike and paprika and bacon and dumplings and sour cream and coffee.

Fisherman's Inn

Tokay is like one of the provincial towns in Russian novels that burn themselves into the memory by their very plainness. And indeed Russia is only forty miles away.⊙

That was the Soviet Union; now, thank heaven, it's Ukraine.

THE FAR EAST The vine travelled west from its earliest home, conquered the Mediterranean, and has ever since given its best performance in Western Europe. But it also travelled east, across India into China. The vine was known to gardeners in China – who called one variety 'vegetable dragon pearls'. They knew how to make wine with it, and did so. Why then did it not become part of their way of life⊙, as it has in every Western country where it will grow successfully?

it has now

AUSTRALIA If the first flag to flap over Australian soil in 1770 had been the white and gold of the Bourbons instead of the red, white and blue of King George, it is pleasant to speculate what the results might have been.

But even in Anglo-Saxon hands, winegrowing got off to a flying start. The First Fleet of 1788, bringing the first permanent settlers, carried vines among its cargo; the first governor made wine; the first number of the *Sydney Gazette*, in 1803, carried an article (translated from the French) called 'Method of Preparing a Piece of Land for the Purpose of Forming a Vineyard', and by the 1820s the first of the present-day vineyards in New South Wales was making wine.

ENGLAND AND WALES The idea of English wine is usually greeted with mockery or disbelief. It is commonly thought that England lies too far north for grapes to ripen – and besides that, there is too much rain.

In 1971 this was pretty optimistic; I was being patriotic, I suppose, to include a map of England at all.

The fact remains, however, that in the early Middle Ages the monastic vineyards of England were extensive, and by all accounts successful. Had it not been for England's acquisition in 1152 of Bordeaux – an easily accessible source of better wine – they would probably have continued to this day. But they faded away in the later Middle Ages, and since then only spasmodic attempts at winegrowing in England and Wales were made until recently.

Now there is every sign that a serious revival is afoot; as many as twenty-four vineyards are making wine.⊙

Now there are five hundred or so.

SCOTLAND: THE HIGHLAND MALTS The 'single', or unblended, malt whiskies of the Highlands round the River Spey are to Scotch what château-bottled classed growths are to bordeaux. The highest quality is combined in them with the maximum individuality and distinction. Each of them is superb, recognizable, consistent, and exactly like no other whisky on earth.☺

Most malt whisky is used to give character to the famous blends that sell all over the world. Only a little is sold 'single'. It has much more body, fragrance, texture and usually sweetness than blended whisky – but no two are alike.

A typical Speyside distillery is a quiet place. It seems to have the pace of farm life rather than industry. On a bright cool summer morning or in the almost permanent darkness of a Scottish winter, the same simple processes are repeated by quiet men.

There is endless debate about the sources of quality and character in Scotch. The water is one favourite topic. There is general agreement that it should be soft, since soft water is a better solvent than hard, and extracts more proteins from the malted barley. Traditionally the best water is said to come through peat over red granite – as the burns do that flow down from the hills of the treeless deer forests past the distillery doors.

The World Atlas of Wine, Hugh Johnson, Mitchell Beazley, 1971

WINE (REVISED EDITION)
FOREWORD

The eight years since the first version of this book came out have been the most tumultuous and exciting in the entire history of wine.☺

I am not talking of the upheavals in which the world's wine trade has been largely reshaped, the acres of new legislation, or even the spectacular increase in wine-drinking in countries where only a narrow stratum of society ever used to drink wine at all.

Far more significant than commercial, legal or even social change has been the revolution in wine technology. Eight years ago there were a few individuals, mostly in universities, who fully understood the controls necessary to make thoroughly good wine. Today wine science is almost universal. Eight years ago good wine was the exception: the bulk of the world's wine was mediocre. Today good wine is the rule: a real old-fashioned bad wine is getting hard to find.

Not all the news is as good as this. Some of the very grandest growths have possibly let their standards slip. Their wine has become too easy to sell, even at its inflated price. And the more modest growths of the most famous regions have shared the price rises and climbed out of easy reach. But the wines that matter to most of us most of the time, the daily-drinking wines whether from old regions or new, have never been better, or been better value for money. What is more we can look forward to their quality continuing to improve, and their prices very likely remaining stable.

When I first wrote this book I was a newcomer to wine, enraptured with my discovery. The book has needed rewriting in detail – but not, I am glad to say, in essence. The way the pleasure of wine renews itself bottle after bottle, vintage after vintage, year after year, is the most exciting discovery of all.

Wine (revised edition), Hugh Johnson, Mitchell Beazley, 1974

YEAR ONE: OK

The club has been going for nine months now: long enough for us to get the feel of it.⊕ They have been marvellous months to live through. Everything has gone the way we expected, planned and hoped – only at twice the speed. We now have about 14,000 members, who are drinking very respectable quantities of wine: to all appearances a healthy and happy underground movement in a world that seems in various ways off-colour and fed up. This summer we are laying plans for our second year and our second phase.

Wine Times (newsletter of *The Sunday Times* Wine Club)
Issue 4, 1974

The Sunday Times Wine Club was launched in 1973. I was the paper's former wine correspondent, so they made me President. Forty-three years later, I still am.

ONE MAN'S WEEK

SUNDAY I've been meaning to photograph Mme Cassin's garden.⊕ This is the perfect morning. Lavender, tomatoes, dahlias, cabbages, pears are all strung with spiders' webs and drenched with dew. At one edge the vines tilt down towards the Dordogne and the misty light. There is no pattern about the garden – no paths, even – just rows of everything nourishing or beautiful that an old hand at the game can squeeze in. I think of last night's dinner: the mayonnaise, the *ceps à la bordelaise*, the Cassins' own blackcurrant liqueur (not together I must add) ... and hurry in to breakfast.

Standing room only at Mass in St-Émilion for the start of the vintage. Ripe grapes and a clear sky: the best-looking harvest for five years. The *curé* (Diet by name, by nature I think not) sits at the altar and booms into a microphone – the last thing he needs. Two big improvements on Communion at home: instead of a disc of blotting paper, the 'bread' is a finger of buttery pastry – and the wine is St-Émilion.

The Cassins were Tony Laithwaite's adoptive parents in France, and started him on his career in wine. I stayed the night at their house in Castillon.

To Bordeaux after lunch for a radio interview. Forty-five minutes of French without a breather is gruelling. We talked about wine, food, trees, gardening architecture ... I begin to sound too brainy to be true. How to explain I'm just the reference library's best customer?

Bordeaux is sad these evenings. Most of the wine-trade restaurants are shut for lack of customers. Tony Laithwaite, David Peppercorn© and I, three of a breed that has haunted Bordeaux for the last eight hundred years looking for bargains to ship to England, settle for the only brightly lit café and eat oysters and sausages like our forebears.

omniscient London
wine merchant

MONDAY Where am I? In a sleeping bag in a three-sided coffin smelling of tar. The charterer's quarters (charterers being expendable) are in the forepeak of our brigantine – the bit you hit icebergs with. We sail at nine, high tide. A quick wash at the pump on deck (the last time I bothered for four days) and a dash to market for hard sausage, hard cheese, biscuits and butter. We have wine: two thousand cases of it. The whole ship is one big cellar, which is why we are dossing with the anchor chains and messing (the right word, that) on the engine-room hatch.

The tide sweeps us downriver like driftwood. We reach our first stop, Château Loudenne, halfway down the estuary three hours early. A lighter brings out barrels as deck cargo and takes us ashore to wait for the next tide. The Bordeaux way of waiting is to sit down to a square meal. Our pilot is a winegrower, too. He is impressed by Loudenne's stainless-steel vats (so am I), but prefers his old oak. His wine is 'as good as Rothschild's, maybe better.'

a big prickly tree
with fruits like big
but useless oranges

After lunch we play cricket with osage oranges from what must be Europe's biggest osage orange tree© on the lawn. For a Gironde pilot, our man is a tolerable fielder.

TUESDAY Glassy calm in the Bay of Biscay. Sails limp. We chug along with our 1938 diesels, stop for a swim (the bowsprit is a dizzy diving board) and chug on again.

WEDNESDAY We're going too fast, motoring. We're meant to take five days. We put in to Brest to kill time.

THURSDAY Westerly gales are forecast. We confer with the captain of the *Malcolm Miller* on the next berth. He has a crew of 30 novices to worry about. Is he going to take his schooner out? He is. And the *Winston Churchill* is out there already. Brian, our skipper, is a cautious old sea dog, but all this confidence convinces him.

A Frenchman on the quay tells me this sort of weather is the only reason Britannia ever ruled the waves. She could nip out from behind the Isle of Wight on any wind while the French were stuck in port. If I had any island pride left I'd keelhaul him. But as things are, I suspect he may even be right.

FRIDAY About midnight the wind freshened, as we old salts say when the ship lies right over and waves break over the deck. The noise in the fo'c's'le is awful. Every timber is grunting and grinding. The anchor chains slam to and fro in their tubes. In the quieter bits you can hear the water slapping about outside. Four giant cartons of long-life milk keep charging across the floor. I go on deck for some peace and quiet.

Is it nine or ten on the wind scale when the surface of the sea starts to peel off? Just after breakfast (brandy and biscuits) our single jib splits and thrashes into shreds.

We somehow miss Plymouth. Nobody quite knows which beetling cliff is which. Brian decides Torbay is a nice sheltered spot and heads east. When we get round Start Point it is like shutting the door on a blizzard.

SATURDAY Home just after midnight to a sleeping house. Took a torch to look round the garden. The gale had come and gone, scoring only one sizeable branch off a poplar and a layer of leaves on the pond. The borders stood unruffled in the moonlight. I picked up a cold windfall and took a bite. That is the magic moment, coming home, before the children see you, before you turn on a light or open a letter, you are a ghost haunting the place you love. It is worth going away for that alone.

'One Man's Week' in *The Sunday Times*, 1975

THE CALIFORNIA WINE BOOK
FOREWORD

The discovery of a new vineyard*
does more for the happiness of mankind
than the discovery of a new star.

To any wine-lover with unatrophied taste buds and an open mind, California's wine is the most important development, the best news, since the Romans planted the vine on the slopes of Burgundy and in the sand and gravel around Bordeaux. Quite simply, the vine has found a new home in California comparable with the places in Europe (above all in France) where its best products have evolved over two thousand years of cultivation.

This sounds perhaps as though it were just a matter of location: a simple change of address. It is much more. The elements that produce a bordeaux or a burgundy or a Rhineland comprise first and foremost the soil and the climate (which together dictate the essential character of the wine), but parallel and just as important are the social conditions – in marketing terms, the demand.

It is no coincidence that California is among the intellectual and cultural centres of the world today, as well as the place that has revolutionised wine. Californians believe in present pleasure, and they welcome new ideas. The time, the energy, and the resources many Californians are prepared to spend on refining their pleasures can be compared, historically, only with the ways of a tiny class of aristocrats in old monarchical Europe.

In Europe the great growths developed to answer the demands of the aristocracy. In an English nobleman's cellar a hundred years *in, say, the 1890s* ago© you would find only First Growths: it was logical that the first stratum of society should drink the first stratum of wine. But more important for us, the first stratum of society had very few members; the demand for First Growths was therefore known, and the supply limited accordingly. It is not (saving their graces) that Lafite, Haut-Brion, Latour and the rest were the only fields in France capable of making wine of that quality. Rather, it was an historical accident that they were discovered and developed ahead of their neighbours, or of any of the hundreds of acres which probably, but unprovably, could make wine as good – though, of course, marginally different.

France's wine system modelled itself on the social system, congealed around it, and was sanctified in its unfluid state by a theologically complicated Koran of laws, which attempted to say, once and for all, which field produced better wine than which. Masterly though these classifications are, there is one kind of change they cannot resist, and that is the kind that shaped them: the demand. The aristocracy has gone. Its place has been taken by the affluent society. It is asking too much of France's old vineyards to supply the world's affluent society with the precise wine that was developed for a tiny European aristocracy. Inevitably prices have risen, and just as inevitably standards have fallen. To a point compromise has worked, but if the New World (in its broadest sense) was to use wine as freely and naturally as the old one did, it had to develop its own wine idiom: to reinvent wine in its own terms. Here not only geography, but also history was kind to California. A century ago it was fully realised by the few French winemakers who knew California that her climate was the grapevine's Elysium. By the early years of this century she was on the way to building an industry which, had it grown unchecked, would by now be one of the world's biggest. But Prohibition stood in its path. California was forcibly retired from the race. By the time winemaking really got under way again in the early fifties, there was little in the way of active tradition to hinder a totally new back-to-square-one approach to making wine. That clean slate was the one good gift of Prohibition. It has allowed California to look for quality by scientific means.

This is not to say that winemakers in California don't constantly refer to the European originals of the wines they make. They cannot avoid comparisons – if only because most of their vines come from France. It is a truism that a California (or for that matter a French) wine should be judged on its own merits and not on its likeness to something else. There is nonetheless an irresistible fascination in making the appropriate comparisons, and a lot to learn from them.

1976 was the year of the famous Judgement of Paris, when California 'beat' France.

California wine is at that fascinating stage of its development where the basic grammar has yet to be written and is probably still unwritable. The urge to work on it, however, has hit many people. At this moment, who knows how many contributors to its future syntax are tasting and thinking their way through its components, establishing the grounds for discussion?

Bob Thompson and I have been among them, he for the last twenty years, I (though mainly from the safe distance of Europe) for the last ten. Five years ago we decided to make a joint contribution: to build our discussions into a book that might help get the eventual grammar under way. The giddy lurchings of an industry booming out of control made sure that nothing permanently useful would emerge for four of those years. At last, in a year of uneasy calm, it has held still long enough for us to get it in focus.

I collaborated with my friend Bob on what was the first critical guide to California wine of what you might call the new age. Sadly, we were sued for a hefty sum by a winery that claimed we had misrepresented it. The publishers dropped the hot potato; the winery dropped the suit, but copies of the book are rare.

This book, then, is our report on a formative stage in the early life of one of the world's great vineyards, and on an industry that has already started to give America as much harmless pleasure as any from Maine to Mexico.

* Brillat-Savarin⊖ wrote 'dish' – but who in France in 1825 could have dreamed of such new vineyards as California?

in Physiologie du goût

The California Wine Book, Bob Thompson & Hugh Johnson, William Morrow and Company, New York, 1976

POCKET WINE BOOK 1977
FOREWORD

My Pocket
Wine Book
was born when
James Mitchell,
my publisher,
brandished his
diary at me and
said 'Hugh, you
could get all I really
need to know about
wine into a little
book like this.' I had
to give it a go.

This book is an exercise in crowding angels on a pinhead, or students into a telephone box. It is deliberately the shortest book into which I could possibly squeeze a book's worth of information. Conversely it holds as much information as I could possibly squeeze into a little diary-format book. Hence no prose: the whole work is played staccato.

The arrangement is intended to be as helpful as possible when you are buying a bottle, whether you are on the nursery slopes or an old hand with a bad memory. You are faced with a list of wines or an array of bottles in a restaurant, wine merchant or bottle store. Your mind goes blank. You fumble for your little book. All you need to establish is what country a wine comes from. Look up the principal words on the label in the appropriate country's section. You will find enough potted information to let you judge whether this is the wine you want.

The introduction to each national section will help you to establish which label terms are the ones that count. In many cases you will find you can look up almost all the words on the label: estate, grape, shipper, quality rating, bottling information.

For your browsing moments the introduction contains important background information about grape types; the first of all determining factors for the quality and essential flavour of any wine.

Hugh Johnson's Pocket Wine Book 1977, First Edition,
Mitchell Beazley

FIRST SEE YOUR BANK MANAGER

Facing up to the wine list in an unfamiliar restaurant always makes me feel like a man negotiating a minefield with a hazel rod. It's my careful Northern blood. I hate paying through the nose for a pig in a poke. The twin factors of unpredictability of restaurant wines and their outrageous price make me almost obsessively wary. There are a few, a very few, restaurants with wine lists that *mérite un detour*, let alone *vaut le voyage*. Where the proprietor invests his reputation and a lot of his cash in his wine list I grudge him nothing. I join in the fun (and skimp on the food). But most restaurants in this country see the wine list as the essential second prong of the fork on which they roast the diner.

The conventional mark-up for wine in restaurants is anywhere between 100 and 300 per cent. The average, I am told, is about

140 per cent. Obviously cheaper wines can bear a higher percentage mark-up than dearer ones – a point to balance against the fact that if you pay more you risk more.

When a well-known London restaurateur was asked why wine had to carry so much profit, the surprising reply was that you couldn't slap that much on a pork chop: people know what they cost. The implication that your average bill-footing restaurant-goer (still the man of the party, MCP⊗ that he is) knows the price of pork better than the price of Beaujolais is surprising, to me at least. How much am I offered for this spare rib?

I have detoured. The object of this article is to signpost the parsimonious *Feinschmecker's*⊕ way through the *carte des vins*. He has parked his car, checked his coat, and been told that his table will be twenty minutes. He asks for the menu and wine list. Sir desires an apéritif? Now what?

Male Chauvinist Pig, a breed that snuffled widely in the 70s

German for 'gourmet' or 'gourmand'

Sir can cop out and have a whisky. But this Sir is sort of a wine buff and likes dry sherry.

The trick with Fino (the only real dry sherry) is to get it as fresh as possible. Once opened it needs drinking immediately. Even unopened it loses its first fine careless rapture in a matter of months, so order your obscurer favourites only in places where you know they serve a lot. Tres Palmas is okay at the Connaught – where I was of course an habitué – I even had an account. But the safe stuff to drink at the Rose and Crown or Chez Gaston is Tio Pepe, which comes in a 60-inch pipe direct from wells in Jerez. If you can afford Champagne it is often marked up less extravagantly than some things, is reliably in good condition and is so good for morale that the meal seems better (hence better value) after it. It also causes a pleasant bustle and provides cover for your next move, which is to see how little you need pay for wine fit to drink with your meal ....

Wine Times, 1978

THE PLEASURE PRINCIPLE

I still treasure a long letter written to the editor of *The Sunday Times* denouncing me after a Christmas wine article I wrote. What had upset this correspondent was that I had suggested having both red and white wine on the table at once when one was eating turkey (editors in those days actually paid one to write on such esoteric subjects as 'What to Drink with the Christmas Bird'), on the grounds that turkeys have both brown and white meat, that some people like red, some white, some brown, and so forth.

What editors want this lean Christmas is hard facts about bargains, coupled, if possible, with unmaskings of rogues and ruffians. But since neither bargain, rogue nor ruffian has recently crossed my path, I have come back to the old theme. Whether or not editors are paying for such stuff this Christmas remains to be seen.

The theme is Freedom of Choice. It says down with regulations. It lays bare the sham of white wine with fish, demonstrates the hollowness of red wine with meat. Like Puck, I dart round gingering up the claret with a drop of Châteauneuf-du-Pape; softening the rugged silhouette of the port with a touch of claret; putting the white burgundy through the Sparklets Soda Syphon.© The idea is to establish pleasure as the only arbiter in wine-drinking. There is no duty to like dry sherry. Not even to like Campari. You can think Mateus Rosé knocks every French wine into a cocked hat if you like. You can, if you have nothing to do the next day, drink vintage port right through the meal.

Now the height of retro cool, the Sparklets Syphon can be dangerous. One nearly killed my parents on their honeyoon in Bordeaux – I'll tell you the story another time ...

Best of all, you need never pay a penny extra for a bottle of wine unless it gives you a pennyworth more pleasure. If the pleasure principle prevents boardrooms from drinking up all the Mouton-Rothschild when they would really much prefer Blue Nun, it has done even more good.

Of course there is nothing to say you cannot eavesdrop on other people's pleasures and try them out. You can, if you like (and so that I have the illusion of performing some useful function) have a résumé of mine.

I like hot rum punch on Christmas Eve – just because it is so totally different from anything else one ever drinks. My recipe is one of those you have to start yesterday, and the results are heartily disliked by friends who were hoping for a glass of malt whisky. But, for the resolute, this is how it goes:

You need:
6 lemons, 6 oranges,
2 bottles of rum, 4 handfuls of tea (I use Earl Grey)
½ lb of sugar, 2½ pints of water, 1 pint of full cream milk

About dusk on December 23rd, you gather the family round and start scratching the zest off the lemons and oranges with a fine grater. Allow two verses of *The First Nowell* to a lemon; an orange will take you right through *Good King Wenceslas*. When you have got all the zests off, macerate them in a mug of rum. They want twenty-four hours' soaking.

When the moment comes on Christmas Eve, strain the rum off the zests. Marvellous smell. Mix it with the juice (also strained) of the oranges and lemons, and a pint of water. Add the sugar.

Boil one-and-a-half pints of water. As it comes to the boil, throw in the tea. Then strain it off straight away so that it is strong but fresh. Add this tea to the mixture in a big saucepan and heat it all up. When it is hot, add the two bottles of rum. Heat again. Do not let it boil, but when it is really hot again, add the milk and stir. Serve piping hot.

On Christmas Day, I like sweet sherry. Bristol Cream; that kind of thing. It still tastes good on Boxing Day. Then I can do without it for another year. At turkey time, I like Alsace Riesling and Beaujolais – but not Beaujolais Nouveau, the two-month-old wine that often tastes to me as though one of those famous hailstorms fell directly into the vat.

Then what I find I need is nuts and port. I will happily swap the name of the port for the address of a good supplier of those great big juicy Grenoble walnuts. I will even trust you: it is Croft's.

The Sunday Times, late 1970s

THE FIFTH ANNIVERSARY DINNER
THE WINE CLUB PRESIDENT REPORTS

The three hundred of us who gathered at Quaglino's on November 25th to celebrate the club's fifth birthday had a memorable evening – and not only in the way we had intended.

Our guest of honour was the club's founder, Harold Evans, the Editor of *The Sunday Times*. Nobody was to know when we fixed our date that it was to be a momentous night in the life of the newspaper; very probably (events since I write this will have confirmed or – I hope – denied it) the last production night for a long while.

There was a moment of high drama when Thomson Newspapers, at fisticuffs with the print unions, closed The Times and The Sunday Times for a year.

In the circumstance we were delighted and very proud that the editor should tear himself away from the battle front to have dinner with us. His speech was both so poignant and so funny that when he left to go back to work at half-past ten, the whole company rose, clapping and cheering, to see him off.

Wine Times, 1979

The 1980s

A NOBLE ATTEMPT

Would you read a book that explored at length the question of which wine with which food? This is not a question sponsored by my publishers. I just wonder, that's all. I don't think I would. There are very few books about food that are not either recipe, or reference, or history books – I can think of Brillat-Savarin, Morton Shand, Francis Amunategui, Romilly Fedden and MFK Fisher.©

Especially MFKF (1908–1992). She wrote some twenty-seven books, including a translation of Brillat-Savarin's Physiologie du goût; Consider the Oyster, How To Cook a Wolf, *and* Among Friends. *She had many.*

Generally a little of someone else's appetite goes a long way. Food is essentially a practical matter, with little room for theory. Matching food and wine, on the other hand, is a subject that could do with opening up. Recently I have come across a couple of pioneers who are hard at work on some basic research.

The first was Shirley Sarvis, a San Francisco food writer and consultant who organises 'taste exploration' courses at one of the grand Nob Hill hotels, the Stanford Court. I liked her style, all open-minded and enquiring. Her $100 course consists of four tasting sessions for twenty-five people, each with about six dishes and six wines.

The second test-bed gastronome was a marvellous contrast: the true Germanic mind at work, looking for conclusions. He is Erwein, the twenty-ninth Count Matuschka-Greiffenclau, the recent inheritor of the 13th-century Rheingau estate of Schloss Vollrads.

The tall young count is Jane Austen's Mr Darcy and a computer executive at the same time: a formidable combination to throw at the humble subject of bottles and dishes. But he has an ulterior motive: to save German wine (particularly Schloss Vollrads' wine) from the slur – pushed about by me, among others – that it is essentially a drink to be enjoyed in the intervals between meals. He rejects my view, which is in fact homage to the wine, as calumny.

He rightly held that white wines go better with cheese than red.

He has called in the best chef in nearby Mainz to prove with examples that Schloss Vollrads goes with practically everything.© It is an impressive performance.

Tragically, his efforts failed: his family estate went bankrupt, and he shot himself.

I was not entirely convinced by the German-wine-with-food argument – partly because Schloss Vollrads, with its range of powerful dry wines, is far from typical of Germany as a whole. I failed, on the other hand, to convince the Count that the finest wines can only lose in being pitted against dishes with any real flavour. When I am really enjoying a glass of wine I'm afraid I push the food aside – however Lucullan.

Wine Times, 1980

THE SOURCE OF THE SEINE

I nstead of carrying out my threat to drag you through the subtleties of cellar work and the bafflements of bottling in this issue, I thought a gentle reverie would restore your strength and put you in good fettle for the winter.

Besides, a nice thing happened to me this summer, and recollecting it will be a pleasure. In the winter a wine-man's fancy turns with increasing insistence to the vine-shaded sunshine of his summer hols. Not for nothing do the Sunday papers fill fat issues with travelogues in January. My little story concerns neither sunlight nor the shade of vines, but seems to me to sum up why wandering footloose through France is one of life's very special pleasures.

It was like this.

The Johnson family, in an extended version, numbering some ten souls and trundling about in two cars, was on its way home from the Alps, where it had been testing the effects of altitude on an assortment of wines collected along the way.

The previous night's resting-place had been Nuits-St-Georges. A detachment of the family spent the morning conscientiously checking the wines for the club's October burgundy offer. Red (aged ten) didn't think much of the Beaune Les Chouacheux. Johnny Ross (also ten) liked the Beaune but thought he detected an off-flavour in the Aloxe-Corton. Kitty-Alice (seven) declined to share her tasting-notes. Meanwhile a working party was out foraging. The day was bright and our plan was to picnic. Nuits-St-Georges came up to scratch. The charcuterie in the square provided terrine and saucisson. A pâtisserie down a side street conjured up a dozen new-baked apricot tarts as though we had had long-standing reservations. Bread, cheese, tomatoes all manifested themselves. The smell of our rations in the back of the car had us salivating before we had got as far as Gevrey-Chambertin⊖.

(about thirteen kilometres)

You know how it is with lunch-stops. At around noon the traffic in France begins to melt mysteriously away. A sense of urgency pervades the Routes Nationales (though curiously not the *deux chevaux* in front, hogging the centre of the road, which slows from a dawdle to a crawl). Instantly the inner man recognizes the signals: they are all stopping for lunch.

Where shall *we* stop?

At this moment, so insistent and unreasonable is the instinct of appetite, the congregation of cars outside a restaurant on the right inflicts the idea that we are passing one of France's great tables without even having checked in Michelin. Feverishly we fumble through the map pages. No, no stars. But a *repas soigné à prix modéré* 14 kilometres on.

Hang on. We've got a picnic. I know, but we'll be in England tomorrow night. We'd be mad to pass up a proper French meal.

It's half-past twelve and the thought of a hot dish, the memory of savoury sauces, just won't lie down. Besides, what had been a sparkling morning has given way to leaden clouds. Those are the first drops on the windscreen now.

Shall we just look at the menu of the *repas soigné*? Why not? Only 7 kilometres now. It is a pretty inn, smothered in Virginia creeper, with a dozen cars in the courtyard. The menu is just inside the door.

Bonjour, Madame. Pouvons-nous regarder le menu? All ten crowd to look.

What's ballotine, dad? One of the party wants the loo. Madame tells the waiter to set up a table for ten. Civil war breaks out, the voice of reason (never mine) asking what's wrong with the lovely picnic in the car. In truth the prix may be modéré but it is scarcely an inspiring menu – and 65 francs for a bottle of Beaujolais.

Out we troop, breaking into a canter for the cars as the heavens open. Now what? We can't even continue the debate without getting soaked. Too late, too demoralising to settle for the *repas soigné*. It looks like crumbs in the car, then. We steer out onto the road again, the rain moderating. A bit of shelter, perhaps a wood, just off the main road, is what we want. We splash along for a mile or two with rumbling stomachs. Then a signpost catches my eye, pointing along a very minor road, to 'La Source de la Seine'.[©]

It seemed as good an idea as any to turn left here. No wood in sight, but a winding lane among harvested fields. A hamlet, then hedges and an even narrower road, but at least another sign for La Source. I remembered the source of the Thames: a damp patch in a field in Gloucestershire. But the French do things with more style – I hope.

Indeed they do. The signs of civic activity were unmistakable. Trimmed hedges, and what the French so charmingly call *un bouquet d'arbres étrangers* – in this case Christmas trees – and through the middle of it, winding all rushy and full of circling ripples from the rain, the infant Seine. Its tiny stone bridge coyly announced itself as the first in the series that includes the imperial grandeur of Le Pont Alexandre-III and culminates in the cool span of the Pont de Tancarville, hundreds of feet above the shipping.

The village is now called Source-Seine. Look 30 kilometres north of Dijon. I haven't been back.

Here was a picnic place all right, even if a damp one. Our spirits rose. They soared when we spotted, a hundred metres downstream and across a meadow, the little bar that Parisian pride, not to mention thirst, had inevitably installed. We trooped in with our provisions.

May we bring in our food if we buy some drinks?

But of course, said the old man, seated foursquare at his Sunday lunch, with his wife at the stove behind him.

You can guess the rest – or you can if you frequent lonely little bars in the uncharted no-man's-land between Burgundy and Champagne. Madame's omelettes were perfection; Monsieur's Beaujolais was Villages, the '78 at its peak, ripe and warming. The coffee was strong and succulent. The shops of Nuits-St-George had not let us down, either. By the time we had finished the sun had come out, and the little park was bathed in a soft afternoon light.

Wine Times, 1981

COMING ON STREAM

I don't think phone-in wine programmes are ever going to be a big thing on the radio. I've done a few, and it isn't that my answers are not sparkling, succinct and full of matter. The problem is that the questions are so predictable. Seven questioners out of ten start 'I have this bottle of 1951 Clos des Mouches (or 1947 Champagne) and I don't know when we should drink it. Is it ready yet?' Like an egg, in fact, wine is popularly conceived as being underdone and runny one minute, too hard and with a crumbly yolk the next.

Before you get too excited, Christie and Sotheby, six of my seven interlocutors have only one bottle of wine, won it in a raffle, and have kept it next to the stove for decades. They remember it, in fact, only when they tune in to the phone-in by mistake. And I bet they reject my inevitable advice to polish up a tooth-mug and ask the neighbours in.

But I do sympathise. It's all very well advising loftily that readers should try a bottle from time to time to see how their '70s are developing. If you have only one, or maybe half a dozen bottles, you want to minimise the risk of wasting any of the magic. So we come straight away to a central question, asked more often by Americans (who are more honest) than Brits: shouldn't the winemaker see to it that the wine is in prime drinking condition when it leaves his warehouse, and stays that way ad infinitum?

'Drink before ...' dates are much needed.

The answer of course is no – not because it can't be done, but because it can't be done without filleting the soul of the wine. Wine is a living entity. We have all heard of rich cranks who have themselves deep-frozen post-mortem in the hope that a doctor of the future will know how to start them up again. Wine has no more chance of successful suspended animation than they do.

The method most commonly used in an attempt to preserve it, pasteurisation at the point of bottling, leaves the wine the way deep-freezing leaves a lobster: limp, listless, robbed of all the qualities that made you save up for it in the first place. So we are left with wine as a moving target, and the neurosis of the bottle-watcher murmuring 'Shall I? Shan't I?' as he cradles his uncommunicative treasure with hideous nail-less fingers ....

Wine Times, 1981

ALSACE AMONG THE GREATS

At a grand-slam tasting in Alsace recently I was lucky enough to represent Britain in a gathering of gluttons from all over northern Europe. Three of the leading wine houses of the region, Hugel, Beyer and Trimbach, pooled their resources to convince us once and for all that Alsace is on equal terms with the best.

It is a good start to have one of France's superlative restaurants batting for the home team. The Auberge de l'Ill, in its garden by the placid River Ill at Illhaeusern, has the aura of utter luxury that comes with diamond-bright glasses on inch-thick linen. The owners, the two Haeberlin brothers, are artists (without the final e that cheapens the word). I can't imagine them gripping the televiewing millions. Their art is the deceptively simple one of keeping house perfectly – in every sense of the word.ⓔ

The auberge has had three Michelin stars since 1967.

We sat down to taste, fourteen of us, round a vast table in a new room with pale oak boiseries on three walls; the fourth being entirely window overlooking garden, willows and river. Each of the three hosts had brought three or four of his favourite vintages of each of the three 'noble' wines of Alsace: Riesling, Gewürztraminer and Pinot Gris (or 'Tokay d'Alsace' for as long as the Eurocrats allow) – a total of thirty wines, to be followed by another ten at lunch. The vintages ranged from the superb '76s, still young and vigorous, to a Riesling over fifty years old. There was no spirit of competition about the tasting, no marking or judging. The guests were simply asked to put the wines of each grape variety in their personal order of preference. In discussion we arrived at an informal consensus. But this was almost beside the point. The real purpose was to learn the range and depth of quality that Alsace can produce – and to enjoy it.

... And so we reached the wild strawberries and coconut-milk ice cream and the parting Gewürz, a Hugel Sélection de Grains Nobles 1971 that was still fairly kicking with life. With such a vivid and concentrated dessert wine I could tell Johnny Hugel was feeling he had out-generaled Château Yquem.

If this was the point of the gargantuan exercise it was well and truly made: Alsace massed its forces and made an impression I shall never forget. But in a sense it was wasted on me. I wouldn't have so much Alsace in my cellar, or open it so often, if I had not been converted years ago.

Wine Times, 1981

BORDEAUX AND ITS WINES (LE FÉRET)
PREFACE

If a priest were asked to write a preface to the Bible he would be wise to limit himself to recommending attentive reading.

'Le Féret' has been around for so long that it is universally referred to as 'the Bible of Bordeaux'. Yet there is much for the prefacer to explain: the story of the book and its rise to pre-eminence, its unique status and the enormous task it accomplishes today.

First, though, its origins. Not inappropriately, considering the ancient links between Bordeaux and England, it first sprang from the mind of an Englishman. His name was Charles Cocks, he was born in 1812, he was apparently a schoolteacher (and a Freemason), and he lived from about 1840 to his death in the region of Bordeaux. Not very much more is known of him, besides what can be gleaned from his highly influential work.

Now in its 18th edition, this fat red book has been edited by the same family of Bordeaux booksellers for four generations. Monsieur Féret asked me to write a preface for the 13th edition, the first in English for many years.

His first book, in English, was a guidebook called *Bordeaux, Its Wines and the Claret Country*, published in London by Longman, Brown, Green and Longmans in 1846. Halfway through *Bordeaux* he turns to wine. It is immediately clear that he knows what he is talking about. His accounts of the country, its vines and their cultivation, the different growths and their merits, are detailed and authoritative. On the subject of vintages he makes an excellent observation, which should be heeded more carefully today: 'A considerable period must elapse before any vintage can be finally pronounced upon.' But Cocks is most famous for setting out, partly following the example of his German contemporary Wilhelm Franck (author, in 1824, of *Traite sur les Vins du Médoc*), a classification of the best wines of the Médoc into five classes. This is substantially the list that was adopted by the Chamber of Commerce of Bordeaux nine years later as the famous Classification of 1855.

Cocks's book first appeared in French in 1850, in a much-enlarged edition, with more detail on the wines and a somewhat evolved classification, closer in format to the official version that followed on its heels the very year after Cocks's death.

The French publisher was Edouard Féret, bookseller in Bordeaux, who found that he had an important success on his hands. In 1868 he published a second edition without the guidebook introduction, a third in 1874 and a fourth in 1881, in which he introduced the engravings and descriptions of the properties that have since become its most familiar feature. The 1881 edition was translated into English.

The latest edition, that of 1982 of which this is the translation, is the first to appear without the name of Cocks on the cover, being in effect entirely the work of Féret's grandson Claude, still working at the same premises in the rue de Grassi. Cocks is remembered in this edition by a memorial statement on page four.

This thirteenth edition contains references to no fewer than seven thousand Bordeaux properties: the only such reference work, and the only place in the world where you can look up every Bordeaux château, if only to check on its existence, its owner and the quantity of wine, red and/or white, that it produces.

For a century it has been the custom for the accounts of the more important growths to glow with that enthusiasm that is proper to the proprietor rather than a critic. Bordeaux, strange to say, no longer looks as it did when the Féret engravings were made.

It is the nature of a classic, however, to gain stature from its own idiosyncrasies. *Cocks & Féret* did. *Féret* does. Bordeaux will only ever have one Bible. Here endeth the lesson.

Bordeaux and Its Wines, 13th edition, Éditions Féret, 1982

AT THE SHRINE OF THE WHITE TRUFFLE

The smell had been haunting us all day at the Wine Fair. At about mid-morning a wine-farmer had unwrapped a large brown paper parcel. The evidence that the contents were not knobbly undernourished potatoes crossed fifty metres of exhibition space like an olfactory sonic boom.

It has taken several days and nights of pondering and experimenting, alternately thumbing the thesaurus and gazing into space, to realise that there is no word for the taste and smell of the truffle, no comparison to be made. A list of the rejects is a faint indicator: autumnal undergrowth, sweat (your own), pepper, various cheeses ...⁹ various wines, in fact, is more accurate, because not only are splendid old red wines, especially Barolo, said to smell of truffles, but also the truffle itself seems to have an almost alcoholic warmth of flavour, as though it had also fermented.

I would add garlic to this list, and ... and ...

This is the white truffle, not the French black truffle, which has an elusive fragrance and surprisingly no taste at all. White truffles grow to much bigger sizes, are hunted by dogs in the same way – and fetch an equally amazing price. The market rate last year was £120 a kilo, which puts the peasant's parcel at the Wine Fair into the Cartier class.

Far from being reticent about the dishing up of such fungal gold, the farmer, and every other Piemontese host, hurries up with his little pocket plane to shower papery flakes of it on every dish that passes. They are crisp, grey-brown, prettily mottled and marbled like burr-wood. They are also habit-forming.

Wine Times, 1982

CHAMPAGNE AND COMPANY

The person who comes up with another name for sparkling wine as evocative and snappy as Champagne, without taking in vain the name of a French province and its produce, is my candidate for the next Nobel Peace Prize.

This was written fifteen years before the advent of English sparkling wines, now Champagne's closest rival.

We need it now. It doesn't take necromancy to see that our drinking future is full of fizz. Our taste tends more and more to the sprightly and invigorating: in pastimes, in menus, and in drinks. There are many ways of making wine sparkle, and many wines that can profitably be given the lift of bubbles. To call them all Champagne is absurd. What do you then call the classic French original?

What is the special quality of sparkling wine? Why does the very sight of its bulky bottle, the muffled pop of its cork coming out, act as the starting pistol for smiles and laughter? You can have a biological explanation if you like. Dissolved carbon dioxide carries the alcohol through the stomach wall and speeds it straight to the brain. The better the sparkling wine, the more carbon dioxide is dissolved in its pearly depths.

Don't tell me, though, that the reason I love Champagne is that it's quicker than liquor. I love it, and put it first in my confessional of passionate preferences, because it expresses best of all the vitality in the heart of well-made wine.

Champagne, remember, was the first of all French wines to be given the full benefit of what we would now call oenology, concentrated care and technical experiment, by a brilliant cellar master whose name has passed into legend. The 17th-century monk Dom Pérignon© was working with a wine that already had been one of France's most expensive for centuries. Champagne was famous not for bubbles, but for flavour and finesse. Pérignon's contribution was to intensify these qualities.

it's worth visiting his little museum and the Abbey d'Hautvillers near Épernay

One of the many legends about the monk was that he could tell by biting a single grape which vineyard had grown it. He seems to have been the first with the taste, the resources, and the authority to make a *cuvée*, a blend of wines from different vineyards seasoning the rich with the tart, the meaty with the delicate, until his brew was better than the best of its parts.

During Pérignon's century, Champagne developed from a pale-red wine to what you might call a dark-white one: a *vin gris*, made of a blend of the full-bodied juices of lightly pressed red grapes with slighter but finer white-grape wine.

The tendency to sparkle was incidental and largely accidental, appreciated by some but condemned by diehards as a vexatious frivolity. Not for another century did it become part of the definition of Champagne.

Why is this historical background important? Because it is too easy to assume that the bubbles are the point, that any wine put through the elaborate Champagne method has achieved Champagne status. The method is essential to create long-lasting sparkle. But the fame of Champagne is based on the inherent quality of its raw materials and the unique conditions of their processing.

Champagne's technology is far from being a secret. There is scarcely a wine region in the world today that does not laboriously follow the *Méthode Champenoise©* in the hope of making its own prestigious fizz. Interestingly, some of the biggest investors in the imitation industry are the original Champagne firms themselves, led by Moët et Chandon, first in Argentina then in California. Do they feel so secure that they can happily offer themselves competition – or so insecure that they feel the need to corner a threatening market?

though others must call it Méthode Classique, Metoto Classico *or an equivalent*

The answer, I am sure, is a bit of both. Modern wine technology is so impressive that nobody can be certain his unique quality will stay unique forever. The French Champagne-makers of California (and now Australia) will tell you that their sparkling wine is 'the same quality as Champagne – but different.' Some seem to intend to maintain and exploit the difference. Others seem to be set on eliminating it.

For years, in reality, there has been an overlap in quality between the most carefully elaborated emulators of Champagne and some of the more slapdash versions of the real thing – considerably more of an overlap than the prices might suggest.

First, without any peer that I have ever tasted, come the vintage wines of the top Champagne houses in their maturity, whether or not they announce themselves as *cuvées de prestige*. There are variations of style among them quite as wide as that between, say, Bordeaux's Margaux and St-Émilion, yet all have room-filling fragrance, powerful flavours that make no timid apology and, above all, the rare combination of surging vitality and perfect breeding; the manners, if you like, of an aristocrat. I stress in their maturity. Vintage Champagne is not offered to the world until it is at least three, more often four or five, years old⊕. But the great vintages put on depth and subtlety with longer storing more surely, and even more subtly, than great white burgundies do. The '71s and '73s are perfection today. Rare bottles of '62s are an incomparable experience. The premium for a *cuvée de prestige* should guarantee a super-selection, a fine-tuning of all the qualities. But it follows that your palate must also be fine-tuned to appreciate the distinction.

longer than any other producers keep their wines bottled in their own cellars – sometimes as many as twelve years

California's sparkling wines, with few exceptions, follow as close on the heels of Champagne as they can – which is, in some cases, very close indeed. The front runner for a decade has been the perfectionist Schramsberg which, until this year, has made America's one true *cuvée de prestige*, its Blanc de Noirs.⊕

Now it's Cuvée J Schram.

France is the logical place to look for the nearest thing to Champagne. Of the many regional mousseux (the French for 'sparkling'), those that come closest to the products of Reims and Épernay in flavour are the increasingly brilliant sparkling white burgundies. A new Appellation Contrôlée, Crémant (de Bourgogne, de la Loire, and d'Alsace), distinguishes mousseux made to stringent standards in limited regions.

The most determined of the 'third countries' to achieve a facsimile of Champagne is Italy. For years the Italians, broke as they claim to be, have challenged the British as the most eager importers of classic Champagne. For decades one perfectionist family business on the road to the Tyrol, Ferrari of Trento⊕, produced a very good copy indeed, using vines brought from Champagne.

the top name today is Ca' del Bosco

In the last few years the spirit of emulation has swept through northern Italy. A number of firms both in the alpine foothills and down on the Lombardy plain have produced models of Champagne-style elegance, often buying in the grapes (largely Pinot Blanc) from considerable distances to find the quality they need. These dry, Champagne-style spumanti are by no means to be confused with that totally different and altogether more Italian phenomenon, Asti Spumante. Asti comes firmly under the rubric of 'other flavours'. Its overwhelming sweet-Muscat breath makes it one of the easiest wines to fall in love with … and to grow tired of.

This could be a long catechism of worthwhile wines. Every group of them is worth investigation in depth. We generally come to Champagne when we are already in high spirits. Let us just make sure that we serve it in peak condition: chilly but never icy, in deep glasses so that we can watch the sprightly play of rising bubbles.

Good Champagne, remember, has more character than almost any wine. It is not a go-anywhere, drink-with-anything fizzy drink. Certain canapés that are regularly served with it are fatal to its flavour, running clean counter to its freshness and elegance. Almonds are ideal with Champagne, peanuts anathema. Slightly sugared langues de chat sponge fingers are a favourite in Reims and Épernay. Olives obliterate its flavour completely. Must you eat olives? Then you must drink sherry.

Cuisine©, 1983

Cuisine was a sadly short-lived New York-based magazine that aspired to displace the revered Gourmet. *I was appointed Wine Editor (having had the same role at* Gourmet *some years before). Perhaps we did too well:* Gourmet *took us over in what I imagine was a burst of rivalry, and my job came to an end.*

WINE COMPANION
INTRODUCTION

To live in the Golden Age of one of life's great pleasures is something we all do, but few of us seem to realise. There never was a time when more good wine, and more different kinds of wine, were being made.

A hundred and fifty years ago Cyrus Redding, a London wine merchant, wrote his great *History and Description of Modern Wines*. To him the word 'Modern' distinguished the wines of his time from those of the Ancients, still then reverentially supposed to have been, like their architecture, of a quality that could only be humbly imitated.

Redding asserted the new world of 19th-century wine, based on the technology of the Industrial Revolution. If the great mass of wine in his day was still made by medieval methods, the leaders were setting the styles and standards and devising the techniques that today we accept as classic.

These methods are now old. Our understanding of wine and our techniques for making it have moved into a new phase, led by sciences that were not dreamed of in the last century. It is time to use the word 'modern' again with a new meaning to describe the brilliant new age of wine that has opened in the past generation.

The 19th century closed, and the 20th opened, with crisis and calamity in the vineyards of the world. Phylloxera, mildew, war, Prohibition and slump followed in a succession that prevented most winegrowers from making more than a meagre living. Standards, ideas and technology marked time. For the privileged there were wonderful wines to be had – and cheaply, too. But little that was new or exciting developed into commercial reality until the 1960s. Then suddenly the product and the market rediscovered one another.

There were stirrings everywhere, but it was California that led the way. The coincidence of ideal winegrowing conditions and a fast-growing, educated and thriving population were the necessary elements. A generation of inspired university researchers and teachers in California and Europe (and also in Australia) were the catalysis. In the 1970s, sudden intense interest in every aspect of wine caught on in country after country.

This book is a portrait of this new world of wine: its goals, its methods, its plant of vineyards and cellars, and above all its practitioners.⊕ It is designed to be a practical companion in choices that become more varied and challenging all the time. Like any portrait, it tries to capture the reality of a single moment. The moment is past as soon as the shutter has clicked. The closer the focus and the greater the detail, the more there is to change and grow out of date. Yet the detailed record of a single season in wine's long history is as close to reality as it is possible to get.

The enjoyment of wine is a very personal thing. Yet if you love it, and spend your life among other wine-lovers, you will find a remarkable consensus about which wines have the power to really thrill and satisfy us. Prejudice and narrow-mindedness have no place; preferences are what it is all about. I have not tried to hide my preferences among the fabulous variety described in this book.

A decade or so after publication of The World Atlas of Wine, *a new editor at Mitchell Beazley cajoled me into writing 'the words to go with the maps'. They nearly killed me. Writing to every known wine producer to ask for information was insanely ambitious, but I seem to have started out in high spirits.*

A few samples ...

CHÂTEAU LAFITE-ROTHSCHILD This is the place to study the author's control of his superlatives. This estate has made wine for intelligent millionaires for well over two hundred years, and when a random selection of thirty-six vintages, going back to 1799, was drunk and compared recently, the company was awed by the consistency of the performance. Underlying the differences in quality, style and maturity of the vintages, there was an uncanny resemblance between wines made even a century and a half apart.

It is easy to doubt, because it is difficult to understand the concept of a Bordeaux 'cru'. As an amalgam of soil and situation with tradition and professionalism, its stability depends heavily on the human factor. Sometimes even Homer nods. Lafite had its bad patch in the 1960s and early 1970s. Since 1976 it has once again epitomised the traditional Bordeaux château at its best.

As a mansion, Lafite is impeccably chic rather than grand; a substantial but unclassical 18th-century villa, elevated on a terrace above the most businesslike and best vegetable garden in Médoc, and sheltered from the north by a titanic cedar of Lebanon.[☉] There are no great rooms; the red drawing room, the pale-blue dining room and the green library are comfortably cluttered and personal in the style of a hundred years ago. The Rothschild family of the Paris bank bought the estate in 1868. It has been the apple of their corporate eye ever since.

Alas, a gale destroyed the cedar in the 90s.

the new circular subterranean wine store, built in 1989, is one of the wonders of the Médoc

Grandeur starts in the *cuvier*, the vat house, and the vast low barns of the *chais*[☉], where the barrels make marvellous perspectives of dwindling hoops seemingly forever. History is most evident in the shadowy moss-encrusted bottle cellars, where the collection stretches back to 1797: the first bordeaux ever to be château-bottled, still in its original bin.

ST-ÉMILION As a town, every wine-lover's idea of heaven; as an appellation, much the biggest for high-quality wine in France, producing not much less than is made in the whole of Burgundy's Côte d'Or. Nowhere is the civic and even the spiritual life of a little city so deeply imbued with the passion for making good wine.

Curled into its sheltered corner of the hill, St-Émilion cannot expand. Where other such towns have spread nondescript streets over the countryside, around St-Émilion there are priceless vineyards, most of its very best, lapping up to its walls. It burrows into its yielding limestone to find building blocks and store its wine – even to solemnise its rites. Its old church is a vast vaulted cave, now used for the meeting of the Jurade.[☉]

The elders of the town meet ceremonially in scarlet robes as the Jurade, and have done, they say, since 1199 and England's King John.

The vineyards envelop several distinct soils and aspects while maintaining a certain common character. St-Émilion wines are a degree stronger than Médocs, with less tannin. Accessible, solid tastiness is their stamp, maturing to warm, gratifying sweetness. They are less of a puzzle than Médocs when young, and mature faster, but are no less capable of asking unsolvable questions as they age.

BURGUNDY The best-situated shop window in France, if not in Europe. The powerful, the influential, the enterprising and the curious have been filing by for two millennia along the central highway of France, from Paris to Lyon and the south, from the Rhine and the Low Countries to Italy. Every prince, merchant, soldier or scholar has seen the Côte d'Or, rested at Beaune or Dijon, tasted and been told tall tales about the fabulous wine of this narrow, scrubby hillside.

Whether any other hillside could do what the Côte d'Or can is a fascinating speculation – without an answer. What it does is to provide scraps of land and scattered episodes of weather that bring two grape varieties to a perfection found nowhere else. In certain sites and in certain years only, the Pinot Noir and Chardonnay achieve flavours valued as highly as any flavour on earth.

So specific are the sites and the conditions needed that the odds are stacked quite strongly against them. It is an uncertain way to make a living. So Burgundy has organised itself into a system that makes allowances – for crop failures, for human errors, for frailties of all kinds. Its legislation is a delicate structure that tries to keep the Burgundian one jump ahead of his clients without their tumbling to the fact.

If this is not a history book, it is not an exposé either. It is intended to be a portrait. And the painter is in love with the sitter.

MEURSAULT Even if it has convinced itself that it's a town, it fails to convince visitors looking for amenities – still less for action. Meursault's streets are a bewildering forest of hoardings to cajole the tourist into the cellars that are its whole raison d'être. Levels of commercialism vary. In one property half-hidden with invitations to enter I was told, and curtly, that I could not taste unless I was going to buy. There seemed to be no answer to my mild protest that I could not tell if I was going to buy until I had tasted.

LOIRE It is marvellous with what felicity, what gastronomic *savoir vivre*, the Rivers Rhône and Loire counterbalance one another on their passage through France. For a hundred miles or so they even run parallel, flowing in opposite directions thirty miles apart.

They decline the notion of rivalry: in every way they are complementary. The Rhône gives France soothing, warming, satisfying, winter-weight wines while the Loire provides the summer drinking.

GERMANY I have sometimes wondered why there is no Chair of German Wine Studies at any of our universities. The subject has just the right mixture of the disciplined, the recondite and the judgemental to appeal to academic minds. It can be approached as geographical, historical, meteorological, legislational, chemical-pastoral, pastoral-gastronomical, chemical-comical ... there are enough departments to fill a college.

The German way with wine has a different logic from that of the French, the Italian or any other country.[©] It is highly structured and methodical, making its full explanation a daunting task, but it has a unity of purpose that makes the principle, if not the practice, easy to grasp. In Germany ripeness is all. All German quality criteria are based on the accumulated sugar in the grapes at harvest time.

If only this were still true. It has since become almost Italian in its twists and turns.

SASSICAIA An eccentric wine that may prove the most influential of all in the future shape of Tuscan winegrowing. The Marchesi Incisa della Rocchetta grows pure Cabernet Sauvignon on the coast at Bolgheri, south of Livorno – outside any recognized wine zone. What started as a whim became a sensation. He ages it in *barriques* like bordeaux. His cousin Antinori of Florence bottles and sells it. There is very little of it, but a bottle should be surreptitiously slipped into Cabernet tastings at the top level.[©]

This at least was a fair prediction.

CALIFORNIA The 1970s was the decade when California decisively took up her position in the world of wine. She had had what proved to be a false start, though a very promising one, a century earlier. An adolescent America was not ready for what she (and wine in general) had to offer. The generation of winemakers that followed the repeal of Prohibition did indispensable groundwork for an industry that appeared to be remarkably friendless. Hardly anyone was prepared for the impact when, in the late 1960s, Americans started to change their habits, to look outwards for new ideas, to start thinking about their environment, their diet and their health, and to discover that they had a well of the world's most satisfactory beverage in their own backyard.

From the early 1970s on, growth has been so rapid and change so breathless that one of the observers and critics closest to the scene in California, Bob Thompson, has compared an attempt to follow it to 'taking a census in a rabbit warren'. The figures hardly express the changes. In 1970 there were 220 wineries; in 1982, 540.[©] In 1970 there were 170,000 acres of wine grapes; in 1982, 343,000.[©] But beneath these figures, impressive as they are, everything was in ferment: grapes, men, priorities, areas, tanks and philosophy. They still are.

In 2014, 4,280. In 2015, 918,000!

Predictably the other drink businesses – brewers, distillers and, latterly, soft-drink manufacturers – have moved in to control what they can of the mass-production end of the market, although Gallo, the company that has done most for wine in America and sells an almost unbelievable proportion – one bottle in three – is still run personally by the brothers who started it. Ernest sells the wines and Julio makes them.

At the other extreme, in what rapidly and rather unkindly became known as boutique wineries, fashion has rocketed about from one winery to another as drinkers even newer to wine than the winemakers tried to make up their minds what they liked, at the same time as discovering who made it – or whether he made it again the following year. There are enduring landmarks, but they are few and far between. Essentially this is an industry with no structure and very few rules.

AUSTRALIA It comes as a real surprise to visitors to Australia to discover how important wine is in the country's life; how knowledgeable and critical many Australians are; how many wineries, wine regions and 'styles' (the favourite Australian wine word) this country, with a total population only one-quarter that of California⊕, can profitably support.

it's now about half

Extraordinarily little of the buzz of Australian winemanship penetrates overseas⊕ – largely because her best wines are made in vast variety but small quantities, and partly, I believe, because the lack of any kind of central direction makes Australian labels a pathless jungle.

this changed in the 1990s

NEW ZEALAND'S natural gift is what the winemakers of Australia and California are constantly striving for: the growing conditions that give slowly ripened, highly aromatic rather than super-ripe grapes. It is too soon to judge yet just how good her eventual best wines will be, but the signs so far suggest that they will have the strength, structure and delicacy of wines from (for example) the Loire, possibly the Médoc, possibly Champagne.⊕

This was right: the rest is history.

New Zealanders are wisely determined to develop their own styles of winemaking. So far almost all the emphasis has been on white wines. There is enough demand and enough small and technically proficient wineries now to experiment with every likely-looking grape, blend and technique.

Hugh Johnson's Wine Companion
Mitchell Beazley, 1983

RIOJA RIOTS

Rioja is like a woman with red hair: one quality can distract you from a host of others.

The taste of Spain's favourite table wine is as distinctive as melons are melony or cheese cheesy. It combines a degree of soft fruitiness, ranging from faint to jammy, with the pronounced vanilla flavour and slight astringency of oak.

Because it stands out so clearly in a crowd, it is easy to think of it as something simple, barely worth investigation. A week in Rioja in July for the feast of San Pedro reminded me, as every visit does, that this little enclave in the mountains of northern Spain has a flavour of its own in every sense, but that its winemakers no more agree in style (or standards) than do their opposite numbers in California or Bordeaux.

The flavour came over full blast at the fiesta. San Pedro is the patron of Haro, the old stone-built wine town at the heart of the high Rioja. This day of celebration starts with an early morning trudge of five miles to a hilltop shrine for Mass, dressed (we had been warned) in a uniform of white shirt and trousers, with scarlet sash and scarf. We joined a throng of several thousands on the little path – everyone carrying his *bota*, a soft leather bottle full of red wine. A gulp or two was very encouraging on the way uphill. The younger and beefier element, we noted with interest, carried more substantial supplies: sixteen-litre knapsack packs furnished, unexpectedly, with spray lances.

The reason was not a mystery for long. The moment Mass was over, every *bota* became a wine-pistol, and every sprayer a machine-gun. In a scene from some Fellini epic of Rome in its throes of decline, the huge crowd surged over the green mountainside, squirting and swigging. In a few moments, all our white raiment was sticky, pinky purple with wine.

I climbed a tree in the midst of a thousand dancing, chanting citizens with the air a pink haze of wine and red rivers running down the lens of my camera. Too much of the research in my job is solemn spitting in cellars. Can you really learn the flavour of a country without being soaked from head to foot in it?

Not, I must admit, that the gallons of wine being so cheerfully chucked about were real Rioja. This was strictly the low-grade pallid red of Valdepeñas or somewhere to the southeast. Rioja is a limited area, inclined to shortage rather than surplus. Like all Europe's great wine regions it controls every detail of the growing, making, ageing and distributing of its wine. So limited is the crop, in fact, that everyday bulk Rioja does not exist. Even the unlabelled young wine in a stone carafe in a simple restaurant is a worthy yeoman with the stamp of the country on him, vigorous and mouth-filling.

I often think that in the essential qualities of a table wine, in being appetizing and refreshing, in giving moments of interest and hours of satisfaction, good Rioja scores ten out of ten. What started as a shadow to bordeaux may sometimes have overstressed its singularity, putting too much emphasis on barrel age. But the red hair is less in evidence today; the bone structure more so. That the woman was a beauty there was never any doubt.

Decanter, 1983

Decanter magazine was born in 1975. I first wrote for it in 1976, and started a regular column a few years later.

HAVE FUN COUNTING

L ength of lingering aftertaste is one of the most clearly defined differences between wines that are simply good, and those that deserve to be called great. The longer the full flavour of a mouthful remains clearly discernible after swallowing, haunting your tongue, your palate, and your throat, the better the wine – provided, of course, the flavour is clean and sweet in the first place.

Logical to the end, the French have a unit of measurement for this gauge of quality. Each second on your stopwatch that the aftertaste remains without changing in character is one *caudalie*. (The word derives from *cauda*, the Latin for 'a tail' – as does a musical coda.)

The Burgundian writer Max Léglise has even suggested a five-rank classification: starting with wines with up to three seconds' persistence, or three *caudalies*; then four to six seconds, then seven to nine, then ten to twelve, and finally, for the real showstoppers, more than twelve *caudalies*.

1924–1996, a pioneer oenologist and biologist of Beaune

Some Burgundians claim there is a direct relationship between the ancient hierarchy of vintage wines, Premiers Crus and Grands Crus, and their *caudalie* counts. One would expect – in fact, demand – a certain correspondence. If a Grand Cru is not more persistent than a Village wine, it is not worth the money. But Professor Peynaud, in his great book *Le goût du vin*, is scornful of those who 'use a chronometer and a metronome' to measure the quality of wine.

1912–2004, the ground-breaking oenologist of Bordeaux

In principle, I am with Peynaud. Quality is more complicated than that. But I can recognize a good party game when I see one. What odds will you give me on the 1975 Romanée-Conti clocking in at twelve *caudalies*?

Cuisine, 1983 or 1984

ARE THE CLASSICS WORTH IT?

Three hundred, six hundred pounds a bottle? How much can wine fresh from the producer possibly be worth? A bordeaux from the middling '97 vintage has already hit the £300 mark, and nobody doubts that a rare burgundy will hit £600.©

Today you could add a nought.

There is an Australian (of course) joke about a winegrower in McLaren Vale who finds a genie in a bottle. 'What is your dearest wish?' the genie asks. 'To see the great châteaux of Bordeaux', replies the grower.

'No worries. Concorde will land on your lawn when you're ready.'

'Sorry, mate, I have claustrophobia. Couldn't fly in that thing.'

'OK. *The Ocean Princess* will pop into Adelaide for you.'

'Sorry mate, I'm seasick; you'll have to build me a bridge.'

The genie gulps. 'A bridge from Australia? Perhaps Sir has some other desire?'

'Yeah, mate. Why don't you get them Bordeaux growers to lower their prices?'

'Get real, mate. What sort of bridge would you like?'

If everybody didn't want the same few wines, there would be no stupid prices. Of course the same goes for paintings. You can't answer the question 'Are they worth it?' It is a question of confidence: not just in the quality of what you are buying, but also importantly in its resale value.

With wine this is the determining factor. Hence the overwhelming presence in international auction rooms of the same few blue-chip names again and again. They must be in limited supply, have a clear identity anyone can recognize, and be capable of living, if not improving, for twenty years or more – time to sell them several times over.

Only the top Bordeaux châteaux, vintage ports, and a small handful of burgundies from the top domaines qualify on all counts. Maybe these days you can add Grange, the 'Super Tuscan' Sassicaia, Angelo Gaja's Barbarescos and Marcel Guigal's Côte-Rôties©, but everything else, however fine and rare – Brunello, Chianti, Rioja, Madeira, Tokay and everything German, even Champagne, however much the classic wine of its region, is relegated to the Alternative Investment Market on the grounds that not enough is known about it by enough people.

a remarkably stable list: few changes in thirty years

If top prices are driven more by speculation than by anybody's desire for a specific taste, it is fair to ask whether it really matters what the wine tastes like. Cynically one might say that the millionaires who drink stratospherically priced wines are rarely particularly good judges. They do have their watchdogs, though: Robert Parker above all – a taster never fooled by any prestigious label. If Château Le Chêne blows a vintage he will let you know, and the price will come down to earth accordingly. That's the theory. In practice if you want to stay in with a chance of buying the next good vintage, you have to keep buying anyway.

But what is a blue-chip wine? With very few exceptions it is an established classic with a long pedigree – much too long to be just the flavour of the year, or even the generation.

What is it like drinking a great classic on top form, in perfect maturity? This is where words become as inadequate as they are for describing music. Someone in fact once called a great old wine 'a chemical symphony'. Maturity takes it far from its original taste of grape and oak and yeasts, barrels and fermentation. Countless biochemical reactions and transformations take place unpredictably in the bottle over the years, transmuting pigments and tannins, alcohol and acids into compounds of such complexity that analysis can find five hundred or more in one wine.

References to violets and roses, lime blossom, plums and strawberries, damp moss or leather, game, liquorice, truffles⊖ and just simple gentle sweetness certainly bubble to the surface. But they don't describe classic quality. Quality lies in more abstract characters: vitality, vigour, harmony of flavours, the ability to seize your attention and hold it, to tease and tantalise you with unresolved questions, then to linger in your throat in ghost-like sweetness for a quarter of an hour after you have swallowed.

this was before Parker and others started hyperbolical inflation

Can you put a price on such a performance? The market does: a very steep one. But all good wines have it in them to fascinate anyone who listens to what they have to say. Never to have tasted the transcendental would be a terrible shame – were it not for the myriad consolation prizes.

Cuisine, 1983 or 1984

A CHABLIS PRIMER

Folklore is not to be ignored. In folklore Chablis is the ideal, the model dry white wine. Sauternes is the corresponding sweet one. I would say folklore has hit the button both times.

Why Chablis? Why this until recently minuscule outpost of Burgundy on the road to Paris? There are grander dry white wines in Burgundy with more resounding names: Montrachet, Meursault,

Corton-Charlemagne. Perhaps it is simplicity: everyone can say Chablis. Perhaps it goes back to the time when Chablis, easily shipped down its own tributary of the Seine, the River Yonne, was the best local wine for the bars and restaurants of Paris. (It still is[©], and once more at the height of fashion these last three years.) A third and even simpler reason is that folklore is the ballot of generations of tasters. Time has averaged millions of scorecards. Chablis has the popular vote.

even today, despite Sauvignons Blanc

Or does it? True Chablis is not easy enough to be everyone's wine. If gulpability, softness, reliability are vote-getters, the body, the 'cut', the shifting subtlety, and the evolving flavours of Chablis should make it a minority taste. Also, until very recently, first-class examples were not easy to buy. It's only in the last five years that new plantings, new crop-protection methods, and a succession of big harvests of good quality have snapped Chablis out of an apparent coma and given it the air of a village with money in the bank.

Chablis is pure Chardonnay. New Chablis tastes, in fact, more clearly and thrillingly of the white Burgundy grape than any other wine. The natives call the Chardonnay the *Beaunois* – the vine from Beaune. But their clay soil gives it an aromatic lift quite distinct from its lime-fed roundness on the Côte de Beaune in Meursault and the Montrachets. The local shorthand for this extra aroma used to be *bonbon anglais*, the French for boiled sweets.[©] In some exceptional young Chablis these drown out all other scents.

Now everyone talks about pebbles in a brook.

More often they mingle with scents of grapes, apples, grass, hay, and a certain flinty note, a mineral undertone that emerges more clearly as the wine matures. Good Chablis maintains a positively hard centre, a core of acidity that keeps it fresh while it ages. The best Chablis carries, secured on this firm base, a superstructure of honeyed potency that can even resemble Napa-ripened Chardonnay. Wine like this, from a Grand Cru vineyard and a vintage of sufficient acidity, will profitably age longer than any other white burgundy. A 1923 Chablis Les Clos was a miracle of freshness and vigour at forty-five years of age.[©]

Today fifteen years is getting on a bit.

The name Chablis covers the whole of the 4,300-acre vineyard around the little town and its hamlets, but it is easy to see (much easier here than, say, in the Côte de Beaune or the Médoc) that some slopes are much better exposed than others. The pecking order is clear, visible on the ground and testable in the wine. Unmistakably best, dominating the village from the 400-foot hill to the north, is the solid block of the seven Grands Crus vineyards, 220 acres of vines sloping steeply south-by-west to catch the afternoon sun.

The Premiers Crus vineyards, 1,080 acres in all, are widely scattered wherever the most favourable hillsides are found. The three most famous flank the Grands Crus on the north bank of the Serein. Premier Cru Chablis, no matter from which vineyard, is my advice for learning the singular Chablis quality: light, limpid, luminous, delicate without being feeble or faint-hearted.

Below the rank of Premier Cru, Chablis (with no qualification), is a less predictable proposition. It may be 'declassified' wine from a Premier Cru vineyard, or it may come from ever-increasing vineyards on the valley floor without the tilt toward the sun that in most years is essential to ripen the Chardonnay properly. The trick with sharp Chablis is to keep it. It will develop a surprising amount of flavour and bouquet over three or four years, even if it remains a steely wine that needs the cushion of a plump oyster.

Grand and Premier Cru Chablis accounts for almost half the total production of the region; plain Chablis for nearly all the rest. A very small quantity of a fourth rank, Petit Chablis⊖, is made in vineyards *there has been* on soils that have never achieved the singular Chablis style and *inflation here too* whose wine needs drinking in its first year. Its right to be called Chablis at all is sometimes questioned, but the Paris cafés where it is drunk are happy with it: it only bites like a puppy.

Cuisine, 1984

NATIONAL ANTHEMS

O ur mental repertoire of food-flavour memories is trained from the day we are born. We have no problem reaching for the pigeonholed image of the nip of a lemon, the plump caress of cream, the sea tang of a clam, or the yielding astringency of yogurt.

Not so with wine. We probably all started, as children, not liking it at all. Then one day we tasted a sweet sherry or a flowery sparkling Muscat and were intrigued. Bit by bit we learned how appetizing drier table wines can be. At some stage we learned that low-price wines are usually thin in their flavours, or at best monotonous; that extra quality consists of a more satisfying depth of taste under taste, a certain definite 'attack', and a lingering sweetness as you swallow.

To go on from here to associating particular flavours with individual grapes, countries, regions, or even individual winemakers takes time and, above all, practice. It is an effort that most people never make. It will never come just by drinking, however much you swallow. It will come only with deliberate awareness; each time pausing for a second to concentrate, to sniff, sip, think, and memorise before settling down to relaxed enjoyment of the glass. How you seize it, how you approach it, and what you expect from it depends on your upbringing.

American wines should be easiest for Americans to understand. The basic syntax of California comes easily enough. A California wine education uses grape varieties as its building blocks. The highly aromatic Muscat or Gewürztraminer is usually the first grape to make an unmistakable impression. Sauvignon Blanc should be simple to spot by its blackcurrant-leaf scent and bold acidity. Riesling is more variable, but can quickly be learned. Chardonnay is more variable still: the clue is often in the potency and balance of the wine it makes – that and the expensive smell of oak added by the winemaker.

Once you have grasped the grape, the first layer of stylistic complication is the producer. Producers are perceived as delivering up to a certain quality level. Often the image is deceiving: Gallo's new varietals, for example, go far beyond the public expectation of Gallo quality. And certain highly praised waiting-list-only Chardonnays are just as surely overvalued.

Grape flavours, frank and fruity, however blended for complexity, overlaid with oak and modified by maturity, remain the hallmark of America's best wines. But ask a Frenchman, a Spaniard, or most Italians which grapes they prefer and they will be uncomprehending. They don't drink grapes; they drink wines – wines that express the landscape, the people, the gastronomy of the province ... you can hear it all pouring forth.

The roots of the Appellations Contrôlées of France and the Denominazioni Di Origini Controllati of Italy are in local pride and jealousy. Identity is what they are all about. They masquerade as defenders of quality. What they really signify are the closed ranks of the regions' producers preserving their birthright.

The chauvinism of France's wine regions is legendary. You risk assault by asking for a bottle of burgundy in Bordeaux. Yet to the outsider what is more striking still is how their wine philosophy is French first and regional second. What makes it specifically French? Its obsession with the table. Just as the pillar of French society is the family Sunday lunch©, with three or four generations filling every restaurant in the land for four hours at a time, so wine gains its merits or demerits by its contribution to *la table*. By understatement, by not dominating the food, it acts as seasoning and whets the appetite.

perhaps in the 1980s, sadly not today

There is little reason, on the face of it, why Italy's wines should have a national identity at all. A country united only within the last century and a half, with one extreme in the Alps and the other nudging North Africa, should have as great a diversity in wines as all the rest of Europe.

What Italian wines used to have in common, it has been unkindly said, was that they were badly made. There is an element of truth in this. The greater part of the country – most of the centre, at least, which the tourists visited – had grapes chosen for easy farming rather than for flavour. Little judgement was used about when to pick them, how to ferment, or how long to age the wine. The better Italian wines of those days were full of rustic character; most were just flat and flabby, in danger of deteriorating into something worse.⊕ *How extreme this* Is there still, then, an Italian identity, now that technology has *sounds, yet how* reached almost every corner of the country? I think there is, but in a *true it was.* French sense rather than in a Californian: in a unity of purpose, that is, rather than organisation or style.

Italian wines are made today in the same spirit as French wines: to be the concomitant of the food at the great Italian feast. There are fresh and faintly fruity whites made now in almost every region, made not so much to interpret the region as to wash down its food. Technology has put colour, punch, and vigour, too, into reds that used to be either pallid or coarse – again, almost regardless of region. More and more French, or 'International', grapes are being planted.

Spain is moving in the same direction as Italy, but from a very *How have* different tradition. Italy used to drink nearly all of her wine at home. *these sweeping* Spain has a long history as an exporter. One or two of her wines – *generalisations* sherry above all, but also Málaga, and later Rioja and the sparkling *aged? Spain seems* wines of Catalonia – were developed as high-quality exports. The *most changed.* others were made expressly for blending: not to be drunk on their own at all, but to give colour and strength to pale bordeaux. The best of the wines that were kept in Spain for home consumption were kept improbable lengths of time in wood. The taste of wood, in fact, became the taste of age and distinction in wine, just as it is in brandy.

You will scarcely taste oak in any of the wines of neighbouring Portugal. They are aged in oak, but something in the Atlantic climate of Portugal and the thick-skinned grapes the Portuguese favour gives them a texture, a balance, and a tannic 'cut' closer to the French style than the softer Spanish.

So it goes round the grape-strewn globe.

What is the most distinctive, unmistakable national style of all? The retsina of Greece, beyond a doubt. Love it or hate it, you can't miss the ancient starting block of the national identity parade.

Cuisine, 1984

REMEMBRANCE OF WINES PAST

Perhaps the ultimate privilege of a wine journalist's job is to be asked to share wines of an era long before his own experience began – and, incidentally, far more valuable than he can personally afford. Great wines made before the coming of modern technology were undoubtedly scarcer. Without the physical and chemical controls available to a modern winemaker, things went wrong far more often. Rot raced through vineyards, fermentations overheated; diseases with vividly unsavoury names struck without remedy.

Great wines were made with a combination of judgement, luck, and great expense in the few privileged areas where natural conditions were near ideal. And then by no means every year, or even in every barrel of a successful year.

So to taste wines of fifty years old and more, and to find them still alive, still individual and true to their natures, is like meeting some exceptional old person, some gifted and fortunate soul whose age is expressed in a gentle sort of sweet vitality never found in youth.

These thoughts justify, for me, telling you about the formal wine tasting and lunch given by the owners of Bollinger Champagne, Christian and Marie-Hélène Bizot, at their home in the village of Ay on the 'mountain' of Reims last autumn. The pretext for the meal was the 'discovery', in the family's private cellar, of some ancient bottles of red wines of France's greatest vineyards. A century ago (and even more recently) it was common practice for proprietors to sell or trade their wines to one another in bulk. Monsieur Bollinger, for so many crates of Champagne, would receive a barrel of Château Lafite from Monsieur de Rothschild, and the equivalent transaction would top up his cellar with the best burgundy.

The lunch was designed around two vintages of Château Lafite, 1911 and 1888, and two great old burgundies, La Romanée 1885 and Corton 1878. To be sure of fitting food, the Bizots had invited the best chef in Champagne, Gerard Boyer, to prepare the meal.

Formal proceedings began with a tasting, standing at a long table in a very cool bottling hall. In front of each of us four glasses were arranged in lines, bubbling with four different vintages of the great speciality of the house. Bollinger's *Années Rares* are not, like most Champagnes, disgorged to remove the yeasty sediment at a standard age of, say, four years. They are kept with the deposit bottled up, imparting its subtle richness to the flavour, until Christian decides they carry the true Bollinger stamp and are ready to drink. These four *Récemment Dégorgés* (recently disgorged, or 'RD') vintages were 1973,

1970, 1964, and 1961. We were asked to taste the four and put them in order of age, which should not have been difficult. But I confused the 1973 and 1970.

I was gently reprimanded for making my first choice the 'least Bollinger' of the vintages. I still swear it is one of the best they have ever made. But it was time to leave our just-tasted glasses, still tantalisingly half-full, and go out into the autumn sunshine to inspect Bollinger's unique little vineyard of Pinot Noir vines that have never been killed by phylloxera.[○] No one knows why these have escaped: because these vines live and produce on their natural roots, ungrafted, they would seem to be vulnerable to attack.

I begged a cutting from one of them. Forty years later it covered a pergola in my garden at home, but its grapes rarely ripened.

... Celestial smells were coming from the kitchen. We took our places at table. This was the menu:

Petite nage de turbot aux langoustines
Dariole de ris de veaux et homard aux truffes
Filet d'agneau rôti, son jus, quelques girolles
Fromages
Assiette de sorbets et fruits de saison

The foodie in me would love to lip-smack through every mouthful with you. The 'little swim' of turbot and crayfish in a light soup, an ethereal sort of fish broth, was accompanied by renewed supplies of the RD Bollinger 1973. There was more Champagne when the silver cover on the dariole[○] of sweetbreads, lobster, and truffles was whisked away, and we were enveloped in a scent I dare not try to describe.

a dariole, for those as grossly ignorant as I was, is a dream turned out of a pudding basin

Now the mood setting was done. There was a sense of expectancy as we were offered the perfect little pink fillet of lamb with wild mushrooms. Time for the red wines. The two vintages of Château Lafite were poured, unconventionally with the older first. The summer of 1888 was poor, but the weather that September was perfect for ripening. Lafite, it turned out, had made the kind of light but utterly complete wine that no other vineyard seems to achieve. Time had faded it to pale brick red, attenuated its texture to a near-watery limpidity, yet it gave off a fragrance of China tea, of woods in autumn, of exquisite old claret that refuses to lie down and die.

By comparison, the 1911 was a disappointment. It looked, smelled, and tasted like the wine of a riper vintage whose stability had gone. The colour was brown and slightly muddy, with scarcely a gleam of red. There was still great pleasure in a scent that made me think of creamy coffee rather than wine. But while the clean, sweet flavours of the 1888 lingered on your palate, the 1911 died away after each sip. Or such were my impressions. Discussion, you may imagine, was lively. One question had been teasing me while we tasted and discussed these venerable relics. How was our host going to end with anything remotely comparable in a Champagne? Surely he would want us to go home talking of Bollinger?

The answer was superbly simple. He gave us the 1914 vintage – Champagne made in the first year of World War I. To our astonishment its sparkle, its pale colour, its intense dry flavour were entirely and unflaggingly typical of the Bollinger vintages we had been tasting that morning. A seventy-year-old wine perfectly expressed the house style of dry, deep, meaty Champagne. It was game, set, and match.

Cuisine, 1984

ALL THAT JAZZ

Burton is a former Editor of the International Herald Tribune who fell in love with Italy and wrote the definitive book on its wines, Vino, *in 1980*

One of my gentle correspondents was moved by Burton Anderson's article© on Lambrusco in the March issue to express her horror and dismay that we were dignifying in print 'the vinous equivalent of rock music'.

I am not a great follower of rock music. Nor of Lambrusco. So they certainly have that much in common. But the implication of the letter went much further. It condemned both Lambrusco and rock as beneath critical attention – too popular, too common, too vulgar, in fact, to be any good.

I can't admit this. To give pleasure to huge numbers is itself a virtue. Follow the argument the other way and eventually nothing that pleases more than a few can have any value at all.

I don't like rock, but I do like jazz. From the first creaky acoustic recordings to the smooth bounce of the big bands, it goes, in the words of *Careless Love*, to my head like wine. Which wine in particular is something I have long been trying to figure out. I have tasted first-attempt Chardonnays from California that were like Dizzy Gillespie's solos: all over the place. And the colour of his trumpet, too.

On the other hand, a 1977 Sterling Chardonnay recently had the subtle harmonies and lilting vitality of Bix Beiderbecke. Robert Mondavi Reserve Cabernets are Duke Ellington numbers: massed talent in full cry. Benny Goodman is surely a Riesling from Joseph Phelps. Louis Martini's wines have the charm and good manners of Glenn Miller. Joe Heitz, though, is surely Armstrong at the Sunset Café: virtuoso, perverse, and glorious.

Cuisine, 1984

HOW TO ENJOY YOUR WINE
INTRODUCTION

Don't look at the label. Ignore (for the moment) even the price. Let yourself be guided by one thing: how much do you like what you have in your glass? This is rule one of enjoying wine, but perhaps more easily stated than applied. 'How do you know how much you like it?' is far from being a dumb question.

The extremes of wine's myriad identities, from most delicate white to most unctuous amber, are as far apart as Alps and Sahara, sonnet and epic, Chopin and Wagner, crocus and rhododendron. The imagery is far-flown, but that precisely is what makes wine different from anything else we drink. It ranges from lace to leather, from glossy to gritty, from insinuating to explosive, in keys, colours and tones innumerable. So how much do you like it?

You can be a technical taster. Makers and traders of wine are condemned, poor souls, to put names to every nuance they detect, to worry about latent faults and not-so-latent price rises. But you are much better advised to drink in simple attentive appreciation.

From mere rain percolating through the soil the roots have collected, the vine transported, the leaves ripened and the grapes matured this magic juice. Yeasts on their bloomy skins have seized on it for food, converting its sugar into alcohol, starting a process of infinite complexity that will end only when the wine is drunk.

I have every sympathy with drivers who don't know what goes on under the bonnet of their cars. Much less with drinkers who never pause to taste what they are drinking. Good wine is as close as we can come to imbibing the very nature of a specific spot on the earth's surface. Do you need to be a mystic to find the prospect at least intriguing? When you learn, as you soon do, that the taste, and hence the pleasure, can change within a stone's throw, the mystery begins to seep into you. Don't fight it. There are too few direct links between nature and art.

How to Enjoy Your Wine, Hugh Johnson, Mitchell Beazley, 1985

How To Enjoy ... *was originally the script of a home movie we made at Saling Hall called* How To Handle a Wine – *I gather wine schools still use it.*

VINTAGE PORT

Wine has many pockets of diehard folklorism, but none so crustily entrenched as the cult of vintage port. See – I have barely mentioned it and you have already summoned up a mental picture of a retired colonel snorting away, his eyebrows and moustache registering one hundred on the Bateman⊖ scale of shock and horror as some cad breaches the unwritten code. The Colonel would have

the cartoonist HM Bateman. His The Man Who ... *series lampooned upper-class social gaffes*

finally popped with indignation if he had been (unlikely thought) at a lunch party in Langon, the capital of the southern Graves and Sauternes, recently. He would have seen Pierre Coste© contentedly pouring his guests vintage port with their Brie, Port Salut, Mimolette and Reblochon. OK – so these cheese-crazed frog-eaters are easily capable of that. But the port, sacré-bleu! The port was purple! The port was stickily sweet! The port smelt of freshly crushed fruit!! The port was new!!!

a négociant at Langon who worked with the now-celebrated oenologist Denis Dubourdieu

Pierre Coste was not concerned with the convention that vintage port is bought for newborn babies for when they come of age. He saw no reason to miss the present pleasure of drinking it as a *vin mute*: as a thrilling, rasping, intensely sweet and perfumed mixture of grape juice and brandy.

So good it was with the cheese, as sweet as peaches and as pungent as a liqueur, that I joined in the orgy with a will. I remembered guiltily those tastings when I couldn't resist letting a drop of the burning nectar trickle down my throat (while officially, of course, spitting it all out).

If it is not what Mr Taylor or Mr Warre has in mind, who cares? I may not be here in twenty years: I may have gout, be begging my bread, be doing time at Her Majesty's pleasure – all circumstances in which I should miss the promised velvet and incense of the '83 vintage at its apogee. In the meantime it may spend a decade or more as a charmless adolescent, a fluid more fit for buying and selling than orgies after lunch. Certainly it will never again be the explosive mouthful it is at present. Gather ye rosebuds ....

Wine Times, 1985

THE GREAT FRENCH APÉRITIF MYSTERY

Sherry in France is like snakes in Ireland. Which of their saints banished it from their borders forever I don't know, but gone it is – if ever it was there. True, at the Paris house of one of the most famous, hospitable, and cosmopolitan of Bordeaux winegrowers, I once had the temerity to ask for sherry and was rewarded by a glass of Oloroso. But the mock reverence with which the butler handled the bottle, the cobwebs about its neck, and the way in which he enunciated the word 'KEREZ' told me before I had even tasted it that it had been bought in an outburst of mistaken enthusiasm for the servants' hall thirty years before. There was Scotch, discreetly decanted, and Perrier on the silver tray. My eccentricity had been indulged, and I found myself, as usual, drinking the *vin d'Écosse*.

What does a Frenchman drink before dinner? Champagne, of course – far more than we do.⊕ France drinks three times as much Champagne as it allows to get away. Krug and Pommery bottles are among the empties every morning at the back door of the unlikeliest-looking cafés. It is not cheap, 35 francs being a reasonable restaurant price, but this completely fails to deter the French diner-out. Looking at my own bill after a modest dinner in France I shudder to imagine the computer-class figures reached by the uninhibited trenchermen on either side of me. Champagne is a perfect apéritif. It animates the taste buds as nothing else can. But this does not solve my problem. I have the rent to pay.

I was wrong here: the French tend to drink their Champagne after dinner – even with their dessert. Dry Champagne with a gâteau? Frankly a revolting idea.

Scotch, then. Scotch is received in the very best circles. It is quite unexceptionable, and not all that expensive: cheaper, indeed, in France than in England at the moment. But I plead against Scotch on gastronomic grounds. Be it never so fine, old, cold, Perrier'd, and served in glasses as heavy as lead with the brilliance of diamonds, it is a spirit, and a spirit made of barley. It dries up my mouth. The sauce in the opening bars of dinner will meet a baffled palate. The Bâtard-Montrachet will be thrown away. Alas, the same must be said of gin.

The most popular apéritifs in France are the branded, wine-based ones – the Dubonnets, Lillets, Byrrhs and Saint-Raphaëls. All, like the fortified wine the French choose as an apéritif – port, and ruby at that – and the *vin doux naturel* of the Midi that sells twelve million (or some fantastic figure) bottles a year, are sweet. Sometimes the sweetness has a strong counterbalancing element of bitterness to it – quinine is an important ingredient in the wine-based apéritifs – but the common taste in France, as it must be admitted it is in England, is for a sweet drink before dinner.

All I can fairly say is that it is not my taste: the sugar and spice of these drinks is too much of an hors d'oeuvre. I still pine for the delicacy without thinness, the flavour without fruitiness, of a glass of sherry.

There is wine, pure and simple, as a last resort. The wine you are going to drink at dinner or another of the same colour, or a white wine before a red, or whatever takes your fancy. But an ordinary wine is not interesting enough to drink on its own, and a fine wine is expensive, and commits you to even more expense keeping up with yourself at dinner. Still, wine is getting warm. If you are in the Jura or can find a bottle of Château-Chalon you will find the nearest the French can approach to sherry. If you are in Bordeaux or Burgundy, Alsace or the Loire there will be so much tasting to do that the question will hardly arise. If you are in the Midi, as I am as

I write this, there is the dry white wine of Cassis© to marry with its namesake, Crème de Cassis, blackcurrant syrup, to make a *vin blanc cassis*. A teaspoonful of syrup in the bottom of a tumbler of cold wine – perfect in sunny weather.

But the fact remains, despite the many pleasant ways of getting round it, that the French, wise and careful, open-minded and scrupulous as they are in treating their favourite subject, have their minds closed to the vital question of apéritifs. It is the only thing I would change in the exhaustless harmony of the French table – but while things stay as they are, I shall continue to smuggle sherry into France.

Wine Times, 1985

A LITTLE ESPIONAGE

We wanted to see how Hungary is coming along, what the Austrians are up to, and whether the rumours are true that the beleaguered Czechs are consoling themselves by making better wine.

The answer to the last question is yes. We crossed the Danube into Czechoslovakia at the border city of Bratislava, expecting to be met by officials who would guide our footsteps and monitor our movements. Perhaps because it was almost May Day, the grey streets festooned with red banners (and cleared for tanks), the officials never showed up, and we had the unexpected experience of driving at will around the countryside, following tips from our most knowledgeable friend in matters Czech, the Dean of Trinity College, Oxford.

Moravia, the central part of the country just south of Brno, was where Dr Milner had tasted the best wine. We tracked down a village he had noted and bewildered everyone, ourselves included, with our attempts to explain who we were and what we were looking for.

Eventually an extremely kind teacher from the local school was sent for to interpret©, and the upshot was a series of happy chances by which we did find wine even better than we had hoped: notably a stunning Sauvignon Blanc, last year's, still in barrel but ripe as a warm peach. Whether we shall ever be able to buy such a wine, get it bottled in the same condition and bring it home for general enjoyment is another matter. At least we established that it is there – just across the Danube from the winiest part of Austria. Now we must try to liberate it.

Wine Times, 1985

SHELLFISH

Sometimes I think I must be a merman, and a half-cannibal one at that, to enjoy browsing on the seabed as much as I do. I remember a particular plat de fruits de mer at Honfleur in Normandy that was quite simply that: a bare-handed predator's banquet on all the stony, scaly or limpid beasts that lie, crawl, or proceed in illogical little flicks among the wrack and the wrecks, stirring up the sand or disguised as pebbles. There were shrimps and oysters, whelks and mussels, cockles and clams. The napkins were sea green with crustaceous designs. The plate was virtually a bivalve in pottery. The wine, palest green from a dark-green bottle, was as cold and as tangy, almost, as the sea itself.

Just a toss of a lobster pot from the harbour wall, where pyramids of tarry rigging were black against the moon, the café-restaurant Aux Deux Ponts was like an extension of the seabed, the only difference being that the water boiled.[⊕] We went back with unabated *Sadly standards are* appetite for grilled sole, steamed turbot, moules marinières night *not the same today.* after night.

The sea itself is an important actor, with all its nautical props. The sight of a tubby little fishing boat, and the smell, stale and fresh at the same time, on the jetty, starts an urgent craving for fish, fish, fish, fish (as Fats Waller put it), fish ....

The Compleat Imbiber, 1980s

THE CELLAR BOOK
INTRODUCTION

The traditional cellar record book was conceived in an age when the range of wines available was very definitely finite: perhaps twenty or thirty if you were lucky. Its object was simply to keep track of the number of bottles drunk.

I have what appears to be the first cellar book on my desk. It was published in the 1750s by R & J Dodsley[⊕] in Pall Mall, London. *(famous as* Beside the spaces for the tally of bottles is a single narrow column *publisher of Pope* headed 'Memorandum'. Two specimen memoranda are given: *and Samuel* 'Claret from Mr——' and 'Lord—— dined here'. Either, I thought, *Johnson)* could make a rather neat title for this cellar book. For it is more about the memorandum than the tally.

The record-keeping problem today is not the number of bottles, *These days* it is the number of wines. A keen amateur may buy several hundred *people use the* different wines, and rarely more than a dozen of any single one. *Internet ....* A tally is still important: bottles can easily be mislaid in crowded racks. But even more vital is the note that reminds you of the taste of the wine, its quality, its value, and the food and the friends that went with it.

This book therefore allots rather more space to small quantities, or even individual bottles, than it does to larger parcels of wine that may make their stately way through perhaps two decades of your life.

Fine red bordeaux bought *en primeur*, at its first appearance on the market, is delivered to you between two and three years old. If you have bought a dozen you may taste the first bottle straight away to make its acquaintance, but the next bottle not for five years, and the next (if it is really good wine) not for another five. Then, when you are convinced it has reached the potential you paid for, you drink all but two bottles – which you probably keep out of nostalgia, or in case you should miss still further improvement. Eventually its page of biography makes wonderful nostalgic reading – not perhaps so useful, though, as the precise name of a miraculous Italian estate wine you found on holiday, brought home, enjoyed, entered in the book and intend to buy again – as soon as you can find it.

The most impressive and unusual private cellar I ever saw was under a dignified stone-built 18th-century rectory in the west of England. It was approached by either of two stately flights of stone steps, shallow in the tread and broad enough for two to walk abreast. They descended into a wide, squarish, stone-flagged chamber, lit by three or four embrasures only, cloistered all round with the comforting arches of bottle bins, arch over arch like the Pont du Gard. The Rector, you might imagine, entered right, conversing, chose the bottles to be brought up, then made his exit left, remarking to his companion how agreeably cool the wine would be.

Stately as it all was, what really fixed it in my mind forever was the evidence of the last incumbent's taste, the names chalked on the slates that hung one above each empty bin. There was no heterodoxy about this parson. Bollinger, the labels read, Clicquot, Moët, Krug. Below them Laurent Perrier, Heidsieck, Ayala, Pommery. On the right were Pol Roger, Mumm, Taittinger. To the left Lanson, Perrier-Jouët, Irroy, Goulet, Roederer, Mercier, Piper, Gratien, Gosset, Jacquesson and Ruinart.

I have often pondered upon this parson. Fond of Champagne, I wouldn't wonder. But how did he make up his mind?

As one who, like as not, goes to the cupboard for a bottle of sherry and comes out with two half-bottles of claret, I admire him prodigiously. 'Gosset!' do you think he exclaimed on waking. 'Is it a

Gosset day?' Or was he constantly distracted in his sermon-writing by the need to decide between Moët and Mumm before luncheon?

The Cellar Book: A Log Book and Guide for the
Personal Wine Collection, Hugh Johnson, Mitchell Beazley, 1986

POCKET WINE BOOK 1987
FOREWORD

This is the tenth annual edition of what I suppose must have become the world's most-consulted wine reference book. These ten years have been the most tumultuous in wine's long history. The trend has been steadily better quality from more and more proficient producers in more and more regions. Some of the exciting themes have been an astonishing run of good vintages in Bordeaux, the most imported wine region of all; the appearance of beautiful new wines from places where ten years ago there were none, and on the darker side some well-publicised (and in one case truly tragic⊙) scandals.

Italian wine tainted with methanol proved fatal

I described this book in its original introduction as an exercise in crowding angels on a pinhead, or students into a telephone box. That was in 1977, when I thought it was pretty ingenious to use symbols and a few abbreviations to make a pocketable encyclopaedia. Looking back at the first edition I realise that I was hardly squeezing at all compared with later efforts. Experience has taught me how to get angels to stand on other angels' shoulders, how to pick pygmy students, starve them and then shove like a Tokyo train-filler.

Hugh Johnson's Pocket Wine Book 1987, Mitchell Beazley

SLUICING THE INTAKE VALVE

My friend Egon Ronay⊙ astonished me the other day by aiming his regular *Sunday Times* column against those who taste and write about wine. They (or rather we) are 'a narcissistic circle', practising 'a barren abstract exercise'. ER is annoyed by the 'cant of the wine clergy'. Don't pause to inhale before you imbibe; not with the Great Inspector around. 'Bouquet' is merely a 'pleasing symptom' to be noticed in passing. What really matters, the only thing that matters, is what wine tastes like with food.

son of a Budapest restaurateur whose guide to Britain's restaurants was the standard reference book from 1957

We have been doing a spot of wine-and-food tasting recently at Reading⊙. The exercise is certainly rewarding, and a lot of fun. But it quickly becomes extremely confusing. How can you be sure that the satisfying combination of smoked trout and Sauvignon Blanc is unaffected by the mouthful of Chardonnay you just swallowed a moment before? What the combined flavours of a succession of

(then HQ of The Sunday Times Wine Club)

wines and foods do to one another is simply too complex for the available software – in other words your palate – to record and analyse in detail.

If you can't use your palate as a test-bench for controlled experiments, what you can use it for, and what wine tasters, Mr Ronay, do use it for, is to compare like with like (or indeed unlike) in the same medium. Is this an end in itself? Indeed it is – and why not? Concert-goers compare musicians, punters horses, philatelists stamps, critics novels, not insofar as they munch up in a satisfying mouthful with, let us say, gothic architecture or road-traffic statistics, but all by themselves, each in its separate compartment. That is what claret means to me: not just an alternative to beer for sluicing the intake valve when I'm masticating roast beef.

It's an odd thing, not often remarked, that the whole notion of matching food and drink, of studying the ways in which they complement (or swear at) one another, is a new invention. It has *(Robinson,* practically no literature. Jancis©, the brave girl, is writing a book *of course)* about it. André Simon wrote a very short one. But think of all the people who might have done and never did.

What is the best-known name in the whole philosophy of the table? Brillat-Savarin, surely. His *Physiologie du goût* is a good-tempered, well digested, thoroughly civilised ramble among the pleasures of eating and drinking. Does he discuss wine and food? Scarcely at all. Never, in fact, in direct relationship to one another. In his day, the first half of the 19th century, a meal was a meal – and not so much square as cubic – but the wine that went with it was required only to be plentiful.

Wine Times, 1987

IT CAN'T ALL BE DOWN TO CROCODILE DUNDEE

An Australian winery I visited in March had cut notches in its barrel for thirty-six Pommie visitors since Christmas. Different visits, that is – not a busload – the winemaker told me with glee, not with the resignation of an Aussie whose path has recently been crossed by an excess of Poms. From which I conclude that business resulted. Still and all, thirty-six is a lot of plane rides.

A great change has come over our attitude to Australian wine. A year or two ago it was still considered a pioneering effort to visit the Barossa Valley. Coonawarra was a funny word (it still is, but it is now also a name you can drop anywhere from the Médoc to Mendocino). What has changed so suddenly? The wines, or our perception of them? I had an ideal opportunity to pursue this question at a tasting in March at the Rothbury Estate in the Hunter Valley.⊛ Eighty of Australia's best wines were teamed up in a sort of Test Match against eighty wines from the US.

Rothbury was Len Evans's creation. He ruled as a benign tyrant – with prodigious results.

I was one of eight judges who had two days to put a hundred and sixty wines in order of merit in eight different classes: sparkling wines, Rieslings, Chardonnays, other dry whites, Cabernets, Pinot Noirs, other reds and sweet whites. It was tough going: the pace so fast that there simply wasn't time to stop and speculate about whether a given wine was from one side or the other. The indication that we tasted reasonably well and accurately came from the unanimity of most of our judgements.

The result? Australia won by an innings. Of the eight classes, Australian wines won five, American only two: Pinot Noir and sweet whites. The eighth class, Chardonnay, was a tie. Re-tasting only confirmed our view that the two best Chardonnays were equally splendid. (We all agreed, incidentally, that we would have liked to have had one or two of New Zealand's best in the match for comparison.)

My plea is for Australia's wineries to help their new fans by making it clear on their labels what the bottle contains, and by sticking to it year after year. 'New releases' with fancy bin numbers will turn off a Pom as rapidly as it will apparently turn on an Australian 'winey'.

If Australia will only make it a bit easier for us we will soon drink the place dry. But of course that is just what the canny Ockers want to avoid.

Wine Times, 1987

RESTAURANT KITCHO

The original Kitcho in Osaka (there are now half a dozen in Tokyo, Kyoto and elsewhere) remains the Mecca of *kaiseki*, the sort of picture-food with which Japanese tycoons follow the seasonal productions of nature without having to inspect her at first hand.

The Yuki family keeps a staunchly old-fashioned house, its threshold stone always gleaming in welcome, a pile of salt by the door to signal hospitality inside. A recommendation or introduction is essential, whether for foreigners or Japanese, before one of the exquisite (and enormous) tatami-floored⊛ rooms is made available. But then the theatre of Japanese hospitality takes over as waitresses in black kimono bring a succession of works of art, while never rising from their knees.

Japan's luxurious and sweet-smelling rush straw matting

I was the guest,
many times, of a
great authority
and teacher, Shizuo
Tsuji, whose École
Hôtelière Tsuji in
Osaka has taught
almost every
classical chef
in Japan.

A November meal started with a whole steamed crab seasoned with rice vinegar and ginger and decorated with pine needles and scarlet maple leaves – the autumnal theme. Next came a quenelle of quail in a delicate consommé, concealed in a lacquer bowl, plain black outside, dazzling with gold chrysanthemums within. The third course was a lobster served all but alive with raw tuna and sea bass, simply dipped in soya sauce.

Then came an intermission, with nothing more than a confection of shrimp and raw oyster and a sea urchin in aspic inside a half lemon, before the fourth and fifth courses: sea bass sashimi and smoked salmon from Hokkaido, presumably intended as an appetizer for the grilled salmon that followed, served only with a cool clean-tasting purée of white radish. End of Act Two.

Pause for a *yuzu* (citrus) sorbet before the introduction to the final Act; a little marvel of shrimp, potato, seaweed, spinach and lemon rind, followed by fingers of beef of melting tenderness grilled momentarily on a tiny charcoal stove (one to each guest) – which in turn introduced the rice-bowl climax of the meal – and its attendant miniature pickled vegetables.

Dessert was sliced persimmon and icy plum-sized peeled grapes, followed by crunchy sugared red beans with an earthenware bowl of thick frothy emerald tea.

The lacquer table, the alcove with its ancient scroll (changed every day) and single chrysanthemum, the succession of lacquer, wooden, earthenware and porcelain plates and dishes were as remarkable as the succeeding tableaux of food.

There would be little, if any, change from $300 a head.

New York Times, 1987

THE DEVIL RIDES IN

(Mitchell Beazley,
1988)

If ever I saw a book that was headed straight for the bestseller list, it was my advance copy of *Jancis Robinson On the Demon Drink*©.

Jancis works with precise calculation where the interest of the moment is. Two years ago, her marvellous book on grape varieties was as timely as it was thorough. And as witty too, which is much harder.

Now she has sniffed a faint fright in the air (not at all faint in America) about what alcohol is doing to us. Although she comes right from the tradition that we wine-lovers hold dear (*wine* is OK; we're safe from booze), she is rigorously honest and she has done her research. The assumption that wine-drinkers are protected is an illusion. Wine, as we all know, has several advantages/benefits: we tend to drink it contemplatively, more slowly than booze, usually with blotting paper in the form of food. But where our bodies are concerned, alcohol is alcohol. Its befogging effect can be dangerous. So can its effect on the liver and the ticker. Especially, Jancis sighs, to women. We should understand it better before we buy another round. And before we get hysterical about it, too.

On the Demon Drink is an important help. Avowed wine-lover and doter on old vintages as she is, she is totally clear-headed when it comes to overdoses. She compares wine with the drugs we don't accept and finds that the Muslim's cannabis is no odder or more antisocial than our Champagne. She has the unusual gift of remaining unbiased while clearly stating her own inclinations. Sometimes unbiased, I would say, to the point of unbalance. But you will know where you stand with this judge. You, the jury, can go and do your own thing with the confidence that the facts have been properly set before you.

I am eager to see what effect this book will have.[⊕] Here, of course, where it will be the subject of many a more-or-less reasonable after-dinner conversation, but even more in America, where anti-drink feeling has gone far beyond propaganda, right onto the statute book.

Perhaps, regrettably, not very much.

It is hard for us to realise just how hung-up America is about drinking today. The fact that the minimum age for buying (or being stood) a drink in public places – even restaurants – is twenty-one only sinks in when you are with young adults whose freedom and judgement are being curtailed and called in question by this amazing law. You can drive (in some states at fourteen). You can marry, have children, vote, kill and die for your country. But a glass of beer, no.

When I first realised this is no joke, trying to buy my twenty-year-old son a beer after dinner one evening in San Francisco, I threatened to arrest myself and go to the sheriff's office to surrender. The manager pleaded pathetically that his job was at stake.

Although this is technically a state law, it was federally imposed: Washington told every state that if they didn't bring it in, their federal highway budget would be cut. The reference to highways is part of the story, of course. MADD (or Mothers Against Drunk Driving) is a very powerful lobby. And, unfortunately, like so many pressure groups, it believes in coercion and rather than education.

Any fool can see, you would say, that if you treat adults as children they will despise the law and break it without remorse. Make alcohol the forbidden fruit, and what do you expect? Binges, surely, followed by drunk driving.

It is an alarming aspect of American society that it has no faith in common sense or in the ability of people to see where their best interests lie, and look after themselves. Americans, as far as their lawgivers are concerned, were all born yesterday.

Believe it or not, the forecourt of every gas station in California is compelled to carry a sign warning you that it sells petroleum products; that petroleum products give off vapours; and that if you take a deep breath it won't do you any good.

California has developed the statement of the obvious into a fine art. Wherever any alcohol is sold, a large sign informs you that drinking alcohol when you are pregnant may cause birth defects. Fair enough. Although, if this is so potent a threat one wonders how the French nation manages to keep going. But there is pressure to go further. Every wine label, say the peculiar citizens who wield power, should carry a warning: 'This bottle contains wine. Wine contains alcohol. Alcohol may damage your health.'

If only. It is creeping in everywhere. The nanny syndrome is peculiarly American.© After the Chernobyl disaster, American friends were aghast that we were actually eating lettuces from our garden.

It is considered antisocial today to stand up robustly and declare that your body is your own responsibility, and that you don't need instructions about how to use it. And yet this is where Jancis Robinson's book is so timely. Surely it is better to know than merely to suppose? It brings the argument right back to education. If we are to teach ourselves and our children moderation, it is no earthly use resorting to the failed weapons of Prohibition.

Wine Times, 1988

A MATTER OF TASTE

The more wines I taste and try to recall, the more I realise that my memory is like a floppy disc in more senses than one. But it's the limited capacity I'm worried about. Unfortunately no 'disc full' sign comes up when it is bursting at the seams with châteaux and vintages. It simply forgets; and not tidily from the top, but patchily in the places that matter most – or so it seems.

I could see that it was time to move on to a hard disc. What is a hard disc for memories? Nothing more IBM-compatible, I'm afraid, than a thick black notebook that lies on the kitchen dresser in which I enter every wine that I open in the kitchen, and most wines that I encounter away from home and jot down in my pocket book. I exclude batches of wines that I taste in more or less formal tastings, which have a filing system of their own (although a rather less fancy one than a disc of any persuasion, floppy or hard).

Most people, I'm afraid, when I mention writing notes on what things taste like, give me a wary look. Anything closer to the bullseye than 'scrumptious', 'fruity', or 'ugh' is widely considered to be a branch of literature only one degree easier than iambic heptameters.

This is where I make my pitch. I've just been reading (as you may have guessed from paragraph one) a word-processor manual, and anyone who can handle jargon at that level is going to find writing wine notes a doddle with three capital Ds.

These notes are valuable. Professionally, to me, of course they are essential. But their value goes far beyond what I need as my stock-in-trade. They represent a unique review of past pleasures (and other sorts of experience) that makes marvellous browsing. Shakespeare had a great line in *Julius Caesar* (Act II, Scene ii): 'Cowards die many times before their deaths; the valiant never taste of death but once.' Turn it on its head and you get the effect I'm driving at. The idle taste a wine but once; those who take notes re-taste it many times after the bottle has been consigned to the bottle bank. (Not quite as snappy as Will's version, I admit; but I'm working on it.)

No note-taker compares with Michael Broadbent. He has been filling little red books since 1952.

Wine Times, 1988

WHEN DID BURGUNDY BEGIN?

I realised this summer, on a trip to Burgundy that had more to do with television than with tasting, that I had never before been there in June.

One tends to get into a habit, in the wine business, of visiting certain places at certain times of year. I know Burgundy all too well in its winter dress (especially in the dampness of early November), and pretty well in autumn. I had simply never realised how lovely the countryside is in the late spring and early summer. The Côte d'Or has wild flowers then on a scale we have almost forgotten in England, and rush off to the Alps or the Pyrenees to see.

The untamed *friches*, the fringes of the upper vineyards where there is too little soil and too much rock for vines or forest, are a tapestry of flowers; the very rocks give birth to clumps of brilliant pinks. Honeysuckle smothers bushes of broom and dog rose (which smells even sweeter under its French name of *eglantine*). Cornfields on the higher ground – no doubt to the dismay of the farmers – are like great soldiers' coats, dyed scarlet with poppies.

It was historical Burgundy I was looking for. We all know its public face in the ramparts of Beaune and the polychrome tiles of the Hôtel-Dieu. Together with the Clos de Vougeot they form a cliché that is no less valid (and irresistible) for being so widely known. But this time I penetrated deeper, to visit the Cistercian brothers who still live their quiet industrious life on the site where their order was founded eight hundred and ninety years ago. I went to look for the traces of the Roman highway that first made Burgundy famous, and to see Burgundy's (perhaps France's) most astonishing treasure from antiquity, the greatest Greek vase that has ever been found.

Nobody knows for sure how old Burgundy is as a winegrowing region. The Romans are usually credited with having planted the Côte d'Or in the first or maybe the 2nd century AD, but there is a school of theory that believes the Gallic tribes from these parts were much too impatient to wait for the vine to come to them, and invaded Italy to fetch it for themselves. These Gauls occupied Lombardy in the 4th century BC, and even made an attempt on the city of Rome, in which they were foiled only by the famous noisy geese on the Capitol.

This line of argument is supported by the certain knowledge that wine was enjoyed and highly prized in Burgundy as early as 600 BC, but unsupported by any evidence that it was actually grown there. The evidence for its consumption is spectacular. In the 1950s the tomb of a Burgundian princess was discovered at Vix, a village near Châtillon-sur-Seine, not far northeast of Dijon. To the astonishment of the finders, the burial trappings of the young lady included a bronze 'crater' – the sort of vase the Greeks used for mixing wine with flavourings and water. But this crater is much the biggest (and one of the most beautiful) to have survived anywhere. Its capacity is 1,200 litres, and its decoration, a frieze of warriors in delicate relief, a marvel. Wild women in contortions form its two huge handles, and it is equipped with a tight-fitting lid, which seems to have served as some sort of strainer.

Its style, scholars say, is Greco-Italian or Etruscan, suggesting that it was made in what is now Campania, around the Bay of Naples. On what evidence I am not sure, but they say it arrived in Burgundy not via the Rivers Rhône and Saône, which seems the least laborious route, but right over the Alps. I have tried to picture this marvel of bronze being manhandled over the treeless wastes of the St Bernard Pass, but I give up. It seems impossible. The Burgundians must have been very fond of wine, or their princess, or both.

Yes, burgundy today is hideously expensive. But those who are privileged to drink it, and above all those who learn its mysteries in its own cellars, are not just buying a drink, however good. Burgundy is a communion with a culture as ancient and as uninterrupted as any in the whole of Europe.

Wine Times, 1988

THE STORY OF WINE
FOREWORD

Farmer and artist, drudge and dreamer, hedonist and masochist, alchemist and accountant – the winegrower is all these things, and has been since the Flood.

I wrote The Story of Wine *after making* Vintage, *a thirteen-part TV series on wine history.*

The more I have learned about wine in the course of a quarter of a century of enjoyment, the more I have realised that it weaves in with human history from its very beginnings as few, if any, other products do. Textiles, pottery, bread ... there are other objects of daily use that we can also trace back to the Stone Age. Yet wine alone is charged with sacramental meaning, with healing powers; indeed with a life of its own.

Why is wine so special? Partly because for most of its history, and mankind's, it has been his one source of comfort and courage, his only medicine and antiseptic, his one recourse to renew his tired spirits and lift him above his weary, saddened self. Wine was the foremost of luxuries to millennia of mankind.

It was the convention, when I began to read and write about wine, to provide each famous growth with a little flourish of history. This one was the favourite of Charlemagne, that of Henri IV, and the other the wine that cured poor Louis XIV of the ague. Classical scholars in particular were fond of referring to the apparently great wines of the ancients, yet never quite explained why their idea of fine wine and ours never matched. I remember thinking how little these anecdotes added to my enjoyment and understanding of what I was drinking, and in my first book, *Wine*, gave them rather short shrift. It was the taste of this mysterious, infinitely varied, infinitely subtle and perpetually inspiring drink that captivated me as a writer, because, first of all, of its utter elusiveness to words.

Of course it is, before all else, a human story. It begins with the worship of wine as a supernatural being: the bringer of joy. It climbs to the heights of dramatic inspiration, and descends to the depths of fraud, drunkenness, betrayal and murder. It involves passionate spiritual convictions, none more so than the Islamic belief that wine is too great a blessing for this world. It visits the physician at his task of healing, the politician in the act of cheating, the monk in his cell and the sailor at sea.

Wine, one might say, gave man his first lessons in ecology. It was at the birth of biochemistry. It has urged man forward in knowledge, and at the same time degraded him in stupor .... All in all, wine is a force to be reckoned with: and never has it been more topical than it is today. The time is ripe, if ever it was, to see it in its historical perspective.

A few opening
paragraphs to give you
a taste ...

the phrase was
coined in 1651 by
Thomas Hobbes
in his Leviathan,
reflecting the
horrors of the
English Civil War

THE POWER TO BANISH CARE It was not the subtle bouquet of wine, or a lingering aftertaste of violets and raspberries, that first caught the attention of our ancestors. It was, I'm afraid, its effect.

In a life that was nasty, brutish and short©, those who first felt the effects of alcohol believed they were being given a preview of paradise. Their anxieties disappeared, their fears receded, ideas came more easily, lovers became more loving when they drank the magic juice. For a while they felt all-powerful, even felt themselves to be gods. Then they were sick, or passed out, and woke up with a horrible headache. But the feeling while it lasted was too good to resist another try – and the hangover, they found, was only a temporary disease. By drinking more slowly, you could enjoy the benefits without suffering the discomforts.

Other foods and drinks had mind- (and body-) altering effects. Primitive people are acutely aware of poisons, but whatever spirit was in this drink, mysterious as the wind, was benevolent; was surely, indeed, divine. Wine, they found, had a power and value far greater than ale and quite unlike hallucinatory drugs. Its history pivots around this value.

Wine has certain properties that mattered much more to our ancestors than they matter to us. For two thousand years of medical and surgical history it was the universal and unique antiseptic. Wounds were bathed with it; water made safe to drink. Because it lives so happily with food, and at the same time lowers inhibitions, it was recognized from earliest times as the sociable drink, able to turn a meal into a feast without stupefying (although stupefy it often did). But even stupefied feasters were ready for more the next day.

Wine ships were
the earliest bulk
carriers: the tankers
of their time.

The catalogue of wine's virtues, and value to developing civilisation, does not end there. Bulky though it is, and often perishable, it made the almost-perfect commodity for trade. It had immediate attraction (as soon as they felt its effects) for strangers who did not know it. The Greeks were able to trade wine for precious metals, the Romans for slaves.

Taking this panoramic view, the discovery that must have done most to advance wine in the esteem of the rulers of the earth was the fact that it could improve with keeping – and not just improve, but at best turn into a substance with ethereal dimensions seeming to approach the sublime. Beaujolais Nouveau is all very well (and most ancient wine was something between this and vinegar), but once you have tasted an old vintage burgundy you know the difference between tinsel and gold. To be able to store wine, the best wine, until maturity performed this alchemy, was the privilege of pharaohs.

How can a rare bottle of wine fetch the price of a work of art? Can it, however perfect, smell more beautiful than a rose? No, must surely be the honest answer. But what if, deep in the flushing velvet of its petals, the rose contained the power to banish care?

WHERE GRAPES WERE FIRST TRODDEN It is late October in the steep-sided valleys of Imeretia⊕. A mist hides the slow windings of the Rioni, gorged with the noisy waters of Caucasian streams. Jason put in to the river mouth with his *Argo* and called the river Phasis. The land he called Colchis – the land of the Golden Fleece. They used sheepskins to filter the specks of gold that shimmered in the river shallows.

the western part of Georgia where it faces the Black Sea

At intervals all through the subtropical summer, fogs have invaded the Black Sea coastline in the afternoons of hot still days, softening the air in the tree-choked gullies where the streams run, and shading the rambling grape vines from the burning sun. Grape vines are everywhere: in stream beds, thick as dragons climbing forest trees, flinging themselves over pergolas, through orchards and against the walls of every wooden-balconied farmhouse.

Shaded by laurels among the vines beside the house, each farmer keeps his *marani* – his wine cellar. It is a mystery: there is no sign of wine, of barrels or vats or jars. A series of little molehills in the well-trodden earth is the only clue. The family bring the grapes here, in long conical baskets, and empty them into a hollowed-out log. When the log is half-full, the farmer takes off his shoes and socks, washes his feet with hot water from a bucket, then slowly and deliberately tramples the bunches until his feet feel no more resistance.

The molehills cover his wine jars, his *kwevris*⊕, buried to their rims in the ground. With a hoe he carefully opens one, chipping at the hill until it reveals a solid plug of oak under the clay. Into the *kwevri*, freshly scoured with a mop made of corn husks, he ladles the crushed grapes until they almost reach the brim. They will ferment in there, in the cool of the earth, slowly at first, then eagerly, then very slowly, popping single bubbles through a crust of floating skins.

the kwevri *is suddenly back in fashion, used to mature natural (and other) wines by experimentalists worldwide*

In the spring the wine is ladled out again, with a hollow gourd fixed on a pole, into another *kwevri*, leaving the skins – a potential source of fiery *tchatcha*, the grappa of the Georgians. Sealed up under its molehill, the wine will keep almost indefinitely. When the time comes to open it, there is no need to send out invitations.

KOTTABOS In about 600 BC some light-headed Sicilian colonist from Greece, leaning on his elbow at an after-dinner symposium, bet his friends that he could hit the lamp on top of its stand with the dregs in his shallow two-handled wine cup. Whether he put out the lamp or not, it was just the sort of Drones Club© idea that would catch on among the lighter element. Throwing bread rolls loses its magic after a while.

Bertie Wooster's club; also that of Catsmeat Potter-Pirbright and many other not-terribly-bright young men about town

The new game was baptised as *Kottabos*, and a crafty bronze-merchant designed a special stand, like a lampstand but with a tiny statuette on top, its arm held aloft. On the hand, precariously balanced, went a faintly concave bronze disc. Halfway up the stand he fixed a much larger bronze disc. The idea now was to dislodge the top disc, called the *plastinx*, so that it fell and hit the lower one, the *manes*, which when hit rang like a bell.

Kottabos became the rage. It spread back to Athens and Sparta, and for no less than three hundred years, during the whole period of Athenian ascendency, it remained the fashionable after-dinner game. It is portrayed on countless Greek vases (the only graphic depiction of Greek domestic life we have) and the rules are known from literature.

The best illustration is on an Athenian wine cooler that shows four ladies of the town, whose names might be rendered Slinky, Wriggly, Couchy and Sexy. Slinky, naked on a couch, is flicking her wine cup with the index finger of her right hand. The caption by the cup reads, 'I'm throwing this for you, Leagros'. Other paintings show more decorous players in action, but leave no doubt at all how Kottabos was played, nor how popular it was.

I have had a Kottabos stand made, and practised assiduously. From personal experience I can say it is not at all easy. The best trainers advise a very high arching shot, so that the wine falls onto the plastinx from above. But liquid does not easily dislodge bronze, however delicately balanced. And it makes a terrible mess on the floor.

Have I found a use for all those wet rooms in expensive London basements?

MERCHANTS OF VENICE It is a fine November day in the Bay of Biscay – too fine for the wine fleet: almost two hundred ships spread out from horizon to horizon. Their great square sails, gaudy with dragons and crosses and leopards, are hanging flaccid and useless. The master of the *Margery Cross*, a heavy cog or round ship from the port of Boston on the east coast of England, is looking out from the high sterncastle for any flurry on the oily swell that could mean a breeze.

He has a hundred and sixty tuns of claret before and aft his great chunky mast. It has taken two weeks from Bordeaux to get this far; the weather is unseasonably warm; at this rate he could still be at sea come Christmas, the market past and the wine turning sour.

A dozen of the crew are throwing leather buckets over the sides and hauling them up to the yard to soak the sail, the only effect being that the *Margery Cross* wallows slightly more ponderously as each unhelpful roller lifts her port quarter and trundles on towards England. There is nothing else for the master's forty mariners to do – and not much for them to eat, either. He has his passport for Port St-Mathieu where there should be bread and meat, but until then the rations are bread and claret – and not very much bread.

His eyes follow a gull to the horizon astern. What is that? Three, no four, strange broad ships, very low in the water, their masts bare of any sail, but definitely coming clearer into view, closing the gap at an impossible speed. Once or twice a flash like a mirror in the sun breaks from the water low beside one of them. Oars! He has heard of the galleys that keep an uncanny, an impossible schedule between Genoa or Venice and Southampton. The merchants of Southampton had craftily convinced the king to give them a monopoly on importing Mediterranean wines, which did not endear them to the wine merchants of other English ports.

Now the crew have seen them too, and are crowding to the stern with their foul language and their fouler breath. The Winchelsea cog, groaning as she rolls three chains off to starboard, has suddenly come alive, with half her crew in the rigging, shaking their fists at the galleys. Now clear to see, four in formation, with what seems like a thousand oars beating the water: four brown and gleaming birds flapping their wings.

Within the morning they have passed through the becalmed fleet, all agog at their mechanical propulsion. On each side were three banks of oars, twenty blades to each. The great lateen sails furled on the two masts' booms pulled hard for most of the journey, but when the wind died the oarsmen, each one a small private trader with his bag beneath his bench, bent their backs to beat their famous schedule. A Venetian galley had made the record passage in thirty-one days from Otranto on the heel of Italy to Southampton on the Solent.

As they creamed through the fleet, the archers on the decks of the galleys raised a cheer, then lifted their crossbows and sent a broadside of bolts high through the air, puncturing the impotent heraldry of the sails and here and there thudding with a shock into a mast. The arrogance of the Venetians was not to be borne.

BARCOS RABELOS Today the Douro is a sequence of lagoons between hydroelectric dams, placid except for the waterskiing families of the port shippers, but up until the 1960s much of the journey downriver could still be made by *barco*.© With thirty or forty pipes of port piled high on board, the unwieldy ship cruised quietly enough along calm stretches of water, then became agitated as soon as one of the many rapids approached. In the mounting clamour of river over rocks, with high stone banks closing in to form a gorge, the oarsmen took a deep swig from a big wooden bottle, then with nerve and sinew directed the accelerating vessel towards the main channel, while the helmsman, perched high on a rickety bridge astern to look out for rocks ahead, shouted directions. With a sense of huge weight effortlessly propelled, the boat plunged quivering down the white-water sluice, sheets of spume flying from the bow, then settled calmly among the whirling eddies while the helmsman set her prow straight for the next *cachao*.

AN AMERICAN VIEW In 1784 at the age of forty-one, Thomas Jefferson was dispatched (as Commissioner, then Minister) by the new government of the United States to France – to his considerable distaste. 'I would go to hell for my country', was his reaction; and his journals in France make clear that he found its government diabolical. He was a laconic, not to say terse, journalist. You meet almost nobody and see few sights in his daily chronicle; just statistics, details of the land and its produce, a panorama of more or less starving peasantry, and damning reflections on the regime that was about to pass away.

Among the few moments of (moderate) enthusiasm are when, in his two excursions through France and Italy in 1787 and 1788, he reaches wine regions. Jefferson was eager to learn about winegrowing: not only in order to introduce it to America, but also to supply himself with the best wines he could buy.

MAPPING THE CÔTE If your hot-air balloon were to land you on the hill of Corton, or in the vineyards of Volnay or Chambertin, on a spring day two hundred and fifty years ago, you would know exactly where you were – supposing, that is, that those hillsides are familiar to you now. You would rub your eyes at the strange dense tangle of vines without wires putting out green shoots around you. (The villagers would rub their eyes, too: the Montgolfier brothers, inventors of the Aerostat, had not yet produced their first model.) You would be surprised to see the panorama of vines broken up with so many hedges and walls. But fundamentally, from the church spire in the cleft of the hills at Volnay to the beret of woodland on the brow of Corton, you would be looking at the same vineyards that appear today. And when you found your way to a cellar you would be offered, in your silver tastevin, a not-very-different wine. The rising mint-fresh scent of the Pinot Noir would tell you that this was indeed the Côte d'Or. The scent above all is the clue. In the words of Claude Arnoux, the priest who wrote *Dissertation sur la situation de la Bourgogne* in 1728⊚, the wines of Burgundy have 'sweet vapours'. They are drunk 'in two ways, through the nose and through the mouth, either at the same time or separately.'

he doubled as a wine merchant, and aimed his wares at England

REVOLUTION AND AFTER The glinting wedge-shaped dead weight of the guillotine in its fatal drop is such a powerful symbol of the end of the old regime, not just in France but in all of continental Europe, that it is tempting to think of a new world in new hands at the start of the 19th century.

The wars that followed, as Napoleon came close to turning Europe into a French Empire and the Mediterranean into a French lake, obscure with battle-smoke the petty affairs of the next twenty years. When the smoke clears, it is a surprise to see so much that is familiar still in place; incredible that one-and-a-half million Frenchmen have been led off to more or less glorious deaths and France continues to function: vintage after vintage picked, trodden and consumed.

The bottles are still in their bins at Château Lafite: none for the fateful year of 1793 when the owner, President Pichard, was taken to the guillotine, but some marked 1797, the year Bonaparte chased the Austrians out of Italy, and 1799 when, having declared that 'this little Europe is too small for me', he abandoned his attempt to take the Ottoman Empire as well, left his army in Egypt and scuttled back to France. The bottle of 1803 marks the return to war after thirty months of fitful peace; that of 1811 a superlative vintage and the retreat from Portugal of Marshal Massena, '*l'enfant chéri de la Victoire*'.

In the peninsula the chaos of war raged around the two principal wine-exporting centres, Oporto and Jerez, and to a lesser extent Málaga. Both Oporto and Cádiz were besieged, and yet their trade continued. The fighting spared their vineyards. The war in Portugal, where the Duke of Wellington and the best part of the British army were deeply engaged for three years, was to make a whole generation of British officers proudly familiar with every shade of Portuguese wine – as well as the port they knew so well already. Their entertainment in Oporto alone was enough to addict them to its liquor for life.

The Story of Wine, Hugh Johnson, Mitchell Beazley, 1989

YOUR CALL

Every wine critic should sometimes ask him- or herself the question: what would I do if I were a wine trader? Trader can mean anything from group buyer for a vast multinational to corner liquor-store owner. The question is, where would I stand if I had to make my living by buying and selling wine?

Some of us have an abacus between the ears: everything goes click with the beads at one end or the other. Others don't know how many fingers they have. The world is out there waiting for them. Let's suppose that we are not innumerate, but that what we put first is our pleasure in wine: for ourselves and other people. What would our personal priorities be? What, in other words, do we think is a really good wine merchant?

First, because wine is all about variety, we have to offer breadth of choice. Sure, you can drink Mountain Red night after night and get the basic buzz that wine offers. But are we in the wine business to sell a short one-way trip?

You and I believe, because our senses keep telling us, that wine was made to wake us up to beauty, not to send us into a senseless stupor. Its beauty lies in its variety, its infinite nuances, its trick of never being precisely the same again.

A choice, then. What choice? We can't buy, store, list, handle, every wine there is. Not even this year's releases. So we choose a way to narrow them down. Now comes the testing part: you can narrow by demand or you can narrow by quality. Are your shelves going to be lined with every well-known brand, or by the wines that you have tasted, compared, thought about and liked and want your customers to taste too?

God, how hard it is to be honest, even with yourself. You tasted a glorious, a singing Riesling the other day; then you read that it had scored 63 out of 100 on a magazine panel. Your judgement falters: if that's what they say, maybe I got carried away. Carried away is exactly what you have to be. How did Gerald Asher[©], did Robin Yapp, did Kermit Lynch become wine-lovers' saints?[©] By being carried far beyond averaged scores, by a moment of recognition that the wine they tasted was both true and beautiful, and that unless they said so they betrayed both it and, more importantly, themselves.

Personal taste does not just come into it, therefore; it *is* it. I don't mean that I would buttonhole customers in my store and make them hear what I drank the night before and how divinely it went with whatever it was we were eating with the cilantro. I can't abide slick

Gerald Asher went bust and became a writer; Robin Yapp was a dentist, hence solvent; Kermit Lynch hit the American mood precisely.

patter when I am deciding what to buy. I want guidance, and the best sort of guidance is confidence that the buyer bought what he thought best.

I like specialised stores. In England we have one retailer who sells nothing but Champagne – much of it from small producers who can't afford to advertise, and whose wines are full of village character. Another one-region merchant does only Beaujolais. Beaujolais is a huge region with thousands of growers. Most merchants spare it a day or two, see a broker (or more likely Georges Duboeuf), make sure the label is legal, has a pretty flower on it, and then wait for the wine to arrive back home. Roger Harris spends months in Beaujolais. He knows the growers, their family histories, their foibles, their wives' cooking ... perhaps he has gone overboard for Beaujolais. There are other wine regions. But what a pleasure for him (and how lucky for us) that he finds fulfilment in knowing one region inside out.

Single-producer Champagnes were rare in the 80s.

Which region would I choose? If (and I don't think it will happen) I were to dedicate my declining years to one sort of wine it would not be such a difficult choice as all that. It wouldn't be Champagne – much as I love it. Good Champagne is easy to find, and what Champagnes have in common (bubbles) is in the end more striking than what they don't. It wouldn't be burgundy; I find it too heady to drink regularly – alas. Bordeaux would be the obvious choice, perhaps; but another element comes into it. Bordeaux is commercial, chic, intellectual, snobbish, extremely worldly – but fun is not one of its talents. And fun is what wine is all about.

So what's on the fun list? Robert Parker finds it down the Rhône. Far too earnest for my liking (also too heady). Burton Anderson finds it in Italy, and so do I, though they make me eat too much and I need Burt to explain to me which wine is which. I find it in Andalucia – boy, do I find it! Sherry is my passion: but not for life.

California, then? I love the wine; I love the people. They are just too intense about one another. Australia? Definitely – except that all that relentless enthusiasm would eventually send me up a gum tree.

For a life's work I think I'll plump for Germany. It's a funny thing, but in all the wine world, the Germans (also the Austrians) are the ones who know best how to enjoy their own wine. They invented the flowery terrace, the snug fire-corner, the carousel (that brilliant instrument for centring discussion on a dozen glasses of slightly different wines). They keep barrels separate for the sheer fun of discussing the differences. They store old bottles like a lovely liquid part of their memories. They invented the range of organ stops that makes Kabinett, Spätlese, Auslese, and the bigger pipes complement each other without competing.

They also have the prettiest wine country in the world, and a range from gothic Mosel to baroque Franconia that will keep me happy for as many years as I'm allowed. One more thing: their wines have the least alcohol. Alcohol I don't need.

I won't be part of a Gadarene rush. Not many of us are tuned in to the world's greatest white wines. If I were any good as a wine merchant, though, they soon would be.

Wine Times, 1989

INTO THE NINETIES: A SPOT OF PROPHESY

I confess I never quite know what the media are driving at when they use a decade as shorthand for a mood, a style, or a way of living. We are supposed to nod wisely when a journalist says how very 'sixties' someone is. I'm too dim to get it. To say that some splendid person is a proper '61, on the other hand, or some wretch is a mouldy little '65, strikes me as a very acceptable shorthand. A vintage year and its quality are historical facts that gradually permeate our wine-loving consciousness. The great ones stay there for a very long time.

That said, the decade of the 80s is the exception that proves the rule. If ever there were a vintage decade, this was it – at least in the regions whose successes and failures make most impact and lodge longest in our memories: Bordeaux and Burgundy. Seven (in Burgundy six) good-to-excellent vintages out of ten is, as far as I know, an unprecedented record. And the less thrilling vintages of the decade were all at least good tries: none of the dishwater that disgraced '63, '65, '68 and '72 in Bordeaux, and '74 and '77 in both.

Credit for great vintages goes to the weather. It may well have been a winegrower who first said 'I like the greenhouse effect.' With its summer that wouldn't end, after the winter that never came, 1989 is so fresh in the memory that it is tempting to extrapolate a trend towards sunnier conditions, especially in the late summer and autumn, and especially in the more northerly regions.©

Global warming? How could I have known?

Credit for saving potentially bad vintages, on the other hand, goes to science. Twenty years, even ten years before, a great part of '84 and '87 would have been written off. But prosperity and science have advanced together to provide a safety net. They also lessen the ever-present chance of something going wrong in the vat room when the grapes are super-ripe and the weather still hot: the cause of many disappointing wines in the past. The winegrower's prosperity is the wine-drinker's guarantee. In a historical context I suspect that it will be technology, not sunshine, that will be remembered as the achievement of the 80s. Technology, and the entry into the international arena of two revitalised wine countries of tremendous significance for the future: New Zealand and Chile.

The 90s will also see the long-overdue revival of appreciation of Germany's wines.[⊕] It has been painful to watch German producers cravenly trading down, apparently frightened that if they charge more than a few pence for their product nobody will buy it. They have been demoralised, it is true, by a run of twelve vintages with only one thoroughly good, and none great.[⊕] Germany needs its occasional bumper year of sumptuous Ausleses, and there was none between 1976 and 1988. But 1988 will set the ball rolling again. The very first sniff of it made me realise just how much I had missed the glorious fragrance of truly ripe German Riesling: the most glamorous, eyelash-fluttering, irresistible scent in the whole seductive wardrobe of wine.

I've been guilty of wishful thinking before.

The good one was 1983.

German growers will make their labels easier to understand, let their wines achieve natural dryness, and reconquer with their penetrating flavours and low levels of alcohol their rightful position as first choice for an apéritif bottle, or white wine for the first course at dinner, or the whole of lunch.

So the 90s have a flying start. What can we expect and hope to see between now and the end of the century? Many exciting developments, I am certain – although against a background of steadily falling overall world wine consumption. Wine as a mere commodity, I suspect, will continue to dwindle in importance as it has over the past ten years. Wine as the essential seasoning to meals, as a minor art form, and I'm afraid as a status symbol, will advance strongly, despite determined sniping from puritans and health-fascists. By the end of the century there will be enough medical evidence of the benefits of moderate wine-drinking finally to silence all but the lunatic fringe.[⊕]

Closest to home, the 90s will see the acceptance of English wine as a serious contender. The '89 vintage, the biggest and best ever (probably) in this country, will start a craze.[⊕]

More wishful thinking, I'm afraid.

It's taken twenty more years, but it's happening now.

The excellence of our Reichensteiners and Schönburgers will lead to bolder experiments with other grapes. Already Riesling of first quality has been made in Devon. Once it is widely known that fine English wine, with naturally high acid levels, gains enormously with five years or even more of bottle-age, trade in it will gain confidence. Already we have the heartening sight of brown signposts all over southern England pointing to local vineyards. As wine culture pervades the rural south, we have wonderful times to look forward to.⊕

I failed to anticipate our bubbly revolution of the 2010s.

The advance of sparkling wine is set to continue. Champagne will find ways of expanding and increasing its output. It will also expand its pioneering activities in California, Australia and South America to supply these markets with impeccable local sparkling wine. Champagne money will probably turn up in Italy and Spain, whose potential for excellent mousseux is undoubted, but relatively undeveloped.

Burgundy will be fully restored in the world's confidence, after three decades of doubt. During the 80s new pride and new ideas challenged the old establishment: a new openness and accessibility among young growers contrasted with an often leaden performance by rich and historic merchant houses. Côte d'Or wines will become more and more the drink of millionaires and the most expensive restaurants – and so, alas, will the wines of the northern Rhône, thanks to Robert Parker. Perhaps we should be grateful that he has not yet discovered Germany.

Can Bordeaux climb even higher in the world's regard? Improbable as it seems, I believe the ambitions of its less-privileged proprietors, with their crus bourgeois, are raising the base level all the time. A farmhouse kitchen can produce as perfect a meal of its kind as a grand hotel kitchen can, and that is what hundreds of quite substantial properties are doing.

In the inescapable comparison with the red wines of California and Australia, it remains brutally true that only a relative handful of New World wineries have yet offered wines with the style, the individuality, and the harmony that can be found at hundreds of Bordeaux châteaux. Given the apparent trend in the climate, recent technology and current ambitions, the future is as rosy for Bordeaux as it has ever been – and for Sauternes, with more income paying for greater selectivity with each harvest, it is even rosier.

Nor can I see any reason why the same favourable influences should not work in the rest of France. We are already seeing the relatively obscure appellations of the southwest, Jurançon, Gaillac, Cahors, Madiran, polishing their acts and their images. Even the humble *vin de pays* is becoming a respected world traveller.

Among our other principal European wine suppliers, Italy (like Germany) will go through a wine-law crisis as the impenetrability of its labelling system, or lack of one, seriously hampers the progress of its finer wines. The tendency will be to concentrate more on fewer grape varieties, and improve them by selection. Sangiovese will emerge as the noble variety of Tuscany, and the Nebbiolo of Barolo and Barbaresco will consolidate in Piemonte at the expense of Barbera, Dolcetto and the rest. Piemonte and Tuscany will also see more and more Chardonnay and Cabernet Sauvignon, not used for blending but made, California-style, as 'varietals'.⊖

Spain has a much harder palm to read. Few of her regions have any fine-wine tradition; when an individual initiative produces a splendid result it may be in a moribund region, or a flourishing one, or one with no tradition at all. It is noteworthy that the Torres family remains almost alone in symbolising energetic experiment and production, however good the wines of, for example, Raimat in Catalonia, or some of the most up-to-date Rioja bodegas (Martínez-Bujanda, for example) may be.

I was wrong here. The rise of little-known local varieties is one of the most exciting current trends.

Attention has focused recently on the Duero with its blockbuster reds. Rioja, I am sure, is preparing its riposte, and Navarre will follow. But Spain in ten years will not have joined the international varietal-wine formula as Italy will. The Tempranillo, under its various regional guises, will remain the key quality red-wine grape. Sherry, by concentrating on quality rather than quantity, will have regained some, but not all, of its sadly lost ground.

Portugal presents a clearer picture. During the 80s the long official domination of the quality 'mature' wine market by the Dão region was successfully challenged by Bairrada, the peninsula, the Ribatejo, the Douro and the Alentejo. Red wines of intense character and interest, sold before under neutral blenders' labels if at all, blossomed in the public gaze. Some are still rather rough and ready, but their potential is clear, and their future assured.

Vinho verde is in a less-confident position, unable to trade much upmarket, and probably about to find that cheap sweet fizz has dwindling appeal. Port has no such worries, and Madeira is overdue for a strong revival: ten years hence I expect to see Madeira back in its place as the conventional alternative to port.⊖

It's coming – but it's quite expensive.

One of the most surprising wines I have tasted in the last few months was a Chardonnay made by an Italian firm in Virginia: crisp, elegant, distinctly Chardonnay and a real, if fairly lightweight, pleasure. Nobody is surprised any more by good Chardonnays from Long Island, and even upstate New York. This will be the great development of the 90s in America⊖: the decentralisation of winegrowing from California to likely and unlikely spots all

I was right here: Virginia is on track, and so are many other states.

over the country. Not that California is going to stop expanding its production: national demand will see to that. It is hard to see how anything can stop the mad modishness of Chardonnay©. Perhaps the process will begin at the beginning, as it were, with the realisation that there are far better apéritif wines than a thumping great Golden State Special.

though Sauvignon Blanc is trying hard

'Meritage' is the inappropriately tacky term now officially applied to California's most interesting category of reds: cross-variety blends that are technically neither Cabernet nor Merlot. Despite its name, this group will grow. So will the range and quality of Pinot Noir, although we may have a wait till the 21st century to see the Petite Sirah take its rightful place on the West Coast.

Pinot Noir will become the flagship wine of Oregon in the northwest. But it is in the state of Washington that it will blossom into a full range of intensely aromatic, well-balanced, reliable and versatile wines. Curiously Seattle, its capital, is one of the principal nests of anti-wine agitation in the US. We should see some interesting developments here.

'Cool climate' is the catchphrase of the 2010s, not just in Australia.

The only thing that can stop Australia's progress is its turbulent weather, as its sad vintage of 1989 made clear. All eyes are now turned on the Yarra Valley just outside Melbourne, as the coming region for the 90s. Its 'cool-climate' wines certainly have that delicacy that eludes most of the established Australian vineyard regions; at the same time they often need longer to mature. Whether as estate wines or in typically Australian inter-region blends, they have a brilliant future. By the same token (and especially if the globe really is warming up) we should watch Tasmania – and of course New Zealand.

We have seen the fruit of only young plantations in New Zealand: white wines of intense and luscious aromas, with seemingly ideal acid balance; but not so far wines to mature. This will change as the vines put down deeper roots, and eventually perhaps produce smaller crops. On the present evidence we have not just wickedly tempting, but positively noble, wines to look forward to.

The 1980s saw the emergence of Chile as a significant exporter outside of South America (she has long been the domestic favourite). That Chile could make splendid wines, above all Cabernets, had been known for a century or more. But politics had made her impotent, deprived her of resources and technology, and kept her in the twilight, losing three-quarters of the potential of her marvellous grapes in primitive presses and shoddy unhygienic old cooperage. From the mid-80s all this began to change. Once stainless steel is installed, control and cleanliness can do the rest. We have just seen the first two or three vintages of one of the world's most exciting prospects – not just for Cabernets, but also for every noble grape variety, growing, what is more, on its own roots. Phylloxera has never reached this mountain-and-ocean-locked country.

Argentina had yet to make its bow, and South Africa was still beyond the pale.

Out of all these prospects for future pleasure, which is the sleeper? In my mind, it is one of the least-touted regions of all, the long- (and usually justly) maligned Midi of France. Slowly the French are waking up to the fact that the long haul to the Napa Valley may not be necessary to find warm and wonderful growing conditions. France may have her own, in the Languedoc, the Aude, Corbières, Roussillon ... regions we wrinkled our noses at until only the other day. I'll lay even money on Cabernets and Chardonnays from the Midi winning gold medals before the 90s are up. And by that time gold medals will take an awful lot of winning.

My score, then? Perhaps eight out of ten.

Wine Times, 1989

The 1990s

WINE OUT EAST

L e Beaujolais Nouveau *était arrivé* – at £6 a glass – when I checked in to the Hotel Okura in Tokyo in November. It was on offer everywhere: with the sashimi, the sushi, the tempura, the sukiyaki; in the Chinese restaurant, in the coffee shop and from room service. The tent-card in my room suggested a bottle at £35 as a modest alternative to half a bottle of Champagne at £40.

I'm not sure which surprises me more: Japan's new enthusiasm for wine or the prices that the Japanese seem happy to pay. Despite much rumour to the contrary, not everything in Japan costs a fortune. Tokyo land prices are certainly stratospheric, yet a room in the capital's equivalent of The Savoy or Claridge's is not just cheaper; it is half the price. Hotel restaurants are very expensive (and very good), but a delicious and colourful Japanese meal in a little place just round the corner from your hotel is cheaper than it would be in London.

Some of these paradoxes can be explained simply by what is considered fashionable. It remains, alas, fashionable to eat dinner at seven or even earlier, and then retire to a 'club' in Ginza, which could more or less be described as the West End of Tokyo, to drink and be flirted with by the hostesses whose job (or most of it) is to speed the ebb-tide in your bottle of Hennessy XO or Dom Pérignon.©

It was strictly business that took me to these dens of iniquity.

Not, I should add, that they themselves do much drinking. They just put Coca-Cola on your bill at £10 a glass. But they contrive, while snuggling their little knees distractingly under yours on the crowded banquettes, to pour rapid rounds into every glass within reach. In the limited light (and cigarette fug) you scarcely notice when Mimi from Thailand, whose secret yearnings to be a nurse you were just beginning to learn, removes her knees and Maria from the Philippines slips hers into the vacant slot.

Nobody seems to stay long in these dispensaries. One £250 bottle of Dom Pérignon and it is time to move, via another dim lobby and crowded lift, to another 'club' – where it also happens to be Madame's birthday, and mounds of plastic-wrapped bouquets give the grand piano that half-fills the room all the allure of a coffin.

Am I digressing? It would be a shame to waste my painstaking research merely because some of it has little to do with wine. Wine does indeed have a growing presence in Japanese life, but it is still a commodity viewed with puzzlement, and perhaps a little alarm, by the great majority of Japanese.

April 1st, 1989 was a key date. It was when the government abolished an ad valorem tax of 50 per cent on wine imports, making them able to compete on something like equal terms with domestic wines. Among more expensive imports its impact was spectacular, slashing the price of a bottle of good claret from, say, £35 to £25. The basic retail price of French *vin de pays* is now about £4. So if the Japanese like wine, real imported wine, they can certainly afford to drink it at home – if not in hotels and restaurants.

Much 'Japanese' wine was imported: blended and bottled in Japan.

Yet funnily enough, drinking it at home is just what they are not doing. The evidence is that the real growth in Japanese wine-drinking is in hotels and restaurants – and hang the expense. Japan being Japan, there is also a large and precisely defined (indeed highly structured) 'gift market', in which the exact degree of respect / fear / affection / veneration felt by donor for donee is reflected in the (undisguised) price of the bottles involved. A two-pack of domestic wine is the humble starting point; a limited-edition engraved crystal decanter of Hennessy is cabinet-level stuff.

Hotels and restaurants (but mainly hotels) have the wine initiative because they have the expertise, the Western-style cooking – and the space. It is not easy to give a dinner party in most Japanese apartments, let alone hold an extended family or business gathering. The restaurants and banqueting departments of hotels are the beneficiaries.

Skyscraper luxury hotels are springing up in all Japan's principal cities. Their chefs are trained in France, and their sommeliers in my experience are quite simply the most highly qualified and skilful practitioners of their mystery on earth.

Having lunch last year with twenty-five of Japan's top hotel sommeliers in a sumptuous dining room overlooking Kobe harbour, I reflected that nowhere in Europe (certainly not in France) could you assemble such a broadly knowledgeable and articulate group of professionals to do the job of interpreting wine to consumers. The conversation was on an extraordinarily high level, both as to fact and understanding. (So was the service: glasses, decanting, temperatures and the rest were impeccable.)

I was not only asked why I had chosen a particular wine for the fish or the entrée, but also whether I did not think that a different vintage, or a different grower, or a different wine altogether might not have been a better or more original choice. Ideas came thick and fast; this was postgraduate stuff and no mistake. It was also, I reflected, what the consumer was paying for at prices that made me blench.

A recent research project into Japanese wine-drinking habits produced some perfectly predictable results. That 'wine-drinkers are generally better educated and have higher disposable incomes than non-wine-drinkers', for example. One finding foxed me though: unmarried women in their twenties are the largest group of wine consumers. So that's what Mimi and Maria get up to when they are off duty.

Wine Times, 1990

AARON'S ROD

Then on Madison Avenue, now at 505 Park, Sherry's has been the carriage-trade Manhattan retailer since the 1940s.

To write an introduction to a Sherry-Lehmann catalogue is probably the nearest a foreigner will ever get to delivering a State-of-the-Union message.© The certainty that every person of consequence in the country will neglect his morning *New York Times* until he sees what 'Sherry's' has to offer makes it an awesome responsibility. Knowing that these words will be seen – may even be read – by politicians, financiers, physicians and scientists, men and women of the highest rank (even lawyers) – makes me pick them with more than usual care.

What I am introducing is of course the choicest selection of wines, imported and homegrown, available in New York and far, far beyond. Selection is the key word. We all know liquor-stores (bottle shops might be a better description) that seem to carry one bottle each of every single wine, spirit and beer produced between Tierra del Fuego and the Turpan Depression. We all know the sinking feeling that comes when you walk into a store and find that every one of Napa's 498 Cabernets is in there hollering to be bought.

A real wine-merchant's role, I have always believed, is to do a thorough sorting-out job. The wines he offers should not be competing with each other because all have already won the prize that matters: his approval. Approval, that is, as to quality, character and value for money.

After that it is simply a matter of your personal taste. Amazingly Sherry's even seems to be able to help you with that. I understand that a career diplomat with a master's degree in psychology is the minimum requirement for a place behind the counters on Madison Avenue.

I chanced to be in New York at the historic moment in 1965 when the Aaron brothers, Jack and Sam, absorbed the marginally snootier house of Lehmann. The Aaron presence in the store today is Michael, Jack's son and the present President, who joined the firm in 1958. The state's lawmakers have found that wine consumers have a formidable advocate in Michael Aaron. You couldn't buy wine by credit card, or buy wine books in wine stores, until Michael

Michael retired in 2008.

persuaded them to let his customers have what they wanted. When New York City threatened a wine tax last year, it had an Aaron to deal with – and the tax has not materialised.

Yet this is no time to be complacent. Federal imposts on alcohol are on the way. Anyone surveying the present position of wine in America must be concerned at how deeply entrenched the forces of reaction have recently become. To a European weaned on wine, aware from childhood of its life-enhancing force, it is close to tragic to see the prejudices that can surface in the land of the free.

Every conceivable accusation has been thrown at wine-drinking – often, I suspect, by research teams at obscure universities, certain of a grant-inducing headline if they lob yet another medical misgiving over the parapet. Such headlines are seldom denied and never retracted; the news value is in the smear, not the truth.

Recently a California winery was denied permission by the Bureau of Alcohol, Tobacco and Firearms to quote Thomas Jefferson on a label, because it happens that Jefferson believed deeply in wine. It is the bureau's business, it seems, to protect the citizen from the opinions of former presidents.

For anyone who does not already know it by heart, let me quote a passage from Jefferson once more. 'I rejoice,' he wrote, 'as a moralist at the prospect of a reduction of duties on wine by our national legislature .... No nation is drunken where wine is cheap, and none sober where the dearness of wine substitutes ardent spirits as the common beverage.' He must be turning in his grave about the current legislation.

In the name of sobriety, Sherry-Lehmann, I salute you.

Sherry-Lehmann Wine & Spirits Merchants Catalog, 1990

THE ART AND SCIENCE OF WINE
INTRODUCTION

The rusty cannon gives the Moutardes' yard, divided from the village street by iron railings, its faint air of a comic-opera set. It was last fired in 1964, when a cloud the colour of aubergine and the size of the Muligny vineyards, hanging above the next-door commune Chassard, began to roll towards the Clos du Marquis.

Using a borrowed tractor, Père Moutarde had towed the weapon into the vineyards, loaded it with a canister of grapeshot from c1815, levelled it at the heart of the threat, and plucked up his courage to apply the taper. The explosion was thunderous. Nobody in Chassard was sure whether what clattered down on several roofs was a flurry of hail or straying grapeshot. The cloud rolled on,

I thought my introduction to this book should give a flavour of how things were before science came into the picture. Hence my invention of a true peasant son of Burgundy, Monsieur Moutarde.

menacing but still costive, over Muligny and three more communes before suddenly dumping its humbug-size hailstones on the scruffy oak wood above Beaune.

The oaks were shredded: not a leaf left. But in Chassard relief for the spared vines was tempered by unneighbourly feelings towards Monsieur Moutarde – indeed towards Muligny as a whole. The two villages had never exchanged more than civilities, not in two thousand years.

Things were different then, in the early 60s, in several ways. For a start, nobody had any money – or if there was any cash in the mattress it meant a harvest mortgaged to a merchant in Beaune. The way the Moutardes made wine had changed very little since the Middle Ages. The most evident progress lay in the vineyards which, since phylloxera, had been far more uniform than before: orderly rows of grafted vines that got a good dusting of sulphur and a bright-blue spray of *bouillie bordelaise*© as often as the weather and Monsieur Moutarde's energy and resources would allow.

('Bordeaux mixture', the classic copper sulphate spray against fungal diseases)

The vats in the *cuvier* were Napoleonic, the barrels in the mossy cellar dark with indeterminate age. Only the basket press on its iron wheels definitely bore some relation to the Industrial Revolution. Père Moutarde had a little cache of bottles in a corner of the cellar; no labels, but dates written in chalk that stood up very badly to any handling. In any case he knew the positions of all the bottles, whose vintages stepped back with irregular intervals to before phylloxera and his grandfather's death. To drink one of them was exceptional. The family's daily drinking came in litres from the *cave cooperative*.

In fact the Moutardes had little to do with their own wine at all. They were farmers, on a tiny scale, who picked their grapes, put them through a sort of grinder that tore off most of the stems, then piled them in a vat and waited for the heady stinging smell of fermentation to fill the barn. Then twice a day the younger male members of the family climbed the ladder to the open top of the *cuve*, wearing only shorts (and sometimes not even those), gripped the edge firmly and lowered themselves in. Their combined weight was sometimes barely enough, even with a fair bit of bouncing, to break the thick raft of skins and still-whole grapes buoyed up on the surface by the fizzing fermentation below. Once you got through into the warm half-wine, the idea was to turn the fragments of raft upside down and tread them back in. This way none of the goodness, the colour and flavour of the grapes, would be lost.

Three weeks or so after harvest, with the weather distinctly chilly, the fermentation was finished; it was time to empty the contents of the vat into the barrels below, having energetically scoured the insides with a length of chain and washed them with endless cold water from the well.

That was almost the last the Moutardes saw of their wine. Before Christmas the négociant called, tasted each barrel, told them how bad business was, and named a price. In January a lorry came round, parked beside the cannon, and hoisted the barrels up to take them to Beaune.

Sometimes in good years (meteorologically and financially) Monsieur Moutarde would decide to keep a small barrel in the cellar, taste it from time to time with a neighbour, and at the end of three or four or even five years, round up and wash enough bottles to hold all the dark fragrant liquid. Most of these he would distribute round the family. His own share would be chalked and squirrelled away.

Only he knew the almost celestial satisfaction that lay in the best and oldest bottles: a mingling of plums and earth and game, of heat and cool, of fungus and farmyard, of iron and leather, yet giving off, for all its strength and maleness, a scent as ringing-clear as violets.

This was Burgundy thirty years ago®, the most prestigious and sought-after region in the world of wine, but in a world where even the rarest and finest of wines from the greatest vineyards went for a song. Winegrowers dragged along at subsistence level, faintly hoping that some eccentric might come and offer to buy their burdensome inheritance, yet dreading the loss of their ancient bond with the land and its sweetest fruit. Monsieur Moutarde and his generation, like their forebears, were prisoners of their peasant suspicions and superstitions. By regarding even the next commune as a rival they spurned comparisons, turned their backs on new ideas, rejected progress. But they conserved and intensified the identity of their 'cru'. When they planted a new vine, it came from their own cuttings. Every move they made at vintage time and in the cellar was ritualised. Muligny could be made only in this way.

Frequently the results of such sleepwalking were catastrophic. It was often just as well the négociant took away barrels of faulty wine to treat them as far as possible, then blend them with Rhône or Algerian to produce an approximation the world would accept as burgundy. Occasionally ritual was blessed with luck, and the results were sublime. Certainly there was enough of this elusive sublimity to keep the legend of burgundy alive in waiting for the next generation – and to fire the imaginations of the very few wine-lovers, mostly Americans, who aspired at least to collect, perhaps one day even to emulate, what they considered the loveliest of all wines.

in the 1960s

Monsieur Moutarde's children live in a different world. They have been to technical colleges, even to universities with departments of viticulture and oenology. They exchange views, read trade journals – and openly compete with one another. They even see themselves as competing with other countries. Above all, the peasant instinct for secrecy has evaporated.

The years between 1960 and today have seen the greatest change in the making, the quality and the distribution of wine in its eight-thousand-year history. This is not something to be surprised at. Which art, and which science, has not altered almost out of recognition in the era of technology?

Yet wine and our expectations of it are profoundly linked with age and time. Of all the food and drink we consume, only wine can live (and indeed, change wonderfully for the better) for decades – even, exceptionally, for a century or more. Yet its lifespan is never certain: its ageing process is unpredictable enough to seem to wear a mantle of mystery.

That cars should work better, or microchips have almost magical properties, are things we can accept without surprise, since they are the products of scientific inventiveness. But weren't we always told that the greatest wines are products of evolution, or tradition, or respect for the soil and patience in the cellar? How can technology improve on something that emerges from the womb of time?

The Art and Science of Wine, James Halliday and Hugh Johnson,
Mitchell Beazley, 1992

RESOLVE ON THE RHINE

An event at the end of April is hardly STOP PRESS in November, but since it has not been reported here yet, as far as I know, let me fill you in.

It was a party (again). A four-day riverboat party in perfect warm spring weather on the Rhine, ripping down the current from Strasbourg to Cologne. The idea was for the combined forces of Bordeaux's Union des Grands Crus and Germany's Verband Deutsche Prädikatsweingüter (twin souls in any language) to show their wines to the hundreds of Rhinelanders who poured on board at every stop.

As a tasting it was terrific. The best German wines of the perfect 1990 vintage at the sharp end, coupled with an extremely impressive line-up of '82 bordeaux in the stern. When Cheval Blanc, Pichon Lalande, Domaine de Chevalier, Léoville-Barton and fifty of their top-weight colleagues open their '82s together, the air is heady indeed. But beside this show of Franco-German solidarity when it comes to the best they grow, there was a far-from-hidden second agenda. At a conference begun in the European Parliament Chamber in Strasbourg, continued in the Chamber of Commerce in Frankfurt, and ended at the Chancellery at Bonn, Peter Sichel of Château Palmer and Michael Prinz zu Salm-Salm, the President of the VDP, drafted a declaration on the considered attitude of Europe's best wine-producers to threats from the busybodies of Brussels.

The manifesto was delivered to the German Minister of Agriculture in the historic old chancellery building, among noble trees on the banks of the Rhine.

What it said, in essence, was that the wine each country, or each region, makes arises from its culture. That its winemakers are the guardians of that culture, and that Brussels has no need, no right and no competence to interfere with their traditions, or their interpretations of their traditions. It said more and said it better, but you get the idea.

Has Euro-creep really kept away from wine?

Decanter, 1993

LES CINQ À TOKYO

A few years earlier the idea of a road show of the First Growths would have seemed, to use a suitably stuffy word, preposterous. One did not expect their individual proprietors to do personal appearances with photo opportunities, let alone all five of them together. But few things are sacred today, and in the world of wine, none. Possibly it is the awe-inspiring vulgarity of some of America's wine spectaculars that has dislodged the dignity and reserve that surrounded the great wine dynasties. In many cases a younger generation is in charge. The opportunities for superlatives offered by The Amazing Eighties may also have had something to do with eroding traditional reticence.

Why had the First Growths never overtly collaborated before? The Japan expedition was conceived at the New York Wine Experience, when the five proprietors met in a dismal coffee bar and were persuaded that Japan would be much more fun.

Whatever the reasons, in 1991 Les Cinq, that is the four Médoc First Growths and Château Haut-Brion, dipped their toes in the water for the first time together at a reception at Sotheby's in London. And in 1992 they boarded a flight for Tokyo, preceded by a freighter from Bordeaux carrying the most magnificent selection of big bottles of great vintages ever to have taken to the sky.

Those in collusion were the proprietors, British Airways, your humble servant, and the man who has been described in Japan as five times more important than the Prime Minister, Seiji Tsutsumi, owner of the Seibu chain of department stores, the Saison group of hotels, and a great deal else besides. Of course it is only the wine you want to hear about, so I will not dwell on the hotel where we stayed, the Seiyo Ginza, so richly endowed with staff that every guest is assigned a personal secretary on arrival; and only touch in passing on the dinners that were laid before us.

They began with a private dinner for fifty at Mr Tsutsumi's house. The terrace where we drank more than one magnum of Roederer Cristal '83 put me in mind of Les Crayères, Boyer's great restaurant in Reims, overlooking a private garden so large and well screened that the surrounding city is invisible. Only this one is in Tokyo, where space is measured out in teaspoons – and the garden is a century-old masterpiece of maples, cascades, bridges and lanterns.

I am delighted to report that Japanese high society, once the initial bowing is out of the way, is as gracefully gay, welcoming and entertaining as the best company anywhere. The Tsutsumis saw to it that everyone met everyone, all in a whirl of high spirits.

Let me recount the menu. It was relatively simple, with each dish simply perfect: *pavé de lotte aux cèpes, gâteau de foie gras aux truffes, roti de veau, pâtes aux morilles, fromages* and *Charlotte à la poire*. The white wine for the *lotte* was Haut-Brion Blanc 1989: wonderfully potent with promise, but scarcely mature enough to do itself justice.

The same, incredibly, could be said about the first claret: Latour 1961. Its bouquet was room-stopping, its flavours awe-inspiring – but it must be admitted that foie gras and such tannins are not made for each other. The effect was to emphasise the cut and denseness of the Latour: in fact, its lack of maturity. My neighbour the violinist was reminded of Smetana, and I of Latour '61 with dark cèpes at the château, when its brooding presence had flickered with lambent ... (*do* get on with it – Ed).

Lafite 1959 in magnums broke my reverie. Oddly, at first breath, the Lafite seemed just as solid as the Latour: as massive and impenetrable. But a few moments revealed a depth of honeyed sweetness matched with velvet that filled the mouth at such length that it became almost monotonous. This was utter joy, perfectly set off by the plain pale tender veal. The violinist said Handel. I didn't argue.

The next vintage, the 1953 of Château Margaux, was a huge step toward maturity from the robust fullness of the first two wines. Its nose, I felt, was less a statement than a suggestion; its structure that of lace, delicately sweet with a touch of sharpness in most persuasive harmony. I said Mozart almost before the violinist did. Haut-Brion '49 was as great a contrast again. My notes on this go on and on. I could have mistaken the nose for Latour: a great masculine smoking-room smell. This was ripe but not sweet; earthy, rather. Deeper in colour than the Margaux, and explosively pungent. No wine developed in the glass as much as this. However complete it seemed, each moment added another element of seduction: gathering sweetness, a limpid texture that made me think of cream poured over gravel. As the bouquet unfolded it became more smoky, autumnal, earthy, roast-coffeeish, and finally touched a note of caramel. I was too engrossed to hear what the violinist said, but I was hearing Haydn.

Mouton '45 in a jeroboam was Napoleonic. My notes reveal that I was not as sober as when I tasted the Latour.

A roll of drums, I scribbled: thunder on the horizon. The colour was almost threatening; the nose had such a depth of cutting Cabernet that one almost recoiled. In the second wave came the sweet creamy mushroom smell that I love in a great old Pol Roger. Its bottom was unfathomable, yet the bite of Cabernet stayed young to the end – the smell of the empty glass only growing fresher and grapier. Beethoven, said the violinist and I with one breath.

It appears from my notes that by the time we were drinking the 1980 Yquem I was relying on the opinion of my neighbours. All I wrote down was *Très sexuel, selon la femme du peintre*[☺] – and suspect, as usual, that the tasting note I borrowed was the best.

... said the painter's wife

Decanter, 1993

POCKET WINE BOOK 1994
FOREWORD

R evising this little book every year amounts to a sort of stocktaking of the world's wines. Each year there is even more choice, as the four-hundred-odd new ones in this edition testify. But is there really more diversity?

The answer, I'm afraid, is qualified. The surge of technology that made the 80s so exciting holds dangers for the wines of the 90s. The threat is that modern wines, wherever they come from, will taste more and more alike.

The first reason is the planting of a dismally limited palette of varieties: above all Chardonnay and Cabernet. Winemakers like them because they allow them to believe they are emulating the world's best red and white wines (also because they are relatively easy to grow). And marketing folk like them because by now everybody knows their names.

But it is not just grapes that threaten uniformity. It is a set of assumptions about what constitutes a competitive, marketable wine – assumptions propagated and encouraged by the simplistic American habit of 'scoring' wines as though they were boxers.

A typical modern Chardonnay has a certain soft or sweet fruitiness and a distinctive smell and taste of oak. 'French oak' has become a talisman of a certain level of 'quality'. But we are being cheated. The great wines that provide the inspiration are not oak-flavoured. Any wine that tastes more of oak than of wine (or indeed more of grapes than wine) should be considered flawed.

The best winemakers look forward. They want to make better use of their land: to find its character in its fruit. Happily the challenge of different grapes shows up more and more in these pages. And so does the merger and shutdown of big wineries that let marketing lead them to perdition.

Hugh Johnson's Pocket Wine Book 1994, Mitchell Beazley

WORDS, WORDS, WORDS

Inside every fat book there is a slim volume trying to get out. Or so I thought, until I received Robert Parker's *The Wine Buyer's Guide* from Dorling Kindersley. To do them justice, Dorling Kindersley do not edit Parker's work, they just distribute it. But some editor's input is badly needed, and perhaps when DK next write to RP they might mention this.

Anyone who reads *The New Yorker* is aware of the American tolerance for words, words, words. Do you think of Americans as being yawningly leisured? Henry James says yes; Ogden Nash no. Robert Parker apparently doesn't trouble himself with such concerns. He just lets rip.

Its funny, isn't it, that the man who invented the world's fastest wine-measuring system is so insensitive to overwriting. Length is not enough. His adjectives are super-colossal to match. But then so is his taste, if you plot the fall of superlatives.© To RP big is good; huge is great. What could be simpler? But why does it take so long to say so?

I do hope I'm not repeating myself.

Super-sensitive readers are suspecting by now that Johnson is a bit miffed with Parker. Why otherwise be boring about a bore? Borrow a copy of the brick that passes as his new book and read it for yourself. RP spends two thousand words of his preamble (or loiter) misrepresenting Johnson and Halliday©. I can't remember any other writer since Ruskin slowing down his foreword by rubbishing another, but this is Parker's way. He has bees in his

in The Art and Science of Wine

bonnet (or hood). If he has droned about them in his monthly, *The Wine Advocate*, you'll get it over again in the next book.

Specifically, what he misrepresents is the H & J view on filtration and the finishing of wines. By selective quotation he paints H & J as manic purifiers, squeezing every wine through every sieve in sight. Filtration being his bee, and moderation not a word in his vocabulary, he shows no sign of having read any part – except F for filtration – of what some consider quite a useful book. And then he seems to have read only the part he was ready to fight.

Let me not catch the germ of boring repetition, for heaven's sake.

Review of *The Wine Buyer's Guide*, Robert Parker,
Dorling Kindersley 1993, *Decanter*, 1994

CRISE DE FOIE

O nly ten – or was it fifteen? – years ago, *foie gras frais* was a treat found exclusively in restaurants with pretentions to high gastronomy. Its *hauts lieux* were Perigord and Alsace. The Bordelais opened Sauternes for it, the Alsatians their *vendanges tardives*, and the Parisians pretty much followed suit.

Nous avons (actually *ils ont*) *changé tout cela*⊖. The foie gras experience has moved out of the toqued and deeply napped luxury class to become damn near a dish of the people. If Mitterand had had the wit to remark, in the tradition of Henri IV, that he wished every Frenchman a foie gras on his Sunday lunch table, he would have marked the *époque* with a *mot* that would have endured as surely as 'Let them eat cake'.⊖

from Molière's Le Médecin Malgré Lui (1666)

Today foie gras seems to be made all over France. It appears on *prix fixe* menus at prices as low as 140 francs (at least in the provinces). Usually it is locally produced, freshly cooked and just as outrageously delicious as it used to be when 140 francs was the price of the dish, not the menu.

Horrible to relate, today's meme seems to be 'Let them eat kale.'

'My' part of France – the little-visited Centre – makes foie gras today with the best. The wine is, or could be, the problem. Sauternes and Alsace *vendanges tardives* (VT) scarcely reach the Allier (which is known for its timber, not its vines or its cellars). But we have discovered a wonderful new resource just to the north: the VT of the upper Loire. In several vintages recently growers in Sancerre, and even in Menetou-Salon, have produced luscious wines that transcend the simplicity of Sauvignon Blanc to become memorably dense, concentrated, sweet and creamy, with a sustaining core of acidity that makes them a better partner to foie gras even than Sauternes.

My first encounter with these wines was at the sleepy little spa town of Bourbon-l'Archambault, where the chef/patron of the Hôtel des Thermes serves *foie gras frais* on a green salad with walnuts and a little walnut oil. Lucien Crochet's 1990 Sancerre VT from Bué gave bold structure and lingering luscious sweetness to this already admirable arrangement.

More recently at the Lion d'Or, an old roadhouse at Estivareilles, just north of Montluçon, we were able to eat the preposterously generous slab of *foie gras richissime* only by virtue of Henry Pellé's Menetou-Salon. As in some great Mosel Ausleses there was a barbershop daring in its close harmony of sweet and keenly acid. Foie gras was sublimated – and the range of France's local treasures extended, for me, yet again.

The *moelleux* wines of Vouvray and Anjou are already well known in this context. Jurançon clearly has the wherewithal for another kind of foie gras experience. What other regions are ready to depart from dry orthodoxy and give us sinful succulence?

Decanter, 1994

BRINK OF EXTINCTION

I thought Brussels had tied up (or down) every conceivable expression that could be used on a wine label in every language, prescribed its type size and threatened with excommunication anyone who tried anything funny. To my delight, though, I found a vintner in the Jura the other day apparently getting away with doing his own thing. Jacques Tissot of Arbois labels his white wine *Vin typé*, and *typé* it most certainly is.

It is a wine that would probably be instantly rubbished as oxidised by any laboratory analyst; a white evidently kept in old barrels until it is part-way to being a *vin jaune*. A *vin jaune* is a fairly hard-hitting going-on-sherry sort of wine (and I imagine a very tough sell indeed outside the excellent restaurants of the Jura). The blanc *typé* is nothing so challenging, but just white wine as white wine almost universally used to be made until tastes associated with oxygen went deeply out of fashion.

It went perfectly with the copious entrée of mushrooms and sweetbreads in cream – and no doubt *vin typé* – at a hotel crowded to the doors with sensible holidaymakers who go to the Jura regularly for long walks and longer meals. It also went down with acclaim at a dinner party in another part of France where I put a half-bottle (of the '89) between guests for two to share with little quiches as the first course. It clearly stirred old memories. I wondered whether *vin de nostalgie* was a term that Brussels would proscribe.

I have often banged on about how (in Italy above all) the cleaning up of such old classics as Frascati and Orvieto led to the extinction of their flavours and the near-extinction of their reputations.

The Frascati in the jug up on that enchanted hill south of Rome, or indeed at Sabatini's in Trastevere⊚, has three times the flavour of any that has ever been bottled. The awkward question is how stable is it? Could it be shipped without falling to pieces? This of course is exactly what was meant by the old, and often true, accusation that a wine 'didn't travel'.

over the River Tiber was where you used to go for proper local food. I wouldn't guarantee it is still so

I'm pretty sure the answer is that with modern bottling technology you could capture any flavour you wanted, that decadent local tastes could be gift-wrapped for shipping – if there was a market for them. I'll buy them. If *typé* is the code word for a touch of decadence, of wine living dangerously, let's see more of it. It doesn't taste of grapes, or of oak. It tastes of history.

Decanter, 1994

REVOLUTION AT LAST

Politics is not my scene. I can count on my ears the number of occasions when I have been in a debating chamber or witnessed a vote that really seemed to mark an important change in the right direction. But a meeting in July of the association of Germany's top quality-wine growers, the VDP, finally showed its frustration with the misbegotten populist wine laws that have so humiliated their industry for over twenty years.

The vote was to resign en masse from the main body that represents the industry to the government, the Deutscher Weinbauverband. After a debate which, at moments, almost reached the decibel level of the House of Commons, it was carried overwhelmingly. There was a tangible sense of freedom and elation at the long-overdue end to shilly-shallying and compromise. Now a hundred and seventy-five of the best German estates will fight their own corner, no longer pretending to have common interest with the discredited bulk of their country's wine industry. Their representations to both Bonn and Brussels, but even more perhaps their self-policing, should at last give German wine its dignity back.

My role at the meeting was to read a paper about classification. In the fourth edition of my *Wine Atlas* I have started on a classification of the top German vineyards that seems to me a prerequisite for their worldwide recognition. I looked at the various French variations on the theme, from Bordeaux in 1855 to Alsace today, via the Grands and Premiers Crus of the Côte d'Or and the Échelle des Crus of Champagne, before explaining how I had started in Germany. I certainly don't claim my work is at all complete, let alone infallible. But someone has to start somewhere. At least now the issue is alive.

One super treat my visit to the Rheingau did produce: a visit to the new-furbished Robert Weil estate at Kiedrich, where young Wilhelm Weil showed me a perfect set of '93s from Kabinett to TBA from the Gräfenberg vineyard at Kiedrich, classified in the new atlas as 'First Class'. Of the Goldkapsel Auslese I wrote, 'A ripe apple loft full of sunbeams. Richness of botrytis plays against almost painful intensity of fruit. It invades the cranium with fumes of apples, pears, quinces ... completely takes over the senses and leaves me inhaling my own perfumed breath.' I have censored my notes on the TBA as too near to porn for my sensitive readers.

The intensity, the elegance, the sheer juicy thrill of these sublime Rheingau Rieslings said more than any amount of debate – or indeed classification. Is there finer white wine made anywhere on earth?

Decanter, 1994

FRUIT-DRIVEN

I'm not at all sure who coined the term 'fruit-driven', but as it seems to me to stand usefully for a whole active philosophy of wine, perhaps it merits a word or two of discussion. Where shall we start? Are all wines driven by something, making fruit just one of the possible chauffeurs, so that acid-driven, sugar-driven, oak-driven, terroir-driven or alcohol-driven are valid possibilities? Presumably so; if not, the simple word 'fruity' would seem to cover the case.

In which case what the term is trying to tell us is that the taste of fruit is the active principle in this wine, by implication, therefore, a particular fruit – a grape indeed. Is this a good thing? To some, apparently, it is – absolutely. I am often astonished at the pleasure some critics seem to get from tasting a gooseberry in a glass. Would they attack a plate of gooseberries with the same exclamation of delight? Perhaps the implication of fruit-driven is that you are aware of the grape taste first, then secondarily of the taste of wine? This would make it an excellent description of most New Zealand wines, and some Australian. In fact it would make it the category heading for the squads of me-too Sauvignons and Chardonnays that make a visit to a supermarket such a depressing experience.

Satisfaction, to me, depends (not entirely, of course) on how far the flavour of the grape has been transmuted by fermentation into the taste of wine. This is my argument with such as Cloudy Bay Sauvignon. It simply fails at the first hurdle: that it should taste like wine⊛. A jug of it might be quite at home on the breakfast buffet among the orange, grapefruit and mango juices, but by lunchtime I am looking for the measured, harmonised flavours in their proper proportions that make good wine as much a question as a statement.

yet it set a trend that became a tsunami

I've just come up for air from deep immersion in *The World Atlas of Wine*. It is undergoing a total refit for the Mark IV version to be released next year. It makes you acutely aware of change, poring over the maps of eight years ago and judging what needs changing, what adding; whether they can be revised or need complete redrawing.

It is not just a matter of past changes, but also the changes we can anticipate up to the end of the century and beyond. I'm not going to give away the plot here, but it seems to me that recent developments will seem like plodding round in circles compared with what we are going to see in the next few years.

If the discovery of the 70s was oak, and the discovery of the 80s was fruit, would you like to guess what the discovery of the 90s is going to be?

Decanter, 1994

VIVE LE PARADOX!

Anyone would have thought they'd found a final cure for phylloxera. *Mairies* were draped in bunting, church bells rang, street parties devastated the *circulation*. No, it was not *Jour-J*⊛ either. It was the screening, three thousand miles away across the Atlantic, of a sixty-minute documentary called *The French Paradox*. It was over three years ago, and yet the French in winegrowing communities still speak of it in voices hushed with grateful awe.

D-Day

At last someone had dared to say that wine does you good – and in America of all places. Even to prove it with medical evidence. And America, sweet naive fad-crazy America, had reacted by rushing to the shops and buying up red wine until the shelves were bare.

Red wine, you note. Americans on the whole don't actually like red wine much. They'd much rather drink Chardonnay. But it was red wine they were told did them good, so red wine sales rose 40 per cent. In the land of the lemming two commodities are in chronic short supply: personal choice and common sense.

The French Paradox was a terrific film, though. It asked the simple question: how come that the nation that eats the most saturated fats has the lowest rate of coronary heart disease? And more provoking still, why, in such regions as Perigord that are perpetually greasy-fingered with foie gras and confits of *oie* and *canard*, is heart disease if anything less common than it is elsewhere?

For once a simple question appeared to have a simple answer. According to Dr Serge Renaud, whose researches were cited in evidence, the answer was red wine, and the reason, that the tannins and anthocyanins in red wine have a scouring effect on the arteries of the heart, preventing the build-up of the malignant form of cholesterol. And not only that, but that all forms of alcohol increase the body's high-density lipoproteins – the benign form of cholesterol.

The medical profession is quite rightly cautious about sweeping statements, and very cautious indeed about recommending something that is capable of being abused. It cannot retract or deny Dr Renaud's evidence relating to red wine and heart disease, but on the more general questions of benefits of wine-drinking it has continued to wear a belt and braces.

The weekly ration has even been lowered since – officially. Few are convinced.

On no substantial scientific evidence it has stuck to the assertion that twenty-one 'units' of alcohol for men and fourteen for women are the maximum 'safe' rations. But this proposition has been looking wobbly for years, and any day now is going to be exposed as without any foundation. On the contrary, several researchers are now saying the alleged difference between the sexes is illusory – as far as alcohol is concerned, I hasten to add. Average bodyweight is probably the only reason to make a distinction. And far more sweepingly, that the amount of alcohol the average person can drink regularly without ill effect is roughly the equivalent of a bottle of wine a day.

Serge Renaud himself visited London in May to lecture to a combined audience of medical and gastronomic journalists about recent findings. He is very far from being a sensation-seeker; his evidence took the form of graphs and diagrams of experiments over many years, often presented in ways that tended to obscure, rather than highlight, the mounting evidence in favour of wine-drinking. He was careful to say that you couldn't recommend wine to non-alcohol-drinkers. It was hard to see why, though, in view of his quite startling conclusion that 'moderate wine consumption is by far the most potent drug we have to decrease total mortality – not just coronary heart disease.' One research project in particular that he cited, which involved 17,000 citizens of Nancy in northeastern France over a ten-year period, showed that (leaving out smokers, whose prospects were dismal in all studies) those most at risk were teetotallers and those drinking more than one litre of wine a day. Those drinking between two and five glasses of wine a day were all in a bracket in which the mortality rate was close to 50 per cent below the average.

Other studies involved the effects of 'the Mediterranean diet', in which vegetables and olive oil play a large part, apparently in conjunction with wine, in lowering total mortality. All studies proved that 'binge drinking' is dangerous – but rarely associated with wine. Few had studied the relative effects of alcohol in the form of wine and of spirits or beer – but where they have, the clear benefits of wine are two: the 'scouring' effect of red wine already mentioned, and the quite different question of its context as a mealtime drink. In France, and certainly in Italy – though not necessarily in Anglo-Saxon countries – close association of wine and food is fundamental.

Let me not give the impression that the long battle between puritans, however they classify themselves, and lovers of life and wine is coming – or ever will come – to an end. Where it is profitable for governments to tax wine as a sin they will go on regardless, whatever the evidence against them. And America is not going to escape from the looming threat of Prohibition just because wine is proven innocent – or even an elixir of life.

But the celebrated TV programme was an unquestioned victory in the continuing war – perhaps most of all because it proved to doctors that news does not have to be dire to get headlines. Since its broadcast, research studies with positive conclusions have been published at an increasing rate. I am told that an important, even a sensational, one is due out in *The Lancet* this summer.⊕ The burden of proof may yet be thrust back on the prosecution.

Whatever medical 'surveys' may come up with, though, there is an argument from instinct that we all know, and that we should never underestimate or feel ashamed of. Wine-lovers are aware that their taste for wine is a real contributor to the quality of their life – socially, aesthetically, and not least for its effect on morale. If we smile more, enjoy our friends and families more, digest better and sleep better we are better. But why should I preach to the converted?

Wine Times, 1994

Red Wine Consumption and Oxidation of Low-density Lipoproteins. *A real page-turner.*

POCKET WINE BOOK 1995
FOREWORD

This little book comes of age with its 18th edition. It is irresistible to compare the world it surveys with the one it sketched in 1977. I look back in wonder at the simplicity of the first edition: unhurried little notes rather elegantly laid out on one hundred and forty four pages with handsome wide margins. Today's book is hugger-mugger in comparison: two hundred and sixteen pages carrying so much information that not only space but also grammar and vocabulary are under severe stress.

Of course all it has done is to reflect changing times, improving standards, and burgeoning choice. Wine lists eighteen years ago were usually simple, scarcely straying outside Europe's classic regions except for local interest and a touch of colour. Today the world is the wine-drinker's oyster, and very confusing it all is: too complicated, in fact, for any but near-fanatics to want to master it.

Hence the paradox that at the same time as the choice is wider than ever before, more wine-drinkers than ever are tempted to shrug their shoulders and say 'So long as it's Chardonnay ...'. On this basis professional wine-buyers are free to concentrate on 'price points' and let the most precious attribute of wine, the vitality that comes with variety, go hang.

Who is winning, then: the individualist or the Great Homogeniser? Happily the evidence of this book says diversity is well ahead. It is your job and mine, as lovers of the spice of life, to back the individualist every time.

Hugh Johnson's Pocket Wine Book 1995, Mitchell Beazley

THE GOSPEL OF THE SNAIL

T he very day, in 1986, that the Golden Arches opened its doors for the first time in Italy – worse, in Rome – Carlo Petrini came booming down from the hills of Piedmont to proclaim the gospel of Slow Food. Booming? The man is the Pavarotti of the table: his sotto voce is your mezzo forte, his sips your swallows – and his emblem is the purposeful snail. Everything fast is trash, he incanted (forgetting Ferraris?). The true virtue is to be slow. The wise do not snatch at life's pleasures, they savour them.

I loved the man from the moment I met him, dispensing wonderful country food and broaching endless bottles of vivid artisan wines at Vinitaly©. He was running what appeared to be a three-star soup kitchen in a glade or clearing among the thronging booths.

Italy's characteristically chaotic annual wine fair, held in Verona

Was this really the free lunch that there is no such thing as? Not quite. If Carlo thought he could convert you into an apostle of positive, proactive Slowness, the rations came free. The slightest hint of speed, physical or – worse – moral, and you'd get the bill. Slowness is to do things deliberately, lovingly, careless of time because the act is an end and pleasure in itself. In a world where homogenisation is coming in like the tide at Mont St Michel, it is to relish what is original, authentic, indigenous – and will very likely soon be banned by Brussels.

In the Slow Food philosophy, therefore, a dish that demands long and arduous preparation, long soaking, fine chopping, gentle simmering, patient reduction, is inherently superior to a quick fry-up – never even to think of that instrument from the Inferno, the microwave. The time spent in preparation is life as it should be lived, in full consciousness of all the senses, in patience and concentration, even in a sense that such acts are rituals, binding us to tradition, to our ancestors, to nature.

And equally importantly the time spent in eating is life being lived to the full: each morsel, each flavour and texture revealing its origins, evoking memories, inducing the heightened state of awareness that brings the ultimate sensuous pleasures.

Carlo didn't invent any of this. It is the epicurean philosophy. It was stated and re-stated by the most famous gourmet of this century, the Parisian Curnonsky (*Cur non* being the Latin for 'why not?'). Curnonsky's slogan was *Les choses doivent avoir le goût de ce qu'elles sont*: Things should taste of what they are.[⊕] Doesn't everyone realise this? Alas, no. The gene for humility seems sadly to be rare in modern technocratic winemakers. And of course, the gene for patience was bred out of marketing persons long ago.

Another quote: 'In great quantity, Madame. In great quantity.'

Once it was cool to be cool. Now it is slow to be slow. Would you join the Slow Food movement? To find out more, write to us; we will forward your letter.

This does not, by the way, constitute an offer of a free lunch.

Wine Times, 1995

TO THE BOTTLE BANK

D iary-readers I'm afraid will just have to lump the time lag that brings you the Johnson Christmas wine list in March. But since Christmas is always the time when I reach deepest into the cellar, it seems only right to report, late or not.

Much the most intriguing moment was a comparison between two half-bottles of extremely antique Champagne: Pol Roger 1906. One was brought up from a shipwreck in the St Lawrence River, having lain there for eighty-odd years; the other left Épernay only two years ago. The latter was almost as good as antique Champagne can get: sublime. I make no apology for doting on the unique combination of Champagne finesse and Madeira depth and length that such grand old relics offer. Yes, they hint of mushrooms, but I like mushrooms.

The submarine bottle, alas, was perished. I shall have to ask local experts whether the St Lawrence routinely smells of bad eggs, although the cork seemed to have done its job of keeping the wine in and the water out. The moral, I suppose, must be to avoid major estuaries for long-term storage.

Decanter, 1995

FIVE KILOMETRES OF FRIENDS

There is nothing quite like Vinexpo in the calendar of any industry. But then there is no industry with as many facets as the wine business. What else brings together farmers and fashion designers, aristocrats and communists, statisticians and gastronomes under the umbrella of a single interest, product, passion?

Vinexpo happens in June every second year in the Parc des Expositions by the huge artificial lake just north of Bordeaux. This is no dog-and-pony show: the hall is over a kilometre long and five broad aisles wide, entirely lined with bottles and bonhomie. 'Five kilometres of friends' is how one (exceptionally friendly) visitor describes it.

Along the lake side of the hall are a dozen restaurants in marquees, offering everything from Californian to Burgundian to Spanish cuisine: not cheap, but packed to overflowing.

A second, smaller hall alongside gives the impression of being about the size of Earl's Court. Then there is the Pavillon de Bordeaux, where the local appellations strut their stuff and everybody knuckles down to Arcachon oysters served with fat little *crépinettes de porc*. And, suitably secluded, in an instant garden of grass-carpet, sunflowers and potted cypresses, is the Club des Marques, where the big groups who consider themselves above the common herd hold court (and serve day-long lunches) by personal invitation only.

Something like forty thousand people flock in to be spoilt for the week, representing every nuance of the wine business in every country where wine is drunk. Can there be a theme to such a circus? Is it possible to discern any sort of plot – or just a plethora of subplots and intrigues?

Two subplots spring to mind at once: not brand-new ones, but themes that get a good airing because they concern everyone who makes, sells, or even merely drinks wine.

The first is health. As Dr Tom Stuttaford⊚ has been so forcefully and The Times' *health correspondent* uninhibitedly letting us know recently, the tide has turned in the wine and health debate. Wine advocates are no longer perpetually on the back foot or ducking bouncers from obscure American research groups. The moderate consumption of wine, especially red wine, is now widely accepted as being positive for most aspects of health – especially the heart. Even the concept of 'moderate' has moved along a bit, from the puritanical twenty-one units a week for men and fourteen for women to Dr Stuttaford's 'thirty-five or so'.

The carefully neutral ground where alcohol is alcohol and there is no effective difference between beer, wine and spirit has also shifted in the direction of common sense and experience. The context of drinking is important: we are advised to eat at the same time, and it is wine, not Foster's or a single malt, that goes with food. Above all, though, it is the antioxidant qualities of red wine that give it the green light.

The other principal subplot is our old friend Terroir versus Variety. I sense a change of emphasis here too. The California viewpoint – by no means limited to California, but articulated there longest and loudest – is that anywhere you can ripen good grapes you can produce memorable wine. Apart from its obvious New-World bedfellows in this heresy, Germany has also officially taken this line – to the catastrophic detriment of its reputation.

I have never understood how anyone can argue that a Chablis from a Grand Cru site is not consistently richer, longer-lived and ultimately more satisfying than a Village wine. How many generations have to agree, and agree to pay the premium, before a terroir-sceptic will accept the prima facie evidence that terroir defines character, and usually (though not always) quality, too?

Wine Times, 1995

OFF PISTE

I'm not sure if French autoroute food is as bad as or worse than our motorway food because I've never tried the latter. But the former, in the utterly dismal *relais* of various denominations that crop up every few kilometres on all but the remotest autoroutes, are one of the (many) disgraces of modern France.

Would some kind person like to compile a driver's guide to good old-fashioned dining rooms not more than (say) fifteen minutes' drive from autoroute exits? I will contribute one that I thoroughly enjoy and is handy for all Chunnel users – at Arras, only forty-five minutes from the curiously named Coulougne (did they marry Calais and Boulogne?) and the Big Hole. The Restaurant Astoria Carnot, opposite the Gare SNCF in the most animated part of town, has all the qualities of a great old-fashioned 'ordinary'.☉

Times have changed. This is Memory Lane, not TripAdvisor.

In the sacred hours of twelve to two and again in the evening it is packed with working eaters deeply absorbed in vast copper dishes of turbot *sauce hollandaise* or *choucroute garnie*. All the dishes are reasonably priced and incredibly generous, the staff care, and a bottle of good Muscadet for your moules and sole is only 70 francs – while for 110 or so you can be drinking Trimbach's lovely Riesling.

If you want evidence that quality and value are still a winning combination, tot up the takings from two hundred or so appetites deeply satisfied twice a day.

Decanter, 1995

THE FRAGRANCE OF MEMORY

then Germany's wine magazine

Heinz-Gert Woschek, the editor of *Alles über Wein*☉, has just asked me an unanswerable question: what are the twenty best wines I have ever tasted? Of course I shall do my best to answer it, but my bin is already half-full of crumpled drafts. Unfortunately there is no long-term measuring device like a thermometer for wine quality: only fragrant memories. How to measure the fragrance of a great antique I was lucky enough to taste a month ago against the excitement I still remember in tasting a perfect young wine twenty years back, I frankly have no idea.

If you asked for a list of the ten best cars I have ever driven, or even the ten best bathrooms I have ever visited, I might, by a feat of memory, be able to oblige. Desert Island wines is another perfectly workable category, because the choice is clearly subjective. But Heinz-Gert does not say favourite. He says best.

High on my list, if not at the very top, is a historic Málaga from Molino del Rey, one of the Duke of Wellington's Spanish estates. I bought it from Christie's, who put on it a date of c1835. In my tasting book I noted: 'Perhaps the loveliest wine of my life. Wax, oranges, smoky incense, caressing sweetness with a hint of spirit. Pure magic. Len (Evans) agrees.'

Logically I should put this (unobtainable, not even precisely identified) wine down before the Latour 1929, Cheval Blanc 1947 and the other famous classics that I am sure will be on every contributor's list. But then what about that 1923 Chablis from Avery's that I drank as though in a dream in 1967, or the very old Oloroso from Berry

Bros & Rudd that I have mentioned in this column more than once already? The nub of my argument is that any attempt to rate wines definitively, outside the immediate context of their tasting, is a chimera. And I decline to pretend I can measure the immeasurable.

Decanter, 1995

THE PRICE OF RESPECT

A sherry shortage sounds like a contradiction in terms these days, when most wine-drinkers probably only ever see a sherry bottle on a family visit at Christmas. I have never been able to figure out why what used to be England's favourite wine (it overtook port in the 1850s) has been so deeply relegated. But now two years of drought in Andalucía has made even the reduced demand of the 90s more than the shippers can keep up with. This year there was a fraction of a crop, and the next few years will be short, whatever happens: young vines simply died this summer in the white dust of the parched vineyards.

So the price of sherry will go up. But might this not also help its battered image? There has been new respect for it since the first-ever vintage sherries (of 1963) were auctioned at Christie's by González-Byass last year. Seventy pounds or so a bottle made them suddenly desirable and exciting – as indeed they are.

The argument I have often used, that a Fino is not only more original and probably better than Yet Another Chardonnay at the beginning of dinner, and is certainly more economical, may be upset by the price rises. But then it never seemed to convince people anyway. When did you last drink Tio Pepe, Inocente or Pando with your prawns or smoked salmon? Probably in Spain. Well, then.

Decanter, 1995

POCKET WINE BOOK 1996
FOREWORD

The wine world in 1996 has expanded again; at least if this minimalist annual précis is anything to go by. It takes eight more pages than last year to shoehorn in all the information you might need. I just hope you can follow the shorthand.

Two discernible current trends seem to me to be very much for the good. One is the planting of a much wider range of grape varieties, bringing into use the diverse traditions and flavours of the whole of Europe – experiments going far beyond the me-too 'classics' that have been a depressing feature of the last twenty years.

The other is increasing use of vineyard names for top-quality wines in regions where the only means of identification used to be the brand. It is the inevitable dividend of experience. For years intelligent growers, especially in California, have been observing where certain varieties produce consistently better wine. They have, in fact, been doing exactly what Europeans have done over centuries. It used to be the fashion to decry Appellations Contrôlées and their equivalents as restrictive. How interesting it is to see self-imposed appellations slowly taking shape. The dominance of varietal wines is certainly not at an end; but distant as it may be, its end is in sight.

Hugh Johnson's Pocket Wine Book 1996, Mitchell Beazley

PÉTRUS ON THE ROCKS

When the price of '95 bordeaux started zooming off the chart last summer, the word went out that the silliest prices were being paid by the Chinese. The Chinese?

We all know that Hennessy and Rémy are household names in the Middle Kingdom, and that tumblers of Cognac are de rigueur with a crab in black bean sauce, but who are these mandarins, or princelings more likely, who are suddenly resting their chopsticks to sip Pétrus from Lalique? This reporter dutifully set off for Heathrow and Hong Kong to see for himself.

Hong Kong is even more frenetically wonderful than ever in its last colonial year.© Matchless are the markets, the restaurants the shops and the views. I dined with the Dom Pérignon Association at the Peninsula Hotel, among Chinese bankers and brokers, doctors and tycoons who gave their considered opinions (very sound ones too, I thought) of vintages of Dom P going back to the sublime '75.

The handover to China was in 1997.

It was here I learnt that Champagne is not normally considered such a big deal in China. Indeed bubbles in drinks altogether are regarded more as a cause of flatulence than flightiness. The Coca-Cola Corporation must be scratching its stubble in perplexity as it contemplates the world's biggest potential market. But at least Coke is red(ish) – and red drinks seem to be what the troops prefer.

Onward to Taipei to find more evidence. I found it at Château Angel, a club in what I am told is a fashionable residential quarter, catering for the businessman who casts off his cares at midnight.

The formula for revving up the muse of Karaoke at Château Angel is simple: First Growths. The wine list suggested nothing else – except, of course, Le Pin, and – with a surprising lapse into good sense – Léoville-Barton.

The *maîtres de chai* had better not find out how their masterpieces are being consumed. The Chinese drinking style is celebratory – if not always exactly formal. Round the Chinese table the action is swift. On nightclub sofas, if anything, it speeds up. I didn't see any thoughtful swirling going on, nor contemplative sniffing. The toast is *Ganbei!* and the glass goes down in one. Pétrus, observed one customer when I was there, was improved by a bottle of Sprite.

The prices, on the other hand, seemed to me rather reasonable in the exotic context. Château Latour '82 at £650 a bottle is not much more than twice the present auction price. The Champagne we drank at £275 a bottle was much closer to the sort of mark-up I expected. Was the Latour a loss-leader, perhaps?

Should we be alarmed at this apparently colossal new market for the wines we prize most? Will we ever be able to afford a bottle again? The First Growths themselves will have to puzzle over this problem. They must be the only world-famous brands that leave their distribution entirely in the hands of whatever trader cares to buy them. One day they will surely have to find a way of influencing, if not controlling, where and how their precious bottles are ultimately drunk.

How prophetic this now seems. But having spent weeks in the 80s lecturing about wine in China and Japan, I should hardly have been surprised.

Decanter, 1996

FAREWELL, MY LOVELY

No vintage was conceived under less auspicious conditions than the 1945 was. The world was at war, and the elements appeared to be at their meanest. May saw a series of frosts that devastated the young growth on the vines, June saw hailstorms, the summer was so dry that in July 75,000 acres of the *lande* were destroyed by fire, and in August pines in the Médoc were in flames. In the middle of August it rained, followed by a heatwave; then more rain. Finally, with a tiny crop of not-very-healthy grapes in the vats, the heat returned so fiercely that fermentations boiled over and desperate growers went looking for ice to throw into their wine.

The result? One of the greatest vintages of the 20th century and one of the very few which (as is already being said about the great clarets of '95) were 'saved by the rain'.

For once the sun had shone gloriously and indiscriminately on every part of Europe from Portugal to the Rhine and beyond. The frosts had made a small crop; the summer heat concentrated it still further. The miracle was that with an almost total lack of *matériel*, and a fraction of the workforce on hand, so many wines came through the gruelling vintage and its aftermath with their qualities and character intact. Fifty years on it seemed fitting to salute them, all now in their maturity, on an occasion touched with pomp, if not solemnity.

It is time to say farewell to most of them; all the more reason to recall how they were made under conditions that meant leaving almost everything to nature.

We fielded fourteen wines to represent the vintage at a glittering dinner in the Paris dining room built by Princess Pauline Borghese and bought from her to be the British Embassy by the Duke of Wellington. Guests of the Ambassador© included the proprietors of four great châteaux, a Champagne and a port house – and perhaps more remarkably, the owner of one of Germany's greatest vineyards who as a young man made his first vintage in that year.

in 1995, Sir Christopher Mallaby

Egon Müller told his own story. In the summer of 1945 he was a serving officer on the Russian front. His father died, and somehow he managed to get home to take charge of Scharzhofberg. The weeds, he recalled, were higher than the vines. From seven hectares he could make only 1,000 litres of wine: no question of selection into Spätlese, Auslese and the rest. Of this single wine he had only two bottles left. He gladly brought them both to Paris to drink them with British, French and American friends.

But back to the wine list and an appreciation of what '45s are made of. Christian Pol Roger had brought a magnum of Cuvée Sir Winston Churchill as an appropriate welcome: dense, pungent and creamy. The Pol Roger '45 that followed was amber and honeyed, with its distinctive (and delicious) old Pol Roger taste of creamed mushrooms.

We served two wines with a first course of warm scallop salad: Chablis Grand Cru Les Preuses of Simonnet-Febvre and Chapoutier's Hermitage Blanc Chanté Alouette (Max Chapoutier was a famous Resistance organiser). There were murmurs of disbelief that the Chablis could still be so pale, firm, stony and completely in character: limpid, strong and long. The Hermitage, despite its old reputation of being France's longest-living white wine, had (in comparison) lost a little of its focus. It was round, soft, but also strong.

With the second course of a warm *foie gras frais en brioche* we served two German wines. First the Scharzhofberger of Egon Müller. To me this was the surprise of the evening. Every quality of the Saar was summed up in this pure, pale and steely wine of infinite depth and distinction. It could have been a mere fifteen years old rather than fifty; closest in style to a dry Spätlese – but one of rare intensity. If this is what happens when all the grapes of one great vineyard go into one vat, I thought, would I really rather have an Auslese? The creamy Schloss Johannisberger Edelsüsse Auslese that followed made it a difficult question to answer.

The only '45 left in the Domaine de la Romanée-Conti cellars was the Grands Échezeaux. Aubert de Vilaine could not come to the party but generously sent this crisp, now slightly lean but prodigiously perfumed wine to accompany the lamb. Many Burgundy growers had serious overheating problems in 1945. Not so the DR-C, if this orientally spicy wine is the outcome.

Anthony Barton brought Château Langoa-Barton, Peter Sichel[☉] Palmer, Eric de Rothschild Lafite, Philippine de Rothschild Mouton and Francois Pinault sent Latour. At fifty years (and particularly when conditions for bottling were so primitive) bottles vary. The two bottles that stay in my mind most vividly are the Palmer – a silky perfection of perfume that haunts me – and the regal Mouton, so dark still and dense with fruit that it stands apart even from the classicism of Lafite and the bold rigour of Latour.

the head of the house of Sichel in Bordeaux and co-owner of Château Palmer. He and I organised the wines

Conditions in 1945 were perfect for Sauternes: heat and rain produced noble rot; frost had already reduced the crop savagely. Château Doisy-Daëne made one of the great wines of a great vintage, now on the orange side of gold but with freshness and brilliance in its intense honeyed flavour.

Taylor's '45 did not need to produce any surprises. It is port at its sweetest and most complete: the quintessence of 'the Englishman's drink' that drew warm approbation from the French. The evening closed with an Armagnac de Castarède of '45. Even down in the Gers the small crop has left its mark with amazing flavours.

How to sum up the evening? Eric and Philippine de Rothschild together simply gave three cheers.

Decanter, 1996

AND THE SCORE IS ...

If you can't beat them, join them. I've lived long enough, and tried hard enough, to know that nothing I say will deter Americans from their doggy devotion to the 100-point Parker Scale. (In Parker's scale, you will remember, 0 = 50 and vice versa. Jonathan Swift would have based a whole fantasy kingdom on it.)

Arguments that taste is too various, too subtle, too evanescent, too wonderful to be reduced to a pseudo-scientific set of numbers fall on deaf ears. Arguments that the accuracy implied by giving one wine a score or 87 and another 88 is a chimera don't get much

*the bestselling US
wine magazine
(not known as a fan
of Parker's)*

further. Even when *The Wine Spectator©* appropriates the system to apply it to a whole vintage ('94 = 87, '95 = 94) the absurdity of the whole thing doesn't seem to register. The last word on the subject was said by Michael Aaron of Sherry-Lehmann in New York: 'If a wine's over 90 I can't buy it; if it's under 90 I can't sell it.'

Clearly the time has come to launch a rival system: one that hopefully bears considerably more relation to reality, is practical and easy to use, and (important, this) is less subject to abuse by salespersons who know the discount on everything and the value of nothing.

Here, then, is an exclusive preview of the Johnson System. It is based on many years of self-sacrifice in tasting every wine that comes to hand, then painstakingly analysing the experience in the rather dodgy piece of software between my ears. It is a system that reflects with inescapable honesty the enjoyment (or lack of it) that each wine offered at the time it was tasted or drunk.

The minimum score is one sniff.

One step up is one sip.

Two sips = faint interest.

A half-glass = slight hesitation.

One glass = tolerance, even general approval.

Individuals will vary more widely in their scoring after this (they do with points systems, too). You should assume that you are drinking without compunction – without your host pressing you or the winemaker hovering anxiously over you.

Two glasses means you quite like it (or there is nothing else to drink); three glasses that you find it more than acceptable; four that it really tickles your fancy.

One bottle means thorough satisfaction; two: it is irresistible. The steps grow higher now. A full case means you are certainly not going to miss out on this one. Two cases: you have convinced yourself that this is a wine with investment potential.

The logical top score in the Johnson System is, of course, the whole vineyard.

In *Hugh Johnson's Pocket Wine Book 1996*, Mitchell Beazley
and subsequent editions ...

POCKET WINE BOOK 1997
FOREWORD

This 20th annual edition of my micro-encyclopaedia has put on weight – and I hope regained a little of the elegance of design, if not language – which my shoehorning technique has eroded over the years. It should be easier to read. It is certainly more up to date than ever, bringing news not just of new vintages but also of the continuing headlong expansion of the good-wine world.

A splendid bordeaux vintage in 1995 was the headline-maker, but a huge one in Australia will add just as much to the sum of human pleasure. Chile and Argentina moved perceptibly up in the quality stakes, Germany took serious first steps towards an inevitable classification of its vineyards, Italy made masses of very good wine ... winegrowing is steadily moving from tentative to confident in more parts of the US and Canada. Round the world, in fact, the science of wine made progress, and its appreciation more than kept pace.

Hugh Johnson's Pocket Wine Book 1997, Mitchell Beazley

THE STICKY SITUATION

'A survey' says that we ate 18 per cent fewer desserts in restaurants last year than we did the year before. I can well believe that we ate much more rocket and Parmesan, tuna *carpaccio* and roasted red peppers, but I certainly hadn't noticed the flow of *tartes tatin* and summer puddings drying up. What is more, and I'd like to see what the survey says about this: I'm certain the 'sticky' is entering more people's lives than ever before.

A 'sticky' is the wine-trade jargon for any sweet wine. Not sweetish, as in Liebfraumilch or many Australian Chardonnays, but truly, deeply, madly sweet.

The trend became noticeable in the 80s when no dinner party from Clapham Common to Ladbroke Grove finished without a bottle of Beaumes-de-Venise.⊙ Perhaps there was something empowering about that name. Its suggestions of balm and Venice allowed people who thought dessert wines were old-fashioned, too strong or too complicated to indulge in one of the easiest of all tastes to recognize and like: super-ripe Muscat grapes stiffened with a fair measure of alcohol. Easy to like – but also easy to get tired of.

Fashionable parts of London in the 80s – and still today. But the fashion for the sweet Muscat from Provence passed.

Simple statements always are. It is wines that tease you, that leave you feeling there is something more to be explored, some elusive flavour to be defined, that keep you coming back for more. Once the sticky revolution was on, though, port began to be seen again after dinner on tables that had lost the habit.⊙

More in the US than the UK, strange to say.

Sauternes and its satellites Loupiac and Ste-Croix-du-Mont had a run of exceptional vintages, showed up on the shelves and were given a welcome. So did the lower reaches of the Loire, in Touraine and Anjou, where the white wines of Chenin Blanc are dry in most years but in the best years honey-sweet. The winegrowers of Alsace found themselves more talked about for their sweet late-picked *vendanges tardives* Riesling and Gewürztraminers than for their undervalued dry wines. And at the same time the word 'botrytised', unmusical at best but truly awful in Australian, announced that the New World had found ways of inducing the noble rot that wizens grapes into intense sweetness.

The greatest sweet wines, the most luscious in texture, round and velvety, complex and capable of long ageing, are ones where botrytis (or noble rot) has played a part. Under certain autumn conditions (misty mornings and sunny days) certain grape varieties catch what looks like a fearsome disease. Their skins pucker, turn brown, shrivel and disintegrate, leaving mere raisins, but raisins filled and covered with grey fungus spores. Picked in that state their sweetness is intense – but so is the concentration of flavours and fruity acidity.

The snag is that they have hardy any juice.

The first recorded wine to be made with such grapes was in Tokaj, in eastern Hungary, about the time of England's Civil War. For lack of juice, though, the dry (in Hungarian *aszú*) grapes were added to ordinary wine from the same vineyards and refermented, and the sweet fiery result stabilised by long barrel-ageing in cold cellars. No one, anywhere, had tasted such a marvel. Louis XIV called it 'the King of Wines and the Wine of Kings'. So different was it that one diarist[©] writing about it said that it 'was like seeing a new primary colour'.

it was
AC Benson, son
of an archbishop,
Master of
Magdalene College,
Cambridge, and
indefatigable
scribbler

In due course grapes of different varieties shrivelled by botrytis were used in Austria's Burgenland, on the German Rhine (first at Schloss Johannisberg in 1775) and in Sauternes, though nobody quite knows when. Only Tokaj, though, continues to add them to already-fermented wine. Other regions wait patiently (it can take two years) for them to ferment on their own. You can taste the difference: Tokaji tends to be lighter in alcohol, darker in colour, more complex in flavour, and keep a considerably higher degree of acidity – which in turn preserves it practically forever.

Unfortunately botrytis can never be counted on. If the autumn is too wet, the rot is far from noble; too dry, you just get raisins. Hence the shortcut, used to brilliant effect in California and Australia in climates where botrytis is not natural, of 'seeding' the crop with the fungus spores. The best results in California have been with Riesling, modelled on Germany's all-too-rare Beeren- and Trockenbeerenausleses. In Australia they have been mostly with Semillon, the principal grape of Sauternes.

One final method of sugar-concentration used to be available only in northern Germany in the dead of winter. Eiswein is made by waiting for the grapes to freeze solid, then pressing them frozen to remove the water content. Now Canada has joined in with spectacular success. Ontario's Riesling ice wines are a thrillingly sweet and piquant addition to the sticky repertoire.

Perhaps we are eating fewer desserts. Seeing the swelling 'By the Glass' lists of stickies in restaurants, we could well be taking them in liquid form instead.

Wine Times, late 1990s

THE WINE-DARK SEA

I t's not every week I have the pleasure of leading a landing party up the beaches into the vineyards and saying 'Take me to your winemaker.' This was last week's escapade, on a *Sunday Times* Wine Club's tour of the wilder shores of wine. Our conveyance? A tall ship, indeed a very tall ship – apparently the tallest ship of all. The *Star Clipper* is a four-masted barquentine, three hundred and sixty feet overall, and I'm prepared to bet the most comfortable and best-crewed sailing ship ever to convey sybarites to their pleasures.

Our landing parties were not for lack of supplies on board. The ship's deep cellars were stocked with the best of the Wine Club's list. We had even brought along our own chef, not to mention such essentials as Cornish lobster and turbot. But you can imagine, I'm sure, how the spirit of scientific enquiry had us packing into the tenders at every sight of green vines ashore.

Our course took us to places where such as Sauvignon Blanc and Merlot are wild exotics; the vines are descendants of ancient Greek or Etruscan stock; their flavours new to most of the party and all the more beguiling for it. In the deep bay of Ajaccio, for instance, we were introduced to the fragrant but soft red Sciacarello of the steep west coast of Corsica, and the firmer, more serious Nielluccio of the north and east. But the grape that caught many people's eye was the white Vermentino – here and elsewhere. When we sailed into Porto Santo Stefano in the Maremma, and visited the lordly estate of La Parrina, the question was why does anybody grow the dreary thin Trebbiano, when the Vermentino has so much more style, scent, substance and general power to satisfy?

On Elba, in the harbour of Portoferraio, Napoleon's little ten-month kingdom, the majority concurred with the royal verdict that the Aleatico was the best stuff. In the right hands Aleatico makes a sweet but bracing and not over-heavy red picnic wine with a clear hint of Muscat. Picnics, at least, are what Napoleon used it for.

Up near La Spezia in Liguria, anchored off the tiny Portovenere, where Byron and Shelley swam and sunbathed and Shelley drowned, we were back on the Vermentino with gusto. The best dry version came from across the gulf of La Spezia in the Colli di Luni. With a *fritto misto mare* at Da Iseo facing the fishing boats (molto Jet Set) it scored however many stars a seaside feast is allowed to score.

Our most memorable vineyard visit, though, was to the impossibly vertiginous – and for this reason, alas, almost extinct – sea-bound slopes of the Cinque Terre. Sun-dried Vermentino and other grapes from these alarming vineyards, where a false step when pruning leads to a watery grave, make the heavenly sweet Sciacchetrà. Taste it while you can.

Decanter, 1997

WINE CHARACTERS

DOCTOR CABERNET Authoritative, senior, unmistakable; a strong personality but a good mixer too. Thick-skinned and adaptable enough to make himself at home anywhere. Confident and wealthy but tending to the austere, even astringent, in taste.

MONSIEUR P NONOIR A fragrant personage inclining a little to the well furnished. Sometimes lively and invigorating, even sparkling, but unmistakably a voluptuary by nature and exceptionally fussy about his surroundings.

C RAH A person of substance with misty oriental origins. Of dark complexion, spicy in his taste, at times peppery in his humour; at his best, capable of using his wealth to spectacular effect.

MERLE O A dark-eyed, long-lashed temptress. At her best buxom, generous, open-hearted, cheerful; the natural partner for Dr Cabernet. Can be a little spineless without his support.

THE GAMAY KID Slickest act in town, but a shallow character deep down. Can be captivating with his wide smile and breezy freshness. Easy to have fun with, but further acquaintance often palls.

MADAME CHARDONNAY An aristocrat, of perfect deportment, with the ability to shine in all climes and all companies. She can sparkle with the best, or develop wonderfully in tranquility. Rather reserved in youth, when she sometimes camouflages her personality with barrels of perfume. But her substance is never in doubt, her salons always crowded, her maturity the epitome of good breeding.

SAUVIGNON BLONDE A slinky dasher with a whiplash tongue. Quite slightly built, with not very much in the cleavage area, but can be a head-turner on the catwalk. A surprisingly good mixer, but usually best in her racy moments as a fragrant vamp.

FRÄULEIN RIESLING A very classy act indeed: but the antithesis of Madame Chardonnay. Lissom, intense, nervous – in extreme cases steely and fascinating, at the other extreme almost overpoweringly sweet and yielding.

G WHIZTRAMINER You get the big hullo from this guy. His aftershave comes out to meet you, then his hand-pumping greeting, then his highly credible spiel. Most people find that a little of his company goes a long way.

THE MUSS CAT Like the Cheshire Cat. A disembodied smile of a grape that pops up everywhere. Sometimes dry, usually sweet; sometimes fizzy, occasionally treacly: always unmistakable and almost impossible to dislike.

Found in my desk drawer, late 1990s

ENGLISH WINE

When forty-odd years ago a handful of eccentrics started planting vineyards in England and Wales, the popular view was that this thoroughly un-British activity could come to no good. Yes, perhaps the Romans had had a go in desperation, and monasteries – well, monks are not expected to be gourmets. But with the Continent so close, with the best wines in the world on our doorstep, and with our famous English summers, clearly it was a waste of time.

It was certainly an act of faith. The faith was (and is) that all good wines are made in marginal conditions. Give the wine-vine all the heat and moisture it can use, and its wine will be gross. The finest aromas, the crispest, most tingling flavours, the subtleties to die for result from slow ripening, cool nights, grapes hanging on far into the autumn.

Yes, Britain is further north (just) than any other winegrowing country, but we have the Gulf Stream. Look at our gardens – able to grow a wider range of plants than any other country. Why not vines?

Vines grow fine here. The question is, do they ripen grapes? The main inhibiting factor is the short growing season. A vine needs, on average, one hundred days to turn its fertilised flower-clusters into ripe bunches of grapes. For success, therefore, flowering must happen at least a hundred days before the autumn weather turns nasty. In Bordeaux the usual period is mid-June to mid-September. If flowering is delayed until, say, mid-July, a hundred days takes you up to late October.

August makes the flavour

Late spring frost is another worry – one we share with most of France. Low August temperatures are more our speciality (and *août fait le goût* © is an axiom you hear everywhere). Of course, with our distaste for shooting songbirds, we have a far higher number of hungry clients for the ripening grapes as well.

So we take precautions. Bird netting is expensive and laborious, but it works. Choosing varieties that ripen early, but preferably don't start out early in spring, is the most essential. Up to a point you can delay the emergence of the fragile spring shoots by pruning late, as late as April. But there are so many vagaries in our island climate that trying to anticipate them leads to nervous exhaustion.

happily no longer

Our pioneer winegrowers started gingerly, planting cast-iron hardy varieties. Extreme cold is not a problem here as it can be in Germany, let alone Canada, but 'hardiness' includes resistance to fungal diseases. The favourite variety was, and is, Seyval Blanc©, a hybrid between a European vine and an American one. Unfortunately, and infuriatingly, European law asserts that hybrids cannot produce quality wine – 'quality' being a term freely used for wines that are anything but, but whose vines have the right parents. Relegation to table wine status is one of the complaints most often heard among English growers. They should wear it, as ground-breaking Italians do, as a badge of honour.

Seyval wine is satisfying but has little scent. The temptation is to spice it up a bit with something more aromatic. There are plenty of candidates: mostly German crosses intended as easier alternatives to the late-ripening Riesling. Names such as Reichensteiner or Huxelrebe appearing on English labels mean more (and sometimes too) aromatic wines. Confidence has grown with experience. At first nobody knew the best way to trellis, train and prune for our climate. As the industry moved from hobby to profession things have become clearer, and the potential far wider than it first appeared.

The discovery that gives most confidence for the eventual standing of our wine is that we can grow the 'noble' varieties after all: above all Pinot Noir, Pinot Meunier (alias Wrotham Pinot) and Chardonnay – the grapes of Champagne. Champagne is the nearest vineyard region to southern England. It has chalk soil identical to that of the North and South Downs and the Chilterns. Granted, Champagne has a more continental climate and slightly less cloud cover, but this is hair-splitting, as recent English sparkling wines have proved. Certainly the best English wines I have tasted have been uncannily close to Champagne, and it may well be that this is the way to invest in the future.⊙

I was right on the money here for once.

Since British Airways started serving quarter-bottles of English wine at the back of the plane and full bottles at the front, there have been few sceptics left. Except perhaps among the Club World passengers in the middle.

Wine Times, 1997

FRANCE ON THE ROPES

How many times have you heard or read that France is on the ropes, punch-drunk before the onslaught of Australian wine technology, South African bargains, New Zealand Sauvignon, Chilean Merlot ...?

There are one or two newspaper columnists who make a weekly practice of slagging off everything French. A piece I have in front of me raves on for a hundred lines about the New World and dismisses Bordeaux and Burgundy in three. Francophobia is a potent force, never dead on these islands and doing especially nicely as E-day approaches.⊙ Yet France remains, despite all the massed expectoration of wine writers, the source of most of the wine we drink, both as a nation and as a club, and of almost all of our best wines.

January 1st, 1999, when francs, Marks, lire and everything except pounds sterling was converted to Euros.

So brainwashed have we been, indeed, that we (some of us, anyway) fall for a truly bizarre sales pitch: Australian wine made in France. Worse still, this claim has been made not by transplanted Australians but by French producers. Morale is at zero when a grower of a famous white burgundy feels he has to put 'Chardonnay' on the label to catch the public eye. Can you think of anything more suicidal than to abandon a unique appellation and claim to fame in order to become just another Chardonnay?

France has all sorts of problems – mostly self-inflicted. If the health of the pound and the dollar have taken a bit of pressure off the franc, the mood of the country is still dour and uncertain,

So I characterised the EU. We still await the dénouement.

heading timorously towards a wedding with Germany that everyone knows will end in tears.© The habit of cosy protectionism, whether of train drivers or any *fonctionnaires*, is another chronic problem. It has recently been revealed in the very heart of the appellation system, where the authorities, it seems, have been routinely covering up for sloppy winemakers.

That is the gloomy side of the picture. But let's look at the other. There is a worldwide shortage of top-quality wines, especially reds, which puts France, above all Bordeaux, in a stronger position than she has been in for years. The first hint of a good vintage last year sent prices into orbit. What will the producers, who saw their farm-gate prices doubled within weeks, do when the bell rings this year?

France is in fact fighting back on several fronts, nurturing what strangely now turns out to be her secret weapon: wines of such unique character that nobody has ever come close to imitating them. I gave a glass of Muscadet recently to a friend, who was completely flummoxed. 'This is amazing,' he gasped. 'What incredible flavour. It can't be Chardonnay, so what on earth ...?' Precisely.

Muscadet – so long despised and neglected – has everything that should make serious wine-drinkers happy. It is a total individual, its tang of the ocean (it should have a faint suggestion of trawler-bilge about it) perfectly matched to its ordained role as the seafood wine par excellence. And it has just had two of its best vintages within memory, so the shopping is easy and results almost guaranteed. If anything is against it, in fact, it is the low price that makes us feel like skinflints when we order it.

Dismiss such feelings. Let your eye go no further down the red-wine page than Beaujolais. There is no Australian or South African Beaujolais, no Oregon Beaujolais – nothing from anywhere else that speaks so warmly and eloquently of its terroir and its blessedly unambitious grape. Beaujolais and its Villages are a deep well of carefree drinking, with the unique smack of French soil.

So long as you buy them in England.

Wine Times, 1997

POCKET WINE BOOK 1998
FOREWORD

Surveying the near-third of my life since I first started this exercise in compression, it seems to me that the biggest change is in the consumer: in expectations, knowledge, demands and willingness to pay more© for better wine. In 1977, the wine countries of Europe were full of gross drinkers with, frankly, only the sketchiest knowledge.

(but not much)

Britain was still mired in Edwardian attitudes; hardly anything beyond 'the classics' was considered worth investigation. America and Australia were just waking up to wine.

They (America and Australia) became its motors. Their uninhibited experiments made science-based winemaking first possible, then the norm, in every country that could afford it. Their influence brought first Italy, then Spain and Portugal, into the modern wine world, and has now so permeated France that it almost passes without comment there.

Without geographical traditions and stylistic conventions, the New World coined varietalism, giving the grape variety pride of place. What started as a sales tool became an invaluable learning aid as millions learned the tastes of Cabernet and Chardonnay and Pinot Noir. They also learned the taste of oak, universally adopted as seasoning for fruit flavours that were often a bit too plain.

Varietalism was a direct challenge to the concept of terroir, the notion that each situation and its soil give a wine a specific character – and that some are inherently better (for the appropriate grapes) than others.

This rivalry has now been pretty much played out, as experience has shown that the effects of terroir are inescapable, and winemakers and grape-growers of the New World are discovering the secrets of their own. The consumer, therefore, is being offered the best of both worlds, in all senses. There has never been a better time to enjoy wine in all its variety.

Hugh Johnson's Pocket Wine Book 1998, Mitchell Beazley

OUR MAN IN BEIJING

*D*ecanter keeps all the tough assignments for me. Last year they packed me off to a Taipei nightclub to see if it was true that Pétrus was the 'in' drink in karaoke bars. (Answer: yes.) This time round it was to Beijing to track down the astonishing quantity of bordeaux that Hong Kong has imported (but certainly not drunk) in the past twelve months. The figures suggest that shipments between January and June 1997 were four times the already heady figure of the same period in 96. One point six million cases, that is, against 400,000. (I suspect that 1.6 million figure, by the way. If China has 1.6 billion people they would get more than a bottle each. In Beijing, at least, there was little sign of it.)

What I did find plenty of, and tracked down all the way to the vineyard, was the local wine. This was the kind of frontier reporting

I was born for. A two-hour journey through the yellow-grey haze that seems to cover lowland China in winter took me to Tianjin, Beijing's port city (and even bigger than the capital, to my surprise). There, skirted by a mega *zone industrielle*, stands the Tianjin Heaven Palace winery of Dynasty, the pioneering joint venture between the Chinese government and Rémy Martin. My hosts were Gao Xiao De, the President of the Board, and Jean-Yves Romagnani, the young Sino-Frenchman who hints at The Way Forward. To remarkable effect, I should add. There are two hundred hectares of vines at the winery: dead flat, immaculately tended, with tall hand-cut granite trellis posts to die for. Not a vine in sight, though: they were all buried for the winter, leaving the land free for a shepherd and his flock. Another funny thing: large parts of the vineyard were flooded: apparently an annual rinse to get rid of salt in the soil.

inox (inoxydable) is a word you often hear: French for stainless steel

The winery differed from hundreds of fairly modern inox-full© plants mainly in being awash with staff. At least fifty workers in blue womanned the bottling line. The bulk of the wine is white, and very easy to swallow. The red is not very – red, that is; but I had no problem drinking that either. As for the Chardonnay, fermented in Allier oak and designated as Wine for Heads of State, I wondered unworthily where the grapes had been grown. Further north near the Great Wall, I was told. It is a bit oaky but of fair Calif/Chile standard.

The only thing that fazed me was the vast carved and painted restaurant building just being finished in front of the winery, with enough private rooms for the whole cabinet. The gold leaf on it, someone hinted, cost enough to build another winery.

Decanter, 1998

BY REQUEST

I wrote this sketch of my patron's life with emotion.

It was not the beat of a butterfly's wing in the Amazon forest, but the Egyptian sun blazing on the head of a painter that started the chain of events. Sunstroke killed Ernest Simon as he sat with his easel facing the pyramids. The indirect results were his son's career as the founder of wine education in Britain, and of the first organisation to publish and proselytise on behalf of higher standards in food and wine. Even Slow Food was foreshadowed on that day in 1895 when the sad news reached Paris.

Ernest Simon had eight children. In the tragic days of the Franco-Prussian war he had had as his junior officer the young Guy de Polignac. The painter's death was a shock in Paris society. Polignac heard of it and offered his help to Simon's widow. 'Yes,' she said, 'my little André has no prospects. He loves books, but not exams. Perhaps you can think of something for him to do.'

The prince in this story had done something princes in other fairy stories never think of. He had married the heiress to one of the richest houses in Champagne. Polignac wed Pommery, and there was no problem offering a desk to his old comrade's child. André Simon moved to Reims, having done his three years' national service in the French artillery. Not aiming cannons, however, but sub-editing the *Revue d'Artillerie*. And having fallen in love with an English girl.

That was in 1899. A year later André and Edith married. Two years after that the young Frenchman, whose English was now better than most of his countrymen's, was sent to work in Pommery's London office.

Selling Champagne in the Belle Époque was a vocation. As André writes: 'The Champagne shipper must be a good mixer rather than a good salesman: neither a teetotaller nor a boozer, but able to drink Champagne every day without letting it become either a bore or a craving.' His unusual national service had made him a scribbler. No sooner was he installed in London than he was researching articles on his new subject. Twelve were published in *The Wine Trade Review* in 1904, and a year later as André's first book, *A History of the Champagne Trade in England*. More than a hundred books later André recalled with amazement how, at the age of twenty-six, he had written in English on English history and been read. Within five years he had founded The Wine Trade Club, been made its Trustee in perpetuity, and launched the first courses of wine education in London, the city of wine merchants.

The Egyptian sun had already influenced the thinking of British wine merchants about wine. Precise knowledge of what you were selling had never before been considered important. There were distractions, of course, two world wars among them, but when the Institute of Masters of Wine took shape in 1952 it was the direct descendant of Simon's Wine Trade Club. Meanwhile he and his friends had written a whole library of textbooks.

André wrote *By Request* to 1957, at the age of eighty, as a record of his career for members of The Wine & Food Society. The society was his second great initiative, his reaction to the Depression of the 1930s. In 1933 his Champagne career was over. People were hungry, restaurants empty and the never-remarkable state of British catering at its lowest ebb. His response: an association for the education of the public in matters of eating and drinking. It consisted of a magazine,

Wine & Food, and meetings, which were either lunches or dinners. The first meeting, in October 1933, filled London's Café Royal with two hundred members and their guests for a simple model menu and three Alsace wines. In January 1934 nearly four hundred came to the second model meal: a dinner at the Savoy Hotel. Looking at the programme, and turning the pages of the quarterly *Wine & Food*, it is impossible not to have a premonition of Slow Food.

My own meeting with André Simon came many years later, when he was eighty-four© and a great public figure. I loved the story he told about a visit to New York that was announced to the newspaper with the headline 'Europe's Greatest Eater With Us'. He was tall and strong, with a mane of snowy hair and huge warm hands. I was a green young journalist when I was sent to interview him and fell under his spell. Evidently he took a liking to me: within a year I was organising Wine & Food Society meetings for him, and within two years starting to edit his magazine.

I was twenty-two

I can hear his warm, exotic voice as I write this. His Maurice Chevalier accent never left him.

There was a theme in his message to the world that appealed to me then and still does today: it was simplicity. He was concerned with ingredients rather than recipes. His model meal was oysters, grouse and cheese, but an omelette and a steak would make him happy. He entertained Elizabeth David and James Beard, the leaders of taste at the time in Britain and the United States, with a roast chicken and a bottle of Lafite. Even as I write it I can feel the sacramental quality of such a meal.

Menus from his earlier life are very different: it is hard to believe the capacity that consumed fourteen courses at a dinner among friends in 1907. But experience – perhaps the Depression, certainly the fine-tuning of his tastes – ended with sublime simplicity and convinced his young disciple. When he chose, described and explained wine it was the same: directness, no more than was necessary, and often an image that stuck in the mind long afterwards.

Wine and food were by no means his only passions. His blood, he used to say, was a blend of wine and printer's ink. He collected a famous library of early books that included a treasure he showed me many times: a single page from Gutenberg's Bible, Europe's first printed work. I can still picture the crisp black impression. Has its quality ever been surpassed?© Gardening was his other love. In the glory days of the Champagne trade he bought a property in Sussex, south of London, that included a considerable lake. The gardens he made around it included rare plants and smooth lawns. They also included an open-air theatre and a cricket field – something few Frenchmen possess.

As André said, printing is the one art that started with a perfection that has never been improved.

Gardens, books, a cellar of good wine ... and a marriage lasting over sixty years. André was a complete man, devout and robust, no business genius but a shrewd judge of taste in every sense, and an unstoppable communicator.

At the age of ninety-one his eyesight began to fail. My wife and I visited him on a rainy day in the country. He was trying to read a book. But even worse than not being able to read, he said, was not being able to see the food on his plate. He was not looking forward to a long dark winter.

We suggested that he write more memoirs, using a dictating machine. He tried. When we next spoke he sounded triumphant. 'Dictating is no good,' he said, 'but I can still use my old typewriter' (a machine as upright and nearly as large as the Vittorio Emanuele Memorial).⊝ His manuscript came to me, with many marks jumbled and half-lines missing, with the request that I put them in order for a book. The result was *In the Twilight*, mixed memories of ninety years of a life devoted to life's blessings, printed in fine type on thick paper and bound as good books used to be. André's story should conclude with the grace he always used before meals, simple or grand: '*Que le bon dieu nous bénisse, et toutes les bonnes choses qu'il veut nous donner.*'

Rome's most vainglorious monument, in shining white marble.

Wine & Food, 1998

POLICING THE VINEYARDS

The French official mind is a fascinating study. It runs along tramlines of what is 'normal'. The 'normal' is what is codified, *reglementé*, sanctioned by the proper authorities, and of course policed by an ant heap of *fonctionnaires*.

Grape varieties are hardly likely to escape. Probably varieties of grass for golf courses have their code too. But a case has come up this year to test the rigidity of the system. Jean-Louis Denois, a go-ahead grower in Limoux, the high Languedoc area celebrated for its fizzy Blanquette, planted an experimental patch of Riesling. Also Gewürz. And L'Institut National des Appellations d'Origine was not amused.

'Pull them up', said INAO. Jean-Louis demurred. He had just made a rather promising first wine. He was quick to point out that the Chardonnay and Pinot Noir he was (legally) growing were not exactly Corbières classics. Indeed that the revived fortunes of Blanquette were due entirely to the addition of Chardonnay.

At this moment, or rather after some months of stand-off, Denois suddenly found supporters. The Syndicat of Limoux producers wrote to INAO and the Douane, the state regulatory police, to say that they would make his experiments official. A *protocol d'expérimentation* would avoid *tout débordement anarchique*. Sure enough, a few months later the Chambre d'Agriculture of the Aude wrote to say they were putting in a patch of Riesling and Gewürz at the official vine research station. They wanted data on these strange Alsatian varieties with a view to their possible authorisation in the department at some future date. Conceivably, they added, they might even form part of the future exports of the region in competition with wines from Spain, California and Australia 'that are not subject to rules'. And by the way, they added, a shade mysteriously, there is nothing in the rule book against top-grafting to change varieties in the vineyard.

If INAO was not impressed by that they must certainly have been by an editorial in the *Revue des Oenologues* in October. The Revue is not an INAO fan club. It blew the whistle on the preposterous 98 per cent pass rate of all wines officially tested by the Institut for their appellation 'labels'. The author of the piece is Pierre Galet, professor at Montpellier University and France's most distinguished ampelographer. Galet is old enough to remember when there were no regulations.

The debate still rages: the New World boasts of its freedom, France insists on the virtues of discipline. But the former discovers new terroirs and the latter gradually compromises. One day there will be a meeting of minds.

'Up to 1930,' he started his article, 'the French winegrower was a free man.' He goes on to say: 'I personally have always regretted that the best quality varieties are not allowed everywhere in France, leaving it to private initiative to experiment.' Why forbid Frenchmen to plant varieties that French nurseries are busily exporting to the competition abroad?

The answer, he writes, is jealousy. Traditional quality regions didn't want 'their' varieties planted in the Midi for fear of competition. And Alsace, a region with no varieties of its own, depending on either German ones or imports from Burgundy or even the Midi, was most jealous of all.

Decanter, 1998

A TRIP ROUND THE BAY

There are moments in my million-megabyte memory of the club's history that stay on the desktop come what may. A remarkable number of them belong in the folder headed *Star Clipper*.

They flash up in random order. The long comfortable beam-reach out of Bandol, still salivating from the rich reds of Château Vannières, into the night towards the high coast of Corsica. Hoisting sail in Ajaccio Bay in a blaze of fireworks on July 14th. Teaching the ship's parrot the rudiments of wine tasting. The night alarm of a

May Day signal in the Bonifacio Strait; the desperate calls of a yacht on the rocks and the Nordic cool of our frogmen, ready to scoop up the survivors .... These memories crowd together with spume-flecked recollections of running before a force nine gale stuffed to the gunwales with claret. Remoter memories, too, of the SS *Ithaca* in Dubrovnik (a nasty gale, that) and the late and much-lamented barque *Marques*⊛ taking shelter in Torbay. They add up to a powerful subplot in the history of our club: a habit of putting to sea in the most spectacular craft at the flimsiest excuse.

having also starred in a TV series as Darwin's Beagle, *the* Marques *sank during the Tall Ships Races in 1984*

There will surely never be a more spectacular ship, though, than the *Star Clipper*. Every statistic about her and her sister ship, *Star Flyer*, is superlative: the tallest sailing ship ever built, the first Sailing Passenger Vessel to be registered at Lloyd's since before World War I. And maybe more alluring for the pleasure-seekers we seem to have as members these days, a splendid table, soft bunks, two pools, and all the things they couldn't have had when sail was a necessity rather than a luxury.

The first sight of our great white bird was in harbour at Cannes, towering above the shipping, reducing our tenders to mere beetles. It was evening. Veterans of club cruises will know that we get down to business without delay. If John Kemp⊛ finds anyone wine-glass-less without good excuse he starts fidgeting with his yellow card. I can't honestly remember how many wines we tasted that first night; but neither then nor later did I notice anyone at muster risking John's disapproval. We worked hard, all one hundred and forty of us, at emptying the innumerable bottles that kept appearing on the tropical deck from shortly after breakfast until long after midnight.

(Club Secretary)

No ship, though, not even a 3,000-ton cruiser, can hold the range and variety of wines that our rules of engagement called for. We had hardly hoist sail from Cannes when we were dropping anchor along the coast at Bandol to be bussed to our first vineyard excursion.

The sight of 36,000 square feet of canvas, spread over four masts and curved taut by a stiff breeze, is something to crick your neck for. A barquentine (the technical description of *Star Clipper*) has four headsails (triangular) from foremast down to mast-like bowsprit. The foremast carries the most picturesque tower of canvas: from bottom to top the forecourse, the size of a tennis court, topsail, upper topsail, lower topgallant and upper topgallant.

But most remarkable of all, all this weight of spotless nylon was donned and doffed with a few quiet commands, the whirring of hidden electric motors, and what looked like a token amount of tugging and winding by the beaming stripe-shirted crew.

Wine Times, 1998

TERROIR
INTRODUCTION

Jim Wilson, a wine-mad former geologist in the US Army, asked me to introduce his magnum opus.

A few years ago, and in some places still today, it was considered somewhere between foolish eccentricity and serious heresy to talk about where wine comes from.

I don't mean its address, geography and postcode. The price, the prestige of the name, its very saleability depend on that above all. I mean the unseen dankness where the vine roots suck: where the liquid in your glass is teased out of the soil.

By physical processes that are still partly mysterious, a white shoot no thicker than a hair nudges downward through soil, sand, close-packed clay, even into hairline fissures in rock. The fuel that drives it is produced by leaves in the sunlight above. But they in turn depend on the capacity of roots to keep sipping successfully, sometimes where there seems to be almost no moisture at all.

Grape varieties, their training, cultivation, ripening, picking and processing have all been under the spotlight. The fruit itself has recently been given the starring role, sometimes almost as though the difference between Cabernet and Syrah were all there was to say about a wine.

This book is different. As far as I know it is the first to investigate the primary source of the wines we know as such distinct characters: the soil. Even recent technical publications in wine countries outside Europe give only fleeting mention to soil. If it keeps the plant upright and lets excess rainfall drain away, its duty, we are given to believe, is done.

Yet soils are more various than vines. They are formed by an infinity of different processes from raw materials as different as seashells and lava. In their physical makeup, their chemical reactions, their interactions with each other, in whether they are willing or grudging to release the elements they contain, from water to metals, they encompass wide, sometimes contradicting, differences. If Chablis tastes different from Meursault, Margaux from Pauillac, the first place we must logically look for the difference is underground.

Terroir, of course, means much more than what goes on below the surface. Properly understood, indeed, it means the whole ecology of a vineyard: every aspect of its surroundings from bedrock to late frosts and autumn mists, not excluding trellis systems and pruning regimes. Not even excluding the soul of the *vigneron*.

From the introduction to *Terroir: The Role of Geology, Climate, and Culture in the Making of French Wines* by James E Wilson, Wine Appreciation Guild, 1998

DE GUSTIBUS ...

W hen your mind starts to turn towards an evening glass of wine, how does the prospect present itself to you? Is your first concern the odds of a heart attack, and the golden opportunity of lengthening them by a micro-fraction if you choose red rather than white?

Neither is mine.

What do I consult? My companions. My dinner prospects. My tasting duties. My bank balance. Most powerfully, though least palpably, the crystallising image of thirst, the anticipation of winey pleasure, forming in my mind as evening approaches. It is, strange to say, quite specific.

The funny thing is that it rarely, if ever, forms itself into the thought 'I feel like a Cabernet'. Or a Merlot, a Syrah, or even a Pinot Noir. (My subconscious doesn't really do varietals at all. I think places, countries, regions, growers, vineyards. I think sweetness, fruity uplift, gripping tannins, scouring acidity or inspiring bubbles before I think grapes.)

There is a list of wine flavours in my unconscious, just as there is an ingrained food menu. You are just the same: lamb, fruit, an egg, salmon, a jam sandwich are all there in your mental menu. For one reason or another (you may even believe it is your body chemistry issuing instructions), one or other takes priority and becomes what you want. The wine I want, in this first recognition of specific thirst, is almost always white.

Bruno Prats⊙ once memorably said 'White wine is what you drink before you drink red wine.' I would put it the other way round. More and more I find that we use Riesling or Silvaner or Pinot Blanc (either German or from Alsace, but more often German) to open the session: a glass before dinner while we bustle round the kitchen, then probably another with some fishy or meaty appetizer. *then proprietor of Château Cos d'Estournel*

People tend to react to Riesling as though finding food to match it is a puzzle. In a recent *Harper's*⊙ supplement, trendy chefs were thinking of daft things to do with Riesling: throwing soy sauce and ginger at it, for heaven's sake. Have they forgotten (or not been told) that it is the perfect match for almost all sorts of cold meat? The *kalte Aufschnitt* of charcuterie is an irresistible accompaniment. Cold game birds (as a rule tastier than hot) are never better than with a crisp Spätlese. *the increasingly lively wine trade organ*

Judy and I then often leave bottle A in the fridge for the next evening and move to bottle B for the main course, which as often as possible is fish, hard as it is to come by out here in the country. We'd be sunk without our deep freeze. Out comes another bottle of white wine: usually something of more weight and substance – even Chardonnay. We are Chablis freaks, but a bit of everything crosses the Johnson threshold.

And red wine? It is always the centrepiece of a dinner party, but alone at home we find it makes the perfect contemplative sipping when thirst has been quenched, with a book by the fireside.

Decanter, 1998

POCKET WINE BOOK 1999
FOREWORD

I'm not sure when wine made the transition from agreeable, even inspirational, beverage and foodstuff to top fashion item. Within the past few years, certainly. Probably I had my eye too close to the viewfinder to notice. But there is no mistaking the signs now. The once crusty establishment of bankers and aristocrats who ruled the wine world for so long now shares it with actors, singers, designers, sports stars – and colossal corporations.

Does it matter? Does it affect the wine we drink? On balance I think we all benefit. Big egos want steep prices, of course; but they also invest heavily in best practices – and sometimes in regions where scientific vineyard management and modern cellar technology were unknown.

The yeast leavens the whole loaf.

The world tour of aspirants to prestige can make you giddy. In a hotel in Wales recently I drank wine from Tasmania, Mexico and Hungary; each a distinct and worthwhile character. The threat of homogenisation – of everyone planting Chardonnay – is still with us, but there are clear signs of the pendulum swinging the other way as alternative, even unknown, grape varieties are given an airing. Meanwhile even the most varietally led regions are learning rapidly that you need more than just a grape name to sell wine these days. The demand that will shape the future is for a sense of place in what we drink. The game is up for those who turn their backs on terroir. The earth will open and swallow them up.

A DECLARATION OF INTEREST Readers should know that I have interests in the Royal Tokaji Wine Company in Hungary, and Château Latour in Bordeaux. (It's hard not to be interested in many friends' vineyards, too.)

Hugh Johnson's Pocket Wine Book 1999, Mitchell Beazley

THE SLOW SHOW

I've touched before on the Slow Food movement and its founder Carlo Petrini. (I once referred to this beaming giant of a man as the Pavarotti of gastronomy – only to be told that the tenor enthusiastically occupies that place himself). 'Zló', as Carlo pronounces his favourite word, was his deeply felt reaction to the threat of the first McDonald's to appear in Italy, it must be fifteen years ago.

Last year the movement put on its most ambitious show to date, the Salone del Gusto in Turin. Over a long weekend almost eighty thousand members of the public turned up at the former Fiat factory (c1920), which is now Turin's exhibition space, its roof a test-track, with the Agnelli helicopter pad still in use. (Plenty of Slow jokes here.)

It was like no other gastro-show I have ever attended: a giant but genuine fair for Italy's artisan makers of all the succulent varieties of *salumi*, breads, fragrant cheeses, prosciutto, chocolates, olives and oils to strut their stuff, surrounded by a humungous wine bar with two-and-a-half thousand wines available for tasting by the glass.⊖

There were scores of events, workshops, tastings and seminars all struggling to make themselves heard, but the nub of the show was the great taste-in sandwiched, as it were, between the wines and the *salumi*, where whole families got to grips with Italy's most delectable produce in an atmosphere both earnest and genial. You felt there was a subplot here – as indeed there was. Carlo put it like this: 'Big business' (I wish I could do his French accent – English is beyond him) 'tells Brussels what to do. Every regulation threatens the small producer, the artisan, who sets standards inconveniently high for mass production. It's the same for food and wine. But it's no use just saying this, it sounds elitist. We have to produce a genuine mass movement to have any political weight.' It looks as though Carlo's point is being taken. Why else was the agriculture minister there?

Not that elitism was entirely missing. Carlo hosted a dinner for sixty under the title *Il Giocco del Tre* or The Game of Three. With each course Dr Franco Martinetti, one of Italy's great amateur wine-lovers, had selected three wines: the first an obvious choice (such as Chablis with oysters); the second two contrasting challenges. With the oysters, and also a scallop dish, to my surprise and delight he was proposing two different Manzanillas: La Gitana from Hidalgo and El Roccio from González-Byass. What's more they got the popular vote.

Sherry served at a French dinner in Italy? Things really are on the move.

Decanter 1999

You just pointed to any bottle and the bartender opened it for you, climbing a ladder if necessary to reach it.

WHERE TO BE ON DECEMBER 31ST

All the chatter at the moment seems to be about where, how, with whom and with what we are going to see the nineteen change to twenty. Some of my cannier friends have already started looking for really hot parties where they can hire themselves out as butlers or waiters, be paid a small fortune and enjoy the privileged rave-up at the same time.

I of course am open to offers.

But meanwhile a few daydreams: favourite winey places where the millennium switch would be without pain. Where indeed one might almost forget that time ticks on.

Of course anything happening in December is best seen in the southern hemisphere, if only on the grounds that you can't see much of anything in the dark. On the other hand, most of the bottom half of the globe being water, there is a relatively limited choice of dry bits, and some them are not dense with amenities.

Except for Australia.

Doyles on the Beach in Watsons Bay

Wing me down to Pete Doyles'© sand-between-the-toes seafood restaurant on Sydney Harbour, get Pete and Len Evans and assorted mates round the table, start with the Krug that seems to fill the air in Evans's vicinity, and let the oysters and the bay bugs roll. Bay bugs are those strange New-South-Welsh crosses between a crab and an oversize beetle that offer more and sweeter flesh than any other shellfish. You start eating them with an old Hunter Valley Semillon, Lindeman's maybe: the wine that convinces with a lighter touch than any other in Australia. Then you hesitate between one of Di Cullen's Margaret River Sauvignons and a Clare Riesling – ordering both. Then comes the Meursault-Charmes you are keeping in the icebox. Then the '85 Montrachet in a magnum. Pete provides delicately fried, then more artfully prepared fishes, salads, and finally a steak for the tarry old Hunter Shiraz that's been lurking in the shade. A carpetbag steak©, why not, stuffed with Sydney rock oysters. Before a glass of Mick Morris's unctuous Liqueur Muscat, sipped with Sydney Harbour round your ankles and no notion of hour, day, year or century.

inspired: a fillet steak with a pocketful of oysters

That's Scenario A. For a less sophisticated, but much closer, shot at the same seaside nirvana I would hope for a warmish day in Sanlúcar de Barrameda. The Sanlúcar Beach, where the Guadalquivir issues from Seville to the sea, was the Cape Canaveral of the 15th century. Magellan and Columbus both pushed off from here on their voyages into space. Magellan's ships carried more sherry than armour[9], and who can doubt that his last meal before leaving Spain was under restaurant Bigote's shelter on this beach? A few tapas: olives, Manchego, grilled squidling, with several glasses of pale, salty Manzanilla Fino. Then a broad dish of prawns, amber and orange, charred here and there by the grill, in oil scented with garlic and chillies. The sacramental wine with Sanlúcar prawns is Manzanilla Pasada, the stinging tawny Amontillado of the bodegas by the sea.

according to Mauricio González-Gordon, Marquis of Bonanza and head of González-Byass, who had the precise figures

I can't shake the sea out of my daydreams. In France I shall have a table at the America's Cup – not the race but the sail-shaded restaurant overlooking the harbour at Sète. I shall drink the ultimate Mediterranean white wine: the softly dense, garrigue-scented, crisp-finishing Château Hospitalet from La Clape, that strange wild extrusion of limestone on the coast near Narbonne.

Will nothing drag this man away from the sea? Not Paris on a winter evening? I'm too late by about five years to get a table at Taillevent. But to be eased from one millennium to another by Jean-Claude Vrinat[9] would be the ultimate pampering.

owner of Taillevent, who died in 2008

J-C's great gift is to lead you through his sensational menu and bewildering wine list, letting you believe that you have made the decisions while composing the perfect menu around you. Is the *mousse d'oursins* too rich? Then the *huîtres tièdes au fenouil* before a *fricassée de homard au châtaignes*. I would see if he still has a bottle of Raveneau's 1983 Chablis Vaillons, and the '88 Pape Clément for a melting dish of *foie de canard au pain d'épices et gingembre*. If the 1937 Château Gilette is still there to perform its unctuous glissade over and around the *moelleux au chocolat et au thym*, the millennium will be immaterial.

In Italy you will find me, for a change, halfway up a mountain: Monte Amiata, the southernmost bastion of Tuscany. The best food in Italy is in simple places. At La Cantina (I have disguised the name; I want to keep it simple) I shall start dinner with the pure-tasting *zuppa di verdura*, coiling a green-gold filament of olive oil on the surface .... The porker that nourished the huge milk-white chop has clearly never done a day's work: it melts between palate and tongue; teeth are redundant. And then there is panna cotta, *vin santo*, coffee, grappa ... which century did you say it is?

If I am found, which is very likely, in England, I shall smuggle two or three bottles from home (all utterly predictable: Chablis, claret, Tokaji) into an estuarial pub whose sea bass is as fresh as its oysters, where they don't bother you with the brown meat of the crab, and where the lambs can look in through the kitchen window.

And in Germany, where thoughts of the seaside are rarely uppermost,
Kriebs, perhaps,
at Brauneberg I shall be snug in the *Stube* of a Mosel-maker© drinking Rieslings, starting with featherlight refreshment, '97 Kabinetts, and moving by degrees through a dinner of blue trout, creamy mushrooms and baked ham, into the sublimity of ancient Ausleses.

Wine Times, 1999

THE DISCOVERY OF AUSTRALIA

I had a glass of Yalumba FDR1A 1974 to my lips when it clicked. The date, not the glass. The year I first went to Australia, according to the notes 'the worst Australian vintage in the last thirty years' and, great Scott, a quarter of a century ago. Very creditable, the FDR1A, all things considered. FDR stood for Fine Dry Red, a right-on name for a Cabernet-Shiraz blend of a lousy year that runs a quarter of a century and still tastes of fruit; 1A, presumably, meant A1.

It was one of the historic rarities at a tasting earlier this year to celebrate a hundred and fifty years of the Hill-Smith's Yalumba Estate. London's wine establishment packed the Delfina Gallery in Bermondsey, agog at relics going back to the 19th century.

That was what was so hard for most in the crowd to comprehend: what you might call the pre-history of Australian wine. The ancient humour (ditto), chippiness (now almost extinct) – and bottle after bottle of incredible, different, utterly special and unlike-any-other wine.

Loving them was easy. Cracking the variant on Enigma that gave them all bin numbers and their labels arcane references to people and places unknown took a bit longer. The rules sounded simple. Much the best sellers were 'port' and 'sherry'. Table wines were red (usually classified as burgundy or claret – sometimes as both) and white (Riesling, Chablis, white burgundy or Mosel).

The categories referred exclusively to the makers' intentions. There were famous regions, starting with the Hunter Valley near Sydney, the Barossa Valley near Adelaide, and Coonawara and Rutherglen in the middle of nowhere. So distinct were their wines (and others from such outlying spots as Great Western, the Goulburn River; Langhorne Creek and Clare) that I was astonished to learn it was common practice to make 'interstate' blends. In fact top winemakers' reputations were based more on their cocktail-making skill (with wines) than faithfulness to their terroir.

Shiraz was King Red – and for that matter still is. Shiraz made the burgundy, claret and the port. And white wine was just as simple:

there was Riesling and Semillon (also, in most cases, called Riesling), almost no Sauvignon Blanc, and no Chardonnay at all.

Yalumba's giants of the past, then, you would think would be in a pretty narrow range. Predictable, yes, but astonishing all the same: they were so good. And none, to my surprise, had the kerosene smell⊖ that is now considered normal in even half-mature Oz Riesling.

It was wines like these that I tasted on that visit twenty-five years ago – wines that scarcely anyone in Britain knew existed. I went on a shopping spree, buying cases and cases just to show the folks back home. I asked Penfolds – indeed Max Schubert himself – how many cases of Grange I could buy and was told twelve: I believe the first Grange ever shipped to England. Lucky Wine Club Members who bought them.

it takes many years for German Rieslings to acquire the forecourt pong

I was so excited that when my trophies followed me home I persuaded Michael Broadbent to lend me Christie's tasting room to show them off to the world. My wife Judy designed an invitation: the outline of Australia, saying 'Come and taste some ripper wines'. The club has never looked back from that first meeting with Australia. For me, looking back, that evening in Bermondsey in May was a pretty poignant moment.

Wine Times, 1999

COUNTING THE EMPTIES

A long the top of the bookcases lining my study I keep a rather dusty collection of empty bottles; each one the container, in its day, of a wine that gave me an exceptional thrill. A few of them are extremely old and rare – the 1840 Cape Constantia, for example, or the 1870 Castle Johannisberg – but most are simply wines that I chose luckily or well, kept in my cellar for a while, opened in their prime, and loved.

I look at the bottles along the bookcase. A motley lot: no prejudice here. In random order comes first a *vin santo* from Tuscany, stored five years in little 100-litre *caratelli* under the roof tiles of the Avignonesi Palace in Montepulciano. Wine that had become almost a liqueur, so intense was the savour of mingled raisins, oak and – oddly – oranges.

Next is the empty bottle of a Chablis Premier Cru of 1971, drunk in 1980 when all the qualities of a supreme Chablis vintage were knit in majestic austerity. Beside it the Trefethen Napa Chardonnay of 1977, drunk in 1982. This wine won famous prizes in its youth. It seemed a different breed from the Wagnerian style of Napa

Chardonnay; closer to the harmony and understatement of the Côte de Beaune. In its sixth year it was no less fresh and delicate – only infinitely more complex: an adult pleasure.

a grape then rare in Napa, I think his first, and wonderful in 1979

There are bordeaux, burgundies, Mosels, Champagnes, the 1974 Joseph Phelps Pinot Noir© Rioja reds, Australian Rieslings, the rare Vega Sicilia, a '73 Chianti Riserva from Fattoria Saulina which in 1979 seemed to me to epitomise the paradox of warmth and astringency that makes Chianti's best wines unique. There is a very rare Rèze, the golden alpine wine of the Swiss Valais, densely concentrated by brilliant mountain sunshine and infinitesimal crops.

The bottle of the 1962 Stony Hill Chardonnay I brought back empty all the way from California, so moved was I by the vitality of a twenty-year-old wine. I did the same from Portugal with the '27 Quinta do Noval vintage port.

For each good wine there is a season (for great wines sometimes as long as a decade) when all its elements are resolved into a unique personality. At its height, wine can be the most complex pleasure, both sensually and intellectually, within our human grasp. I have often tried to explain to myself how a smell and taste can seem to reach so deep into our subconscious minds, evoking memories and stimulating responses as not even a perfect flower can. We sniff a rose with pleasure, fondle it for a few minutes, but our attention wanders.

What gives the perfume of wine such power that it can tease us, sometimes for half an hour, showing us new facets of beauty every minute? When I sit into the small hours reading, or enjoying the night air in the garden, the ripe Riesling in my hand has the near-divinity that made the ancients carve images of Bacchus. Only music shares this power to move.

I hear the sceptic say it is merely the alcohol carrying the fragrance straight to his poor soft brain. A kinder (and more scientific) explanation is that the olfactory nerves in the brain – the ones that perceive smells – are immediate neighbours to the memory lobe. Whatever the physical reason, men and women of culture and intellect have prized wine above all other foods, and other stimulants too, since the era of prehistory, when it first emerged on the slopes of Mount Ararat.

It is forty years since I first realised how much wine has to offer anyone whose senses are awake, whose mind is open, and who appreciates the interactions of man and nature. Every bottle I open is still a new lesson, in a subject none of us will ever master.

Decanter, 1999

The 2000s

POCKET WINE BOOK 2000
FOREWORD

I t is a well-established convention that every thousand years (and indeed every hundred), writers of reference books do a little stock-taking and crystal-gazing. But wine calls for much shorter intervals.

You don't have to look back more than twenty-five years to see a totally different wine world: one where France was in firm control, indeed virtually the only producer of fine and luxurious wines. California and Australia were only just beginning to understand their potential. Italy and Spain were so little exploited or understood that their exports were limited to two or three wines apiece. Germany alone was held in more respect than her wines receive today.

Look forward twenty-five years and what do we see? Wines of good to fine and even luxurious quality from almost every country that makes wine at all.

This is the pace and extent of progress. What a joyous prospect. Are there no snags? Only for people with long memories and those with a passion for the distinctive and authentic. For clearly there is a risk, and more than a risk, of all these good, fine and even luxurious wines resembling each other. They will not become identical, or even indistinguishable; but already we see certain characteristics praised by the critics in one region being imitated by producers in another. Big fruity red wines tasting of oak are only the most obvious example.

Once a region discovers that it can raise its price by abandoning its individuality, it becomes a mere fashion item. Fashions change; terroir is the one immutable – the anchor of character.

supermarkets
above all
There are other changes, too. The ever-present temptation to over-produce, resulting in watery wine, is encouraged by better disease control in vineyards. Wine merchants© encourage it too, by haggling for unrealistically low prices.

But the overwhelming majority of the news is good; there is scarcely a country or region in this book without aspiring and dedicated producers leading it on to higher ground.

Hugh Johnson's Pocket Wine Book 2000, Mitchell Beazley

ARE THERE ABSOLUTES?

W hat marks out this millennium, this turn-of-the-century, this decade, even this year from all other moments in history is the universal chat-line that suddenly links us all. The wine world is as much affected by it as any other trade, craft or market. More so, in fact. It was only in the past generation that its principals began to network, meet and bond across the globe. Now there are few secrets at any level: the race is to the swift (and ruthless).

The question in my mind is whether the true values (or what I consider the true values) of wine appreciation will survive the deluge of modishness that comes with the new global market. Put it another way: are there absolute qualities that are bound to re-emerge, as oil floats on water? The gobs-of-fruit syndrome, the sickly taste of oak, the thick mouthfeel that too often get the points today – are they passing fads? Or will the essential values be reinterpreted by each generation? Or each country?

The American taste for the sweet and not precisely subtle is predictable. I can't speak for what the Chinese might ask from wine, if they ever came to dominate the market (bubbles, for example, are not their thing).⊖ I strongly believe that certain attributes of good wine are essential and universal, even if the words to describe them call for a little reflection before they mean very much.

Perhaps a famous name has priority, but bordeaux was the flavour of the decade.

The first is life, liveliness, vitality, vigour – however you want to express it. There is no good wine without it. Wine that is either stolid or limp-wristed is no good.

To arrive at liveliness the components have to be in balance. The flavours must dance – and an unbalanced dancer falls over. Given these two essentials, the third follows as Saturday follows Friday. You want a second glass. A second bottle even. Overstuffed, over-oaked, over-heady wines are one-glassers. They can win competitions (they shouldn't if the judges are awake) but they can't win your heart.

To keep our interest we need variety. It was what drew me to wine in the first place: the fact that grapes can give you Champagne or Hermitage, port or Mosel. I believe the new global market has already learned the limitations of the me-too approach. Not that we can do without gushers of formulaic wine. Thank God for Australia. But tomorrow's wine-drinkers will want novelty and distinctiveness as much as we do today. And in wine, distinctiveness comes from the earth. I predict we will hear more and more about the earth. At the biodynamic extreme, sure. But also from every grower whose heart is in the business. And who would make wine if it weren't?

Decanter, 2000

A FOUR-LETTER WORD

Now that you can be sent up the river for using the p-word⊖, chic traders (like me) are offering 'a demi-kilo, darling'. I have better news, though, about another p-word you had almost forgotten.

a stallholder was convicted for offering his apples by the pound

Only grey-haired readers will recall the pint of Champagne. The ideal size, it was, for the lonely diner, and good for four glasses in the interval. There used to be countless occasions – or so it seemed – when a bottle was a bit too big, and a half-bottle a bit mean. More seriously, half-bottles of Champagne are notoriously bad keepers. The case of twenty-four halves is a risky proposition; the last few in my experience almost always taste tired.

Then Those Who Know Better in B******s decreed that Champagne in pints was too – what? Dangerous? Decadent? Untidy? Anyway they banned it. The near-as-dammit half-litre (the difference is sixty-eight millilitres: a small half-glass) is legal in Europe for still wines, but not for bubbly. Whether you felt outrage or merely irritation, it was one of those many decrees that build up resentment. But now there is hope.

My first pint-sighting for ten years was in Switzerland. Being shrewd enough to avoid massive stitch-ups like the Communauté européenne, the Swiss remain free to order what size of bottle they like. The glassmakers of Champagne only wait for an order to get blowing. Now a trickle of half-litres is coming back on the market. In 1999 only about 12,000 dozen, but it's a start. America took some;

Again, I'm afraid this was just wishful thinking.

Japan a few.[©] And apparently the EC does not ban them from tax-free outlets. I give notice, here and now, that I'm going to smuggle some, if that's what it takes, to have them handy for my lonely evenings, theatre intervals and *déjeuners sur l'herbe*.

Decanter, 2000

ATHLETES OF LIQUOR

A little bottled history ...

'Athletes of liquor' was one description of the legendary English topers of the 18th century. Their habit of drinking three bottles of port at a sitting left other nations in awe – and perhaps unsurprised by our lager-drinkers today.

Are we just flattering ourselves, then, when we claim that our national expertise goes further than merely lifting the elbow? Not according to the figures. The wine we buy is the evidence. In value we easily lead the world: in 1997 we bought 18.4 per cent of all French wine exports (Germany bought 15, the US 15.8). We were the biggest importers from Germany, too; from Australia and New Zealand by far, and in the top two or three for Italy, Spain, and almost everywhere else.[©]

In 2015 Germany was Number One in volume, the UK in value.

What makes us, in a land until recently without wine of its own, such conscientious wine-drinkers? Is it something new, born of the supermarkets and Oz Clarke? There were signs of it much, much earlier. A 'negotiator Britannicus' was spotted on the Bordeaux waterfront in the 1st century BC: excavations of Roman Colchester have revealed wine amphoras from sixty different sources. Wine fleets sailed into Saxon York from the Rhine and most famously, in 1153, the future Henry II of England married Eleanor of Aquitaine, uniting the crowns of England and western France for three hundred years and giving red bordeaux an English name it has never lost: claret.

England's capital in those days

But Bordeaux was lost, and we turned for our supplies to Spain. Sherry or Canary 'sack', also Rhenish from the Rhine, were the wines of Shakespeare's time, enormously boosted by Sir Francis Drake's freebooting raid of the Armada stores in Cádiz. He brought home 2,900 butts of sherry. One can imagine the blackboard in every pub offering 'Drake's Authentic'. And Shakespeare seems to have been a shareholder: no wine has ever been more loudly plugged than sack by Falstaff: 'If I had a thousand sons, the first humane principle I would teach them should be, to forswear thin potations, and to addict themselves to sack.' His 'thin potations', of course, were such light wines as claret and Rhenish.

Henry IV Part II, Act IV, Scene ii

But then it was the Dutch who ruled the waves. With three-quarters of Europe's merchant fleet, their traders called the tune for half a century. They commercialised spirits (gin and brandy) as rivals to wine, browbeating winegrowers to grow the white wine they liked, its fermentation stopped with sulphur to keep it sweet.

It was in despair at the dim outlook for claret that the President of the Bordeaux Parliament looked to London as the natural outlet for a superior product; indeed he sent his son over to start a tavern in the City for the *gratin* of the day. Samuel Pepys gives us our first glimpse of 'Ho Bryan, that hath a good and most particular taste.' Château Haut-Brion, the first of the First Growths, became the rage in early Georgian England.

upper crust

An English grandee in the first age of English ascendancy was rich and curious, open-minded and greedy for novelty – a Grand Tourist in every sense. The class is epitomised by the Duke of Chandos, Handel's patron and perhaps the first great English wine-buff – or wine collector – of any nation. His cellar was supplied from every part of Europe, if necessary by smuggling. More surprising still is his cellar book with his own tasting notes. Port he considered 'a very ticklish purchase.' Yet port, to spite the French and Spanish, was what the government wanted the whole nation to drink, and by mid-century all but the mightiest had become compliant – to the extent, in some cases, of three bottles at a sitting.

The rest is down to differential duties. For nearly two hundred years British governments manipulated popular taste away from natural table wines (above all French) towards port, then increasingly in Victorian times sherry, then the products of the Empire: 'port' or 'burgundy' from Australia and 'sherry' from the Cape.

Not until Prime Minister Gladstone's budget of 1860 were these distorting tariffs removed. In the 1860s British consumption of French wines multiplied eight times. But the social mould of wine-drinking in Britain had been formed too rigidly to change in a hurry. The British are said to organise everything along class lines. It was certainly true of wine-drinking. The habit of drinking table wines remained an upper-class preserve for another century.

In the 1960s the old wine trade was living on borrowed time. To find a wine merchant who even spoke a foreign language was rare. Scores of highly conservative London and provincial merchants (their lists virtually limited to bordeaux and burgundy, German wines, port, sherry and Champagne) were gobbled by breweries – which usually then lost what remained of the plot. It was thought revolutionary (and certainly didn't pay) to look even as far off-piste as the Rhône or Loire, let alone Italy, let alone the New World.

What rekindled the business was the sheer inherent interest in the vast variety of wine, the possibilities that younger people found as they extended their trips in Europe and beyond. This was what Britain brought to the party: not so much crusty tradition as eager open-minded curiosity.

And the other wine-buying countries? The heavyweights are Germany, the US (though not in proportion to its population), Belgium, Switzerland and Holland, with Japan catching up last, and Denmark punching far above its weight.©

Now we're all looking at China. We may not have long to wait.

Where Britain is right out in front is in critical authority. Our Institute of Masters of Wine sets the international professional standard. More wine books and better magazines are published here than are in all the rest of the world. We crave information. We are certainly seduced by the folklore, but we don't want to be fooled; if anything sharpens discrimination, it is paying some of the world's highest excise duties. Wine has always had its political dimension. Nothing has changed. The government has even managed to revive the ancient resource of smuggling across the Straits of Dover ....

Wine Times, 2000

TUSCANY AND ITS WINES
INTRODUCTION

At the end of the 20th century Tuscany had become half the world's icon of Arcadia. For millions it epitomises the pleasures of *villeggiatura*: the dreamed-of escape from the city, however historic and adorned by art, to a villa in an idealised countryside ... countryside captured in the glowing colours of the Renaissance, but familiar from far further back in our faded memories of the classical world.

Virgilian is a lovely word. Tuscany is Virgilian. The *Georgics* are the poet's specific instructions for attaining and maintaining this idyll of country life, from the dressing of vines to the olive harvest and the proper management of bees. But far beyond Virgil, in the time of legends, we picture the smiling Etruscans tilling the same land, sitting under the same trellised vines, looking out on the same blue receding hills, glowing inwardly with the same oil and wine.

The oil and wine are the foreground of this happy picture, as much now as they were then. The mythology of Tuscany gives them the role of milk and honey in this Promised Land. If the myth and the reality were often far apart, the endless stream of tourists were usually ready to forgive. As Henry James wrote, 'The fond appraiser, the infatuated alien'[⊙] dotes on a 'mellow mouldering surface, some hint of colour, some accident of atmosphere ... just because it is Florence, it is Italy.'

It is the Tuscan paradox that this cradle of creativity, a culture whose instinctive artistry has inspired the world ever since, has, until recently, been relatively backward when it comes to the arts of the table. Compared with the French genius for exploring the savours of every terroir, the Tuscans took their lovely land for granted. For all their intensive cultivation of the landscape, their stately villas and ingenious gardens, even the proudest rulers of Tuscany were, with few exceptions, happy with simple rations, and rarely seem to have bothered overmuch about their wine.

A Florentine feast under the Medici was a spectacle, but scarcely epicurean. 'An Italian banquet,' said Michel de Montaigne[⊙], 'would be a light meal in France.' Tuscany's foremost chefs to this day repeat as an article of faith that they are wedded to rustic traditions, that they merely refine the *casalinga* classics – farmers' food. And indeed a Tuscan meal is defined by its predictability: bread, oil, beans, roast meat, vegetables, *funghi*, cheese.

To see crostini, angular morsels of hard unsalted bread moistened with oil, as an exciting appetizer day after day demands dogged conservatism. The same undemanding standards have historically applied to Tuscan wine. But the past quarter-century has seen the greatest change in its whole history. The straw-covered Chianti *fiasco* has all but disappeared. Wine has become chic, winemakers public figures. Tuscany now plays to an international audience. You would not expect her to cut less than a dashing figure.

Times of change are always the most exciting. Over the last generation Tuscany has turned a peasant culture of suspicion into a fluid and affluent society, translating ideas from round the world into its own inimitable tongue. Tuscany today makes some of the world's most original and resounding red wines, and serves them with deeply satisfying vernacular food. Progress with white wines is slower. The simple seafood wines are there already; adding something finer is top of the agenda.

'Supertuscans' emerged in the 1970s.

But does the visitor, watching the nodding fishing boats and their rippled reflections from a table on the harbour, really care? When the waiter brings you a grilled *bistecca*, maddeningly savoury with salt and oil, are you still indecisive over the wine list – or just revelling in being there, as infatuated as Henry James?

Perhaps no agricultural landscape has ever been so poetically lovely as the *cultura promiscua* of Tuscany just those few decades ago. Mixture was at the heart of it: trees with vines, olives with elms and poplars, cabbages with corn, figs, sunflowers and chickens. And in the vineyards the noble Sangiovese growing alongside a dozen other grapes, indifferently black and white.

The fields were more populous than the silent streets of villages – the black-clad *contadini* planting, cultivating and cropping with hardly a pause. At vintage time families followed the ox cart into the fields, a single white beast or a yoked pair pulling a wooden vat on wheels. Wide-based ladders were propped against the trees to reach vines draped in baroque festoons. As the ancient vat filled with grapes, black and white together, their green stalks still attached, the farmer stood beside it with a thick stick, plunging it in like a cudgel to break the bunches and allow room for more. The inky mixture began to ferment in the sunshine, beaded bubbles appearing among the gleam of skins and tangle of stalks.

At breakfast the farmer passed round an old *fiasco*, its straw purple with use, to fill thick tumblers with last year's wine. It was black as night, bitter, sour and sweet at the same time. It washed down hard bread and sweet grapes in handfuls. It was impossible not to think of the *Georgics*, the countryman's calendar of two thousand years ago. What little change there had been, you felt, was hardly for the better. Virgil's slaves may have been bound to the land, whereas these peasants might have cousins in America. But a sharecropper has the minimum motivation, the narrowest horizons. The Tuscans, wrote Henry James, have 'the faculty of making much of common things and converting small occasions into great pleasures.' They have been taught by long experience.

As Virgil, whose love of the land is as clear in his poem as the spring smell of growing grass, acknowledged, 'The dressing of vines is never finished ... admire a spacious vineyard if you like, but farm a small one.'

FLORENCE The capital of Tuscany is in no sense a wine town like Bordeaux or Beaune. The city that six hundred years ago reawakened the arts, gave us back classical learning, and can almost be said to have invented modern thought, straddles the Arno with a bridge that seems almost a parody of worldliness – a street of goldsmiths. You are aware of the joy of wealth, the feeling for everyday luxury, in Florence's clothes, its handbags and shoes and innumerable touches of vanity. The markets are rich with every sort of food. Wine seems no big deal. If there are wine warehouses in Florence they are not evident. But in a Florentine trattoria the marriage of wine and food is so fundamental that you realise Tuscany can no more run without wine than a truck without diesel.

At the most basic level is the *fiaschetteria*, a bar serving wine and panini or simple dishes. At the other, one Florentine establishment has a worldwide reputation for pampering rich wine-lovers. The Enoteca Pinchiorri is installed in the grander ground-floor rooms, the courtyard and cellars of a palazzo. Wine is more temptingly displayed here than anywhere on earth – such a cornucopia of abundance and variety, reaching far beyond Italy, that it is impossible not to be seriously tempted. Waiters may be as professional in France, but here their agile omnipresence is almost feline. The familiar Tuscan insistence on peasant roots for every dish is stretched beyond credence in the midst of such deep napery, such tinkling crystal, such gleaming silver, such a profusion of flowers.

SIENA Is there a more perfect medieval city than Siena left in Europe? Siena formed its character earlier than Florence, built its uncompromising brown-brick buildings in the Gothic spirit, and fell from its height of prosperity before the gaiety of Renaissance architecture could make its mark. The narrow streets between six-storey palaces are utterly unadapted to modern life.

In its early 14th-century heyday Siena was a greater banking city than Florence. Its Monte dei Paschi bank is the oldest in the world (the name conjures up shepherds tending their flocks in the hills; the *monte*, though, were the heaps of gold in the counting house). In the Palazzo Pubblico the fresco of Good Government by Ambrogio Lorenzetti gives a graphic picture of the brief glow of an enlightened republic before the Black Death quartered its population. The palazzo itself, indeed, in its perfect proportions, with a tower infinitely more graceful than that of its rival in Florence, seems to symbolise a rare moment of harmony between centuries of mayhem.

It is hard to believe that the glorious scallop-shaped Campo was finished and paved at the same time, nearly seven hundred years ago – the division of its brick paving into a nine-part fan representing the Council of Nine, the best government the city ever had. A 16th-century visitor recorded that Mass was said daily outside the Palazzo Pubblico while the citizens went about their shopping and gossiping in taverns, with a trumpet to hush them for the moments of solemnity. Today the Campo is known worldwide for its summer horse races, the Palio, when centuries-old scores between the *contrade* are brought out,to be put back after the race, as unsettled as ever.

Tuscany and Its Wines, Hugh Johnson, Mitchell Beazley, 2000

AUSTRALIA AT LEISURE

Cocktail of the day, says the notice in the Bougainvillea Bar: A glass of Riesling wine. So I have lived to see it, and on the Barrier Reef. Move over, Singapore Slings. Australia, I salute you.

No, I am not criss-crossing the wine regions of Victoria or South Australia this time. For once I'm in Resort Australia – and learning just how far Oz has come as a wine country in the last few years. A wine-drinking country, that is.

We used to laugh about the statistic that the average time between an Australian buying a bottle and drinking it was twenty *I didn't make it up* minutes©. Now when someone says 'Let's have an old red', he means something he's been hanging on to for ten years. Well, five anyway. And once you've got the taste for what time will do, there's no going back. No need to go back, either; there's more and more old stuff out there growing as gamey and leathery as its proprietors.

Ten days to go to the Olympic Games and Sydney was sparkling. Not that its harbour is ever less than an exhilarating, wind-tossed and dazzling, splashing and bumping free-for-all. The trick is to order a water taxi to the nearest jetty and work up your appetite in the sea air, heading for Rose Bay, Balmoral or Commissioner's Steps. San Francisco and Hong Kong may have been at it longer, but in the restaurants-on-the-harbour stakes Sydney has taken a convincing lead. And for restaurants-with-great-indigenous-wine-lists-on-the-harbour they will have to reconfigure France to dislodge it. (Cross Bordeaux with Sète and Deauville, perhaps?)

It helps if you like oysters. Sydney Harbour is the ultimate oyster-pond. The tang of Sydney Rocks focuses the appetite as few things can. Oysters don't demand fine wines: just simple tasty ones with a bit of bracing acidity. Which is why Muscadet works so well. Come to think of it a Mornington Muscadet or Geelong Gros Plant mightn't be such a bad idea. I expect someone is working on it. Chablis for oysters should be just Chablis – maybe Premier, certainly not Grand Cru. So forget buttered-toast Chardonnays. Young Semillons, too: they taste undernourished beside oysters. And so far Australia has not really scored with Sauvignon Blanc. So Riesling it is – though with a thought for a good Marsanne such as Château Tahbilk, or that great all-rounder from Houghton's that used to claim the name of white burgundy.

There was one dish that made me meditate like mad on the oyster. It was the creation of Serge Dansereau, who has converted the Bather's Pavilion, where the bourgeoisie of Balmoral once slipped into their one-piece swimsuits, into a beguiling restaurant on the beach. There were chilled oysters on one plate, some with a Champagne sauce and others with capers and chillies. On a second plate came a little iron casserole with three kinds of clams à la marinière, hot and buttery with garlic and parsley. This was addressing the harvest of the seabed in three contrasting ways at once – and a triumphant appetite-rouser. The wine proposed, yes you've guessed, was Riesling. Tasmanian, Tamar Ridge '99, fairly zinging with limey and apply acidity – Australia's answer to Mosel. Total success, utterly Australian – only one complaint: they serve it teeth-achingly cold. Champagne, too. But aiming off for the climate is a benign fault. And it's the only one I have to report.

Decanter, 2000

ENTER THE MAREMMA

Does anyone else find it strange that it took so many centuries for Tuscany to discover its own best wine region? Only in the past forty years has anyone planted vines in earnest along the coastal strip, where the climate is milder, and ripening much earlier, than inland

and uphill in Chianti. The reason is simple enough: hardly anyone lived there. Barbary pirate raids were one reason; mosquitoes another.

The pioneer of coastal planting has reaped a rich reward. The whole world now knows of Bolgheri and its dazzling Sassicaia, since followed by Ornellaia and others. But south down the coast, the Maremma, the coastal plain and foothills behind the resorts of the Argentario peninsula, was still considered cow country until very recently. The name for such Sangiovese as it grew was Morellino. As early as 1978 a DOC was agreed for the cooperative at Scansano, but Morellino remained a local wine.

Development came in a rush in the 1990s, when many of the big names of Chianti realised that earlier ripening and cheaper land made a seductive combination. The roll call today is almost alarmingly star-studded.

But it won't only be Morellino these big guns plant in the Maremma. Wait for the first Cabernets and Syrahs. There are more 'Supertuscans' ahead.

Decanter, 2000

LOIRE ET MER

I'm afraid it's an occupational hazard of the wine business, having to sit in restaurants reading menus and wine lists, often having to shelter from the sun under vine pergolas, working laboriously through nuances of pleasure and delight.

Earlier this month you could have caught me at it at different points along the Loire, that river that so tediously winds through about three-quarters of France, lined with challenges to gastric equipment every few miles along its placid rural way.

Of its major challenges Sancerre, Touraine and Anjou are all conveniently en route to some other place of work. The trek to Burgundy or Bordeaux almost invariably makes a Loire stop inevitable. Not so Muscadet, which only really comes into itineraries involving the hardships of beach life or sailing; things that occupy the energies of the French along this Atlantic shore.

Muscadet is a small region, not famed either for beauty or variety. Nor is its wine considered by most of us as other than the cheap-and-reasonably-cheerful choice in seafood restaurants from Calais, via Paris, to Brest. On my last Loire trip, though, I drank a score or so of Muscadets, and hardly one failed to please. Something has been quietly going on in a region which will never hit the heights, but need never explore the troughs, either.

At home Muscadets are essential drinking from summer through to Christmas. Most memorably, Judy and I called at the Château du Coing de St Fiacre, the beautiful hundred-acre vineyard estate that lies at the confluence of the two rivers⊕ that give the district its names. St Fiacre, despite being named after a horse-drawn Paris cab, is the patron saint of gardeners. The grey château, decidedly dilapidated, rises from beds of hydrangeas and fuchsias that tell you how soft and Atlantical the climate is.

the Sèvre and the Maine

Véronique Günther-Chéreau is extremely proud of her wines. If you can be superlative in a low-key way, that just about describes her '99. Taste it as a model of classic Muscadet de Sèvre-et-Maine.

Wine Times, 2000

POCKET WINE BOOK 2001
FOREWORD

The wine world is becoming more and more competitive, the consequence of ever-increasing numbers of competent grape-growers, aspiring winemakers and demanding drinkers. Don't think I'm complaining. The net result is better wine for all of us – and logically, one fine day, the disappearance of bad wine from earth. One fine day.

Competition is healthy and productive, but there is a catch. I am getting a clearer and clearer picture of the wine world gradually dividing between the hemispheres. Not north and south, but east and west, with the Atlantic as the dividing line.

The wines that score highest with most American judges (and score is the operative word) are the darkest, richest, strongest, most fruity, most oaky, and usually most alcoholic. They are the wines that win blind tasting competitions by simply smothering more moderate and subtle entries. They are Formula One wines, as it were, unbeatable on a race track, but entirely out of place where wine belongs: on the table with food.

Europeans are impressed, too, by their scale and concentration. It is, after all, the definition of a great European vintage that its wines excel in ripeness and flavour the more dilute productions of lesser years. You can see the trend in the boutique (these days 'garage'⊕) wines of St-Émilion and Pomerol, outdoing the classic First Growths in dense concentration and instant tactile appeal – and overwhelming them in rarity and price. Similar things are going on in Tuscany with certain 'Supertuscans', with Duero and Douro table wines, in Catalonia with Priorato and in South Australia with monster Shiraz. Turning up the volume is not such a hard trick. But

you don't hear the expression fifteen years on

before long, like nightclub music, it deadens the senses. Worse, it can make you forget what wine is for: to refresh your palate as you eat.

There is judgement, and there is appreciation. I have been to tastings of rare old wines, each an individual with the patina of age, a marvellous proof that great wine can grow in complexity and subtle beauty for a hundred years. Three or four noble vintages are poured and some figure of authority says 'The 1870 is clearly the best.' 'You're quite right,' say the other pampered tasters. 'What a nose, what body, what a finish.' And they almost forget the other wines, the unfortunates that don't happen to be 'best' that day. Savoured singly, each of these historic bottles would make a day memorable, linger in the mind's eye, be the stuff of legend. But they were eclipsed. Who remembers horses that came second or third?

The wine world is much more rewarding (and holds so many more possibilities) for those who taste with an open mind, rather than dismissing less obvious wines, or wines that express something they don't understand.

This is my plea for appreciation. If we could put behind us the racing mentality that must always have a winner, we would enjoy so many bottles so much more. Love them for themselves; don't give them marks out of a hundred.

Hugh Johnson's Pocket Wine Book 2001, Mitchell Beazley

WHAT ABOUT THESE 2000s?

Everyone has asked me whether I am 'investing' in the 2000 clarets. There is such a surge of interest in them that the word 'hype' always comes into the conversation. But isn't this just the modern world? Footballers are the greatest. Singers are the greatest. Someone is always top of the charts. That's 2000 for you.

Will it still be in ten years' time? That's the question investors have to ask themselves. Two factors come into it: how good is the vintage, and will better ones come along to challenge its Number One spot? It's not hard to answer the first. The wines are grand. They have that confident richness of flavour that comes from truly ripe grapes that have not been rushed to ripeness by a scorching sun. This is where the best European regions still have the advantage over anything except the coolest in the New World (and why New Zealand has a quality advantage over most of Australia).

The best of the 2000 clarets are about as big in flavour as bordeaux gets, yet with that lovely restraining line of acidity and just-ripe tannins that will give them a ten- to twenty-five-year lifespan.

Question Two is unanswerable. This very autumn we might get a vintage as good, or even better. What it won't have is the hypnotic three 0s. I'm filling my boots⊙.

– and haven't regretted it

Wine Times, 2001

I WANT THEM ALL

If I am pressed to be specific on wines I would really miss deeply, there is no stopping at a mere top five – or even top ten. I need fresh young clarets and also meditative old ones, zingy new Rieslings and multilayered orangey old Ausleses, the minerality of Chablis and the nuttiness of Meursault, the cherry-ripe bite of young Pinot Noir, the velvet tannins of great Merlots and Cabernets, the steeliness of an Austrian Smaragd⊙, the crispness of Barbaresco; the vigour of a great Chianti, the unctuousness and unbelievable length of great old Tokaji *aszús* (and vintage Madeiras, too). I would sooner lose a finger than one of the greatest marques of Champagne. I love Haut-Brion because there is also Cheval Blanc – or, more realistically, Chasse-Spleen because Haut-Bailly is always at hand.

means 'emerald'; top dry Wachau wine. Its symbol is a lizard

Just don't pin me down. Why have I loved wine for forty years? Why the keen anticipation each time I draw a cork? Because, thank God, nature is infinitely various – and in no department more marvellously than in wine.

PS … SEEING YOUR OWN GEESE AS SWANS is all too easy. Can my wine possibly be as wonderful as it tastes to me? I wonder. As it develops in its little barrels, deep in the cold and mossy cellar, it opens vistas of flavour I never would have suspected. You would not guess that it goes to the limits of sweetness: the fresh acidity of fruit freshens your mouth with every sip. Deep, long, perfumed, and penetrating are easy words to use – but how to express the layers of flavour that roll on like instruments in a symphony, flutes to cellos, trumpets to violins? Better not to try, I reckon; just to say that Tokaji, for me, does for the end of dinner what Champagne does for the beginning. I wouldn't know how to say it any more clearly.

Decanter, 2001

POCKET WINE BOOK 2002
AGENDA

You might think that by the 25th edition of a book like this things would have settled down to a more or less predictable pattern. There are, after all, only so many wine regions in the world. They can hardly all change year by year. You would be amazed. Each year brings its own agenda, and 2002 has plenty of novelty for us.

A year or two ago we were lamenting an increasing international monoculture of Chardonnay and Cabernet. But wine-drinkers have quickly familiarised themselves with Syrah, Viognier, Merlot, Sangiovese and they have shown little loyalty towards any particular source of supply.

Chile and New Zealand may have made headlines, South Africa attracted sympathetic attention. Spain produced remarkable value for money, Portugal some highly original flavours, Italy raised its game, and Greece finally joined the party. But it is the best-organised and best-distributed producers who win and keep the spaces on the shelves.

Aside from Champagne, the traditional reference point in regional marketing, it is Australia that is showing most flair and ambition so far. In contrast to those American producers who buy their sales with massive advertising and promotion, Australia has a coherent scheme for doubling its production and hugely increasing its market share. On recent past form it seems their aim is remarkably accurate.

Other points on the agenda for 2002: corks are in the firing line. The number of cork-tainted bottles has gone far beyond an acceptable risk. Yet it is a safe assumption that the majority are not recognized by drinkers for what they are; they just think that mouldy smell is bad wine. At least 90 per cent of wine would be at least as good, *Revolutionary then;* probably better, under a screw cap.© We are far too conservative *self-evident today.* about corks and corkscrews.

Oak. The smell that was once a sign that a wine had been expensively aged, maybe fermented, in small oak barrels now more often comes from a bag of oak chips or even a bottle of essence. A wine cannot be oak-matured without a high price tag. Nor is there any point: it won't get better. It is time for consumers to recognize that oak is a foreign flavouring in wine. Great wines don't taste of oak; they taste of fermented fruit.

Gigantism. Where is it all leading? At the present rate of takeovers and mergers in a couple of years all Australian wine will come from one vast company. How will it compete against itself? And how clever is it, come to that, for the great names in different continents to pool their resources and produce international blockbusters? Not at all, in my book, where diversity is very definitely the soul of wine.

Hugh Johnson's Pocket Wine Book 2002, Mitchell Beazley

BOTTLES AT THE BOTTOM OF MY GARDEN

For someone like me, with one foot in the cellar and the other in the potting shed⊙, the parallel pleasures of wine and gardening are pretty obvious. What they have in common is the exercise of taste: enjoying the productions of nature, and the element of time. Both are moving targets. A garden is as much a process as a place. And the same wine tastes different, is different, yesterday, today and tomorrow – or at least this year, next year and ten years down the road.

gardening is something I do – and even write about. See www. tradsdiary.com

True, the Ruth Draper gambit ('You should have seen it last week!') is not often heard about a bottle of claret. The timescales are rather different. But the wine trade is always using its converse: 'Only wait for four or five years and you'll see. Those tannins will be nicely rounded.' The back label that says 'Delicious now or will improve with two or three years' cellaring' pretty much covers the case.

Or does it? What it does is to encourage the common fallacy that most wines get a little bit better with a little bit of age. Specific wines do, for specific reasons. Non-vintage Champagne because it is produced in a hurry and can taste raw. Rieslings, particularly German Rieslings, because that is the nature of the grape. Many red wines with high tannin levels. Port with raw alcohol .... But the objective has to be clear. A simple wine does not become complex, or even 'mellow'; it just loses its freshness. Back labels, in other words, should be specific, even if it means introducing a sell-by date, to the possible embarrassment of the seller.

And there should be a not-before date, too. There is no point in paying for a fine wine that needs ten years or more to show its quality and then drinking it young. 'Awesome' it may be, but also raw and indigestible. Nor does the wine trade stick to such rules as there are. There is 'late-bottled vintage' port on the market which would be better described as 'early-bottled ruby'.

The fascination lies in wines that break all the rules. Recently the black hole in my cellar produced two ancient Sauvignon Blancs. If there is a grape I would not keep, it is Sauvignon Blanc. But you needn't worry about your Malartic-Lagravière 1983. Malartic (I love the full-rigged ship on the label) is or was a totally Sauvignon Graves. At nineteen years it was pale, gentle but positive, aromatic, buttery; very fine indeed. Nor should your Sterling Vineyards 1976 Sauvignon Blanc cause you concern. It smells of mushrooms and toffee, like old Champagne, faintly leafy as Napa whites do, gentle and harmonious as an old Hunter Semillon. Come to think of it, an ideal garden wine.

Decanter, 2002

AGENDA

Revising this book (and this is my 26th shot at it) is like plotting the swirling Sahara sand. There are, thank goodness, oases here and there which re-emerge each time the sand settles (or we pretend it has settled; the new edition is going to press). But the dunes around them have shifted; the landscape is different, there are new high points, new depressions – and new routes to where you want to go.

For ten years now it has been the New World that has set the agenda. Uninhibited experiments by countries without the baggage of regulation and tradition are more exciting to watch. They make the contortions of appellations and the laws to enforce them look painful. To many the effort seems pointless. 'If you grow Chardonnay, why not say so?' is a question that still shocks growers in Chablis or Meursault. It has only one possible answer: the consistent uniqueness of what the growers bottle.

Two arguments today seem to point in opposite directions. One says that wine is too complicated: that big, well-advertised, often-discounted brands are the only things the public can be bothered with. The other says that a bit of a puzzle is the very essence of wine. Strip it of its mystery, its complexity, even the racy hint of risk, and it's just a drink. Certainly restaurants with wide-ranging wine lists that dip into more obscure regions, suggesting inside knowledge, do well out of it. And producers with successful simple brand ideas are rarely content to leave them alone. They soon complicate them with premium notions.

Inherent in the idea of an Australian Riesling or a California Cabernet is the possibility of a Clare Riesling or a Napa Cab, a closer focus giving a better wine ... until you name the vineyard, regulate the labelling and presto, you have an appellation.

Are all old appellations good appellations? The challenge is thrown down by the organic movement. If what is unique about Meursault (or Margaux or Montalcino) is its soil, you had better not mess with it.© All the fertiliser you chuck on, the effects and residues of antifungal treatments over the years, the stuff you use to kill red spiders – they all alter the subtle biochemistry of the place: the very thing you call terroir. It is a serious case that farmers have to answer. Many are taking self-denying steps, if not to fully organic or 'biodynamic' farming, at least to what the French call *lutte raisonée*: a controlled campaign using minimum artificial treatments consistent with reasonable returns.

'Bio'(-dynamism) was just coming over the horizon.

Hugh Johnson's Pocket Wine Book 2003, Mitchell Beazley

ALIEN INVASION

New at our local supermarket in the centre of France: 'California Wine' (*sic*), bottled in France – the Rhône, I detect from the postcode – *issu du cèpage Cabernet Sauvignon*. It has the plainest of labels, costs the same as a Shiraz from the Pays d'Oc, and is rather pleasant to drink. What do the locals make of it?

The French always start their comments on wines from beyond their own backyards with a cautious *quand-même*. They say it in Bordeaux about Burgundy and vice versa, the Loire about Alsace, Graves about the Médoc. 'All the same' is not merely a throat-clearing exercise. It reflects deeply inbred doubts about whether something foreign, however folkloric, even however French, can truly be safe to swallow.

I expected a chorus of *quand-mêmes* when I proposed a taste of California to neighbours who still find the Gamay from the other side of the River Cher pretty strange stuff. They rather liked it, though. 'Maybe a bit sweet', 'It reminds me of currants' were the lowest ratings it received. If I were the anonymous California exporter I would feel encouraged. And if I were making wine in the Midi, I would be worried.

Decanter, 2003

FAITH IN ROOTS

In a world depressingly risk-averse it is inspiring to meet someone who dares all for his beliefs. (And in the wine industry pretty rare, too.) Henry Marionnet is that man. He believes ungrafted vines make better wine, and risks wipeout by phylloxera to prove it.

I remember when dinners used to end with a rather redundant debate on whether great wines were greater before the louse from America destroyed Europe's vineyards. It was easy to say they were better – but impossible to prove. Conditions were different, yields lower, and the wines were mature. You couldn't compare like with like. And since all vines were now grafted on American roots, did it really matter?

It did to Henry Marionnet. There is enough of the old belief in the air still to stir a romantic idealist. Bollinger still has its legendary Vieilles Vignes Françaises at Ay, unexplained but distinctly different. I went to see the man who plays Canute to the dreaded soil louse, deep in the backwoods of Touraine between Blois and the town of Romorantin-Lanthenay.

He is not the first farmer to plant ungrafted cuttings there. Peasants who couldn't afford to pay a nursery had done it and their vines had inexplicably survived. Recently Marionnet bought a little plot of Chenin Blanc planted on its own roots in 1979, and then, sensationally, a plot of the local variety Romorantin©, planted in 1850 before phylloxera arrived in France and for all we know France's oldest surviving vineyard.

it makes seriously acid wine

In 1992 Marionnet decided to plant his own cuttings of Gamay – not in sandy soil, which phylloxera is known to shun, but in clay. All went well. In 1995 he made its first wine.

The experiment continues. In 2000 he planted Sauvignon Blanc ungrafted, then Côt (or Malbec), and even the almost defunct Gamay de Bouze. They make an intriguing tasting, though I am hesitant to draw any grand conclusion about ungrafted wines. Marionnet is a skilful winemaker.

Stay away, louse.

Decanter, 2003

NO LONGER RACIST

We all know what made us turn our backs on Beaujolais. For a year or two in the early 90s it was fun to follow the crazy race to be first home, by hovercraft or helicopter, with the raw new vintage. We forced ourselves to swallow the pale purple banana-flavoured acid as though it was a once-in-a-lifetime chance. The producers were only too pleased to take our money. One year I went down to film the juggernauts leaving Georges Duboeuf's yard at midnight. They had a ragtime band with a souzaphone whose *oompah-phrrrt* just about summed it all up.

It was a discovery at the time: that any wine didn't have to be kept a year or two to be drinkable. For the wine trade to do anything in a hurry was pretty revolutionary. Strange to think that we now expect most white wines, at least, to carry last year's date. Beaujolais sold almost anywhere beyond the bistros of Lyon used to be a dubious dark-coloured brew. Then suddenly it was party time, a sort of world-wide vintage celebration when you dared to drink wine straight from the vine. In Japan the trick still seems to work. We rapidly lost the taste for it – and sadly, it seems, for Beaujolais of any kind.

There are other reasons, too. We became variety-obsessed at about the same time, latching on to Chardonnays and Cabernets from no matter where. But nobody outside Beaujolais plants the Gamay. If there were an Australian Gamay the name would be on everyone's lips. If Beaujolais grew Pinot Noir it would be in every line-up. But no. Funny grape, funny region. There are no comparisons to be made – so why complicate life? Let's have a Merlot.

I went back to Beaujolais in May on a refresher course. It was hardly higher maths to guess they had had a super-ripe harvest. A neglected wine region after a great vintage is not a bad place to go prospecting. What I found, though, went way beyond a good vintage. It was the whole population rubbing their eyes.

It had not been easy. There was hail to start with, so only half a crop. Nobody was ready for the heatwave of the century. Nobody had ever seen ripe grapes in mid-August. Everyone was on holiday. I heard the story from Guy Marion, right-hand man of George Duboeuf, the unchallenged king of the region. Chancellor (or Chamberlain) Marion has tasted with Duboeuf every day for thirty years, from noon to 1pm and from 6 to 7pm, every vat made in the enormous Duboeuf winery and every vat brought in from one of many hundred small producers. You might say he has a considered view.

We had lunch at Le Cep, the cheerful shrine to appetite in the square at Fleurie, full of merry broad-beamed grey-heads in sports shirts and tans. There were twelve different vegetables with vinaigrette, all fresh, for a first course, then a casseroled pigeon, then endless cheese. We drank a Pouilly-Fuissé 2000, mature and nutty, then Moulin-à-Vent 2000. Nothing evanescent about this.

Guy told me how the alarm bells rang in August when the supermarkets suddenly had empty shelves. They stock up for the picking season and the influx of workers when the holidays are over. A great telephone call-up brought everyone back from the beaches to sweltering labour and emergency rations.

And of course things can go wrong when you pick hot grapes and the cellar is a sauna. Not every vat was a happy story. I was cherry-picking, though; the privilege of a potential customer, and what I tasted were curvaceous, creamy wines carrying the different characters of the different crus to levels I scarcely imagined. Nobody had to chaptalize last year – and natural alcohol is good alcohol.

Beaujolais is one of the world's most beautiful vineyards, rising, falling and rising again into hills that deserve the name of mountains. Considering the modest price even the best wines fetch here it is hard to see the sense of cultivating some of the lifting corners of this huge spread of vines. Yet far up the hills the vines march on, each one an individual soldier keeping his dressing without the aid of wires, on fields that vary from granite chippings to soft friendly loam – without a weed.

It was warm again in May, the sun burning among the fresh sprouting vines and the cool of a cellar a welcome retreat. Winegrowers are rarely at their most enlightening as they squeeze between their barrels, pipette in hand, fetching samples of what they hope are their best wines. They tend to speak in enthusiastic clichés. This year, though, there was a different note. The clichés don't fit. Not only are the wines richer, with wilder and more exotic perfumes, but the Gamay has an unaccustomed element: smooth, silky tannins that can shape and structure its cherry-ripeness into something almost formidable.

My notes on the seriously senior 2003s become lyrical, rising at times almost to hysterical. As happens in hot vintages, sometimes the north slopes and colder soils come into their own, where normally they are at a disadvantage. Perhaps the single most important fact, though, is that the alcohol comes easily and naturally. Nobody has to add sugar.

When you have a naturally small crop of the right grape on the right soil fully ripened by nature you have wine as good as it gets. If you still don't like Beaujolais after a handful of the 2003s – it's your loss.

Wine Times, 2004

THE BURGUNDIAN WAY

Here's a sales plan. You have a little region with red and white wines to sell, you want a worldwide market of high-rollers. What about dividing it into thirty bits, then dividing these again into three hundred or so, then subdividing the three hundred among hundreds of different producers' labels ....

Thanks a lot. Show the next one in, please.

Burgundy gets away with this 'Through the Looking Glass' system. The clients, in fact, love it. There are dinner jackets out there who take rubicund pleasure in knowing their Hudelot-Noëllats from their Confuron-Cotétidots. But why, when branding by broad brush is the Holy Grail everyone else is chasing? And for how long?

It was the second week in January when samples of the new burgundy vintage, the 2002s, hit the London livery halls, clubs, restaurants ... anywhere that can manage a long table and a white cloth. The word was already out: these are ripe, juicy, frank, open, jolly enjoyable wines. Volnay tastes like Volnay and Nuits like Nuits. You can run the scales of Clavoillon, Pucelles, Caillerets or Charmes, Genevrières, Perrières, wondering how each manages to cap the juiciness, raciness, spiciness of the last: that's exactly what burgundy is all about. The clientele rolled up, journos to the fore, chequebooks (not the journos) singeing their suits. Perhaps they feel Bordeaux has let them down recently (they shouldn't: the massed 2001s shown at the Floral Hall⊕ recently were a real pleasure).

at Covent Garden: venue for bordeaux crus classés tastings

As I sniffed and spat and tried to find space to scribble I was wondering, though, why does anybody do this? How many times have we been told that white burgundy is not what it was? Didn't you read how Jancis proved that Grüner Veltliners were much better? And Pinot Noir – if you really want to taste the grape, Central Otago is the place to go. France is so last century ... they tell me.

Success came back to Burgundy when it gave up the whole branding thing. Until quite recently its business was built on the idea that cellar work and bottling were too tricky for growers, and all those names too complicated for drinkers. A few big simple names were what the public wanted. The merchants simplified things all right – the teasing, will-o'-the-wisp flavours included. With honourable exceptions, the top domaine wines of such grower-merchants as Drouhin and Jadot, burgundy became boring and overpriced.

So the sales plan worked. Boring it certainly isn't. As for the prices, I leave you and your calculator to work it out.

Decanter, 2004

WHEREVER NEXT?

Nothing is rasher than prediction. Especially about the future. If you want to make God laugh, tell Him your plans .... Yes, it is safer and more comfortable to look back, to tick off the discoveries and inventions of our first thirty years at the wineface. If we⊕ were the first (and we were) to bring you good wines from Australia, California, the Midi, Bulgaria, Chile – the list goes on – wherever are we heading next? The list of countries and regions where grapes will ripen is finite – though it didn't feel like that when Jancis and I were revising *The World Atlas of Wine* last year.

The Sunday Times Wine Club

At some point we'll have 'done' all the eligible places, and at least prodded the ineligible ones. Is that that, then? Oh no, that's only the start.

The first question, of course, is what do we, and will we, want to drink? A huge variety is the one certain answer. But also, judging by past and present performance, better and better stuff.

If we simply project current trends we will be drinking more sparkling wines: New World ones, of course, but also such

English Wine!
This was new.

Champagne parallels as Crémant de Bourgogne – not to mention the stellar bubbly of the South Downs.© The old mistrust of rosés was certainly evaporating in the sunshine of the summer. And I suspect the simple pleasure they bring will eventually win us all over. Red wines we seem, on balance, to be wanting redder, more assertive, but with softer tannins (and plenty of alcohol).

White wines are harder to call. Clearly Sauvignon Blanc hits the aromatic button with most people, but even in this enlightened age there is still a question mark over the real class act among the aromatic grapes, the Riesling.

Things other than taste can influence fashion, too. Look what happened when a TV programme said red wine was good for your heart. White-wine makers are even trying red-wine techniques, even fermenting on the grape skins, to beef up their antioxidant quotient so they can make the same claims. Since every bulletin brings a new health scare or miracle cure you can be sure some kind of wine or other will soar or bomb on the basis of its supposed effects. Hungarian Tokaji dined out for centuries on its reputed aphrodisiac properties, but now you have to be extremely careful how you mention them.

Altogether more serious is the issue of organic farming and its opposite, the dreaded GM. At present GM seems fairly remote from wine, but who knows what would happen if growers on the damper edges of viticulture were offered a new vine you didn't have to spray against mildew? The trend today is strongly towards more organic vineyards – at the extreme (some say loony) leading edge to biodynamism. You can dismiss what looks like witchcraft in this growing cult, but not the incredibly pure and profound wines of such practitioners as Nicolas Joly© in Anjou and Anne-Claude Leflaive in Puligny-Montrachet.

*at Coulée de
Serrant*

*Anne-Claude
Leflaive died in
April 2015, alas.*

We have seen over the past decade, with huge excitement, what the various countries of the New World overseas (to borrow an Aussie term) can do with modern investment. The grapes they grow are mostly familiar. There are no lurking native grapes in Australia or California; it is predictable Shiraz, Cabernet, Riesling, Chardonnay and the rest. Though South America holds good surprises: juicy red Carmenère in Chile, sumptuous Malbec in Argentina, grippy Tannat in Uruguay, even – and back in Argentina the wild white Torrontés.

The big question in these vineyards is seeing what spin the new growing conditions give to the classic varietal flavours. New Zealand did something explosive to the modest Sauvignon Blanc. Shiraz in Barossa is something totally different from the original Rhône Valley version. When old varieties take on such strong local colouring they almost deserve new names. They certainly add real alternatives to the total wine list, rather than just substitutes for something else.

And when we have tried all the grapes from the newly galvanised Latin Europe of the Mediterranean, brought blinking into the new century by cascades of Euro-grants, what then? Why, the about-to-be-galvanised Eastern Europe, most of which has a winegrowing tradition going back to ancient times, too – and the grape varieties to prove it. Memorise Hárslevelű and Fetească Regală. One day, mark my words, we shall see Romanian Pinot Noir head to head with New Zealand's best. And very probably Burgundy's best, too.

Wine Times, 2004

THE AUSTRALIAN PROBLEM

For a country whose national motto is 'No Worries', Australia was not doing too well when I visited in March. I was taken aback by the long faces. What's up? Can the country that has overtaken France as our favourite wine supplier be suffering self-doubt? Yup, mate, said my host. We've blown it. We can only sell all this wine by promoting brands. You can only promote brands through BOGOFs (Buy One Get One Frees).

I exaggerate slightly. But nobody seems to know if Australia has too much wine or not enough. One winemaker told me growers were driving round with trailers of Shiraz 'as though it was nuclear waste'. And 80 per cent of all this is in the corporate hands of the so-called Big Four. Scary.

The paradox is that Australia's best wines are better than ever. There is no mystery; they come, most of them, from regions long known for exceptional terroir, though every year some new part of the bush steps up with impressive credentials. Their makers have just been uncharacteristically bashful about them, unsure whether the world is ready for the reality of grown-up Australian appellations.

The high points of my visit were very high indeed. We drank stellar wines in the Hunter Valley: delicate Semillons, decadent earthy Shiraz and golden Chardonnays. In Victoria the range runs from crystalline Rieslings and lively, penetrating Chardonnays (not to mention fragrant Viognier and Marsanne) to poised, structured Cabernets, Pinot Noir luxurious with the fumes of cherry brandy ... and to complete the course, from Perth to Pemberton via Margaret River, the wine list from Cabernet to Riesling is stunning.

To choose just one of many dream-like Australian experiences, the restaurant at Leeuwin Estate faces a superlative grove of jarrah trees over a natural amphitheatre, the site of a famous annual concert (this year it was Lesley Garrett). Riesling drank sweetly with little Albany oysters on ice, Chardonnay with Pemberton marron, the plump local crayfish; local cheese with a silky young Cabernet: leafy, gingery, dusty and intense. Margaret River seemed a long way from the real world. Perhaps that's the problem.

Decanter, 2004

POCKET WINE BOOK 2005
AGENDA

Does the world of wine really change in its broad outlines so much from year to year?

It looks the most stable of all businesses: burgundy and bordeaux have been around since the Romans, Alsace since the Middle Ages, and even New Zealand for twenty years now. There are winegrowing families still tilling the same plots as they did in the 15th century.

Yes, but even they live in a different world today. Flavours are no longer exclusive to regions, or knowledge to the experienced. The same techniques are practised round the world. The New World borrows ideas from the Old; the Old promptly returns the compliment. You might think that with so much swapping going on, it scarcely matters any more where your wine comes from: same grape varieties, same tanks, same yeasts, same barrels – what's the fuss?

It is a powerful argument, and regularly aired by powerful buyers looking to save a few pence. Buyers, especially for supermarkets, are paid to be ruthless. The emergence of a new competitor – a new region with plausible Chardonnays, let's say – hands the buyer a stick to beat an established supplier. Healthy competition, they call it. But is it really all positive? It makes producers 'realistic' in their pricing. (Most realistic, of course, those icons whose wines have waiting lists. They can charge the earth.) But not so healthy, for those who love wine, is the pressure it puts on producers to cut costs – which can mean cutting corners.

Of all the foods we buy wine is the one that has the most direct, traceable links with its source. It is, after all, the water from the ground of a real field, with its soil and stones, its slopes or lack of them, its puddles and weeds, transmuted by the vine into sweet juice, and by yeasts into strong drink. Nothing is purer or more alive – alive until the moment your stomach digests it. Why are we so precise about which wine is which? This immediacy, from the vine to you, is at the heart of it.

Hugh Johnson's Pocket Wine Book 2005, Mitchell Beazley

A WINEMAKER'S CALENDAR

A winemaker's work is never done. There is a job outdoors in the vineyard, and a job indoors in the cellar, for every day of the year. They vary with regions and seasons but the rhythm is something like this. We are somewhere in the heart of France ...

JANUARY Pruning is the great midwinter task, cold and wet as it may be. Every vine must be reappraised, its old branches reduced to a few buds, programmed for the next vintage. When it is too wet to prune there is work indoors on equipment and shipments. Barrels of the last vintage must be kept topped up to the bung.

FEBRUARY Go on pruning and overhaul the tractor, plan the year's 'campaign' and order the sprays, take cuttings and get grafting. At the new moon, with pressure high, rack the new wine into clean barrels and begin bottling lighter wines. Taste and 'assemble' blends. See the bank manager.

MARCH Finish pruning. A run on the tractor, cultivating between the rows or out with Dobbin, if an artist is watching. Look out your best samples at the approach of journalists. Finish racking, bottling, e-mailing customers, writing memoirs and other indoor jobs. Spring is coming; you'll be needed outdoors.

APRIL Plenty of visitors this month. Essential to keep the barrels topped up; you may need to go round with the ullage can⁹ two or three times a week. Overhaul stakes and wires in the vineyard; pray for buds to start swelling later rather than earlier: dread of frost sets in.

ullage is the empty space in the top of a barrel that mysteriously keeps reappearing. It can cause oxygen problems unless you keep filling it up from another barrel

MAY Fear of frost at its height. You may be up all night lighting stoves among the vines. Another round on the tractor to kill weeds. First spraying against mildew as new shoots erupt. Plant new vines. Rack the new wines again. Send out finished orders.

JUNE In the vineyard tweaking shoots, rubbing out surplus buds, enjoying the embryo flowers and worrying about the weather as they emerge. This is when the vine takes its shape for the year and the size of the crop is determined. Finish racking; finish shipping.

JULY Spores of mildew and tiny spiders threaten your vines. Most farmers get out their sprayers (usually on tractors that straddle the vines). The biodynamic school uses forefinger and thumb. Trim the long shoots to keep tidy hedges of vines. Keep the cellar as cool as you can. Start bottling wine matured in barrels.

AUGUST Overhaul your barrels; general clean up, ready for vintage; see bank manager about new barrels. Last chance of a green harvest if the crop is too heavy: grapes turn colour mid-month. If you can find someone to patrol the vineyard, take the children to the seaside.

SEPTEMBER Pray for sunshine and activate your cousins and aunts. If you are lucky harvest starts early, about the third week; long hours are endemic, energy infectious. (If you are not you could be waiting in the rain until mid-October). All the cellar gear must be spotless, machinery oiled, visitors discouraged.

OCTOBER The heady smell of fermentation – but keep the doors open: you can suffocate. Keep the red-wine skins immersed and the temperature in check. Time to move maturing wine (bung the barrels tight) to make room for the new vintage. Take the marc (the skins and stalks) out to spread on the vineyard as fertiliser. See the bank manager.

NOVEMBER Fermentation finished, the long process of racking starts again, running the clear wine off its lees into its fresh barrel (new, for valuable wines). Scotch the rumours of a triumphant/disastrous vintage: time will tell. Tidy up the vineyard and plough weeds out and manure in.

DECEMBER You need a break. Start tasting the new wines with old friends. Watch the finishing fermentation, start topping up casks, get on with bottling, brace yourself for weeks of pruning: tradition starts it off as the shortest day approaches. Reward yourself with an old bottle at Christmas – it will give you courage to review your prices next year.

Wine Times, 2005

DOWN TO EARTH

I thought I'd have a reality check the other day. I am always pretty spoilt in my drinking, but I felt spoilt rotten after dozens of beautiful wines of the 1980s and 90s: all essential research, of course. It is all very well, I said to myself, saying claret can be this and burgundy that in glowing terms, but what about the average Joe who pops into Tesco to see what he or she thinks? So I popped, and bought a bottle of claret – Reserve Bordeaux 2002 – for £3.99, and a bottle of Bourgogne Rouge for £5.99. To my delight (and perhaps, to be honest, relief) they did what it said on the tin. The bordeaux was a lovely clear dark red with the smoky/herby nose of not-extremely-ripe Merlot. If the flavour was a bit leafy to start, it finished nicely plummy. Altogether it was dry, soft and had just the right acidity to make it fresh. An admirable drink, which is the whole aim and purpose of claret. The burgundy was perfectly representative of the region too, in the sense that there is nowhere else it could have come from – at least to my knowledge.

Now I have to admit to a shocking crime. Wine-lovers are not supposed to mix the stuff. Not before drinking it, that is. It is one of the wine trade's holy cows: wines are individuals. It is heinous to sully their individuality by tipping one into another. We merchants are allowed to do it, that is, but not you punters.

Judy and I had been enjoying a very grand Barolo of the great vintage of '95 (as part of the domestic spoiling programme) but decided it was still too darn hard to really enjoy. The fruit had all the symptoms of a classic on the way, but the tannin was like a razor. I like crisp wines, but this was scouring. Then my eye fell on the Tesco burgundy. I tried half and half, then one-third Barolo to two-thirds burgundy. The Barolo was still dominant, but a little soft padding made it, dare I say, a better drink – at least for a kitchen supper.

I cracked the candlepower problem, too, in this week of dangerous experiments. The picturesque method of decanting over a candle flame has its atmospheric charm, but I am sure we have all lost sight of the moving sediment when the flame flickers. An ordinary torch is not a perfect answer either: you still get only a partial view of what's happening. But now I've found the answer. It is a fat yellow lamp, £6.99 at the garage between Wapping and the Limehouse Link (and no doubt elsewhere). I don't know about its claims to produce the power of 1,000,000 candles, but it makes blackstrap Barossa as see-through as a rosé.

Decanter, 2005

THE FIRST THIRTY YEARS

Picture a cramped, ill-lit room in a less-than-fashionable part of London. It is 1975. Two men are scribbling, conferring, filling waste baskets with crumpled paper far into the night. Transparencies are scattered round a light box. The smell of Cow Gum© betrays an incipient art department. An advertising manager (also incipient) alternates between hope and despair. You are witnessing the birth of *Decanter*.

Shift your gaze to another part of London. The same night; a similar scene, but I am one of the hopeful hacks, devising a different magazine. Its name? *The Garden*. *Decanter* and *The Garden* have been on parallel courses all this time. They are so well established now that no one questions when and where they began. I have been part of *The Garden* for the full thirty years, *Decanter* for only half of that time, but they represent two great and similar pleasures that fill the lives of a large number of like-minded people.

Why are they similar? Because they follow the nuances of natural beauty. It is hard to argue that the three Léovilles or the three hyphenated Montrachets, Chevalier-, Bâtard- and Bienvenues-, have the status of natural species, or even of natural varieties. How about Gloire de Dijon, Rêve d'Or and Madame Alfred Carrière among roses, or (to prove the French don't have a monopoly) Taihaku, Okame and Shirofugen among cherries? Nobody needs to know these names, or their relationships; there is no evolutionary or even pecuniary advantage to be gained. They are simply the preoccupations of cultured, and – yes – leisured minds, wired to senses kept in practice by observation. Birdwatching, opera-going ... there are plenty of others, but wine and gardening both home in on the finest of distinctions, nice differences produced by man and nature in concert, to take pleasure in them.

The problem with wine, I am always reading, is that it is 'product-led', not designed in response to consumer questionnaires. We have all met wines designed by marketing departments, and generally learn to avoid them. No: our subject is complicated. It is elusive; a moving target, demanding more than a little humility. The pleasure is in the diversity. Man proposes and God disposes. End of sermon. Shall we have a drink?

Decanter, 2005

WINE: A LIFE UNCORKED
PREFACE

My memoirs. I wish I had thought of a better title.

Proust had his madeleine, and I have my claret. And burgundy and Champagne and Mosel and Chianti and Coonawarra. Every bottle, every glass of wine connects with bottles and glasses that went before, leads back in memory, forwards in anticipation and sideways in reverie. The wines I specially love are those that reverberate on more than just my tongue. Some wines simply have more to say than others. Hearing what they say, following up and linking their stories is a pursuit with no end in sight – which means, to me, that it is high time to start.

Wine is a social game first and foremost; only secondarily an interest like music or collecting. It is about human relations, hospitality, bonding, ritual ... all the manoeuvres of social life – and under the influence, however mild and benign, of alcohol. No wonder we talk about its shades of meaning. So here is a memoir written with a corkscrew, a book of tastes and opinions, a few assertions, a few conclusions – and not a single list. Reader, I picture you as having your own tastes and opinions, as having as much information to hand as you can handle (and the Internet beside you for more), and as being eager to understand. We are in the same boat, you and I. I will tell you what I have understood so far.

I STAND AT THE TOP OF MY CELLAR STEPS and the faintest scent greets me: more an atmosphere than a smell. Moist, organic, old – the words are not very attractive, but a congregation of bottles, some of which have lain side by side for decades, is too powerful a presence to send off no signals.

There were five whole rooms of cellar; I never discovered why. There was no bottled wine when they were built.

It is a library down there: a library of different takes on the same plot. The plot starts with vines insinuating their roots into the soils of a thousand different fields, feeding on what they encounter in the ground, rock or sand, wet or dry, lean and hungry or fat enough to grow marrows. It ends with the air in a glass rising through your nostrils and your mouth to leave an impression on your mind. The two are intimately, directly, inevitably linked – via a chain of events that can go this way or that in numberless and ceaseless variations. On some nano-scale of infinite variety everything is recorded. Like the wings of a butterfly in the rainforest, a passing shower or a spore of fungus can tip a balance that eventually makes you decide to order another bottle – or not. Much more, of course, can all the decisions of the farmers, engineers, chemists, lawyers, bankers ... the army of operatives who intervene on the way.

There are generous decisions and mean ones, intelligent ones and stupid ones, good ones and bad ones. Cumulatively they make not just a bottle or a vintage but an identity, and a reputation. The differences between wines are genetically inherited: the vines and the vineyard are the bloodline. They are also acquired: when the vine is pruned, as the grapes ripen, when they are picked, as they are fermented and matured and bottled and stored again. The wine has its memories: of the stony soil where the vine's roots probed deep, of the stone wall that gave it shelter, of the frost in May that reduced half its shoots to brown rags, of the sun that crept up the rows in the morning and left the grapes glowing as it went down, of the sudden cold showers. The wine remembers it: the dry days of August in the sweet jam-like concentration of its flavour, and the downpour before harvest in a flicker of weakness as you swallow.

PRICES AND VALUES It is easy for someone who drinks for a living to become detached from the realities of a budget. It is one thing to work out for yourself whether the colossal price demanded for a cult wine is justified (the answer is probably no), or to weigh up the relative values of two different châteaux, or two different vintages. Abstract valuation, you could call it.

Real priorities are more demanding. The housewife asks 'Is that fair value for the same price as a chicken?' If you are a shopper who hunts down the best and freshest chicken in the market you will have the same feeling about the wine to go with it. You want real satisfaction, not a token. Curnonsky, the first French food journalist, formulated the basic requirement: food should taste of what it is. It is no different with wine.

Saling Hall in Essex was our home for forty-two years.

THE SALING CELLAR Anyone looking around my cellar would have no doubt where my heart lies: claret, red bordeaux, outnumbers all other wines put together. The slim dark cylinders with their white labels are everywhere, tucked away in racks, stacked in bins, standing on the table or the floor looking expectant – opening time must be near. Even more of a presence are the pale pine boxes as yet unopened, a pile here, a pile there, each with a black brand on the end, some quasi-armorial, some outlines of châteaux, some just resounding names.

It was true for a long time, my preference for claret above all red wines. I am more open-minded now, as the slope-shouldered bottles and the cardboard boxes attest. There is a simple reason, though, why bordeaux will always be in a majority down here. It stays longer. The waiting time can be, and often is, ten years or more; thirty years in some cases. So it accumulates while other equally loved wines pass through.

Burgundy came more recently into my life, and into my cellar. There has been a great change in style, in quality and in availability of good burgundy in the past decade or so. And what is true of burgundy is true of almost every other region and country:

it has far more to offer than it did. Does this mean that bordeaux should change too? It is the debate of our time.

White wines by their nature flow more rapidly. The come-and-go rate is higher, but there are exceptions. Some of the German wines have been in residence as long as thirty years. It's time I drank them. The problem has been – who with? For years my friends groaned when I went into my 'Don't you like Riesling?' routine, but things have got better recently.

In reality there is a two-tiered system in operation: the wines I must taste as soon as possible, regardless of when they will be at their supposed best, and those I am hoarding out of passion to follow their careers all the way. The first you might call my professional cellar – but could you separate what you drink out of curiosity from what you drink out of conviction? If there is a difference, it is in giving a conviction wine the benefit of the doubt. It may have seen better days, but it revives old memories. A wine-lover should be a romantic; romance can plaster over all sorts of cracks. And one sip can be enough to register a new conviction wine.

Which raises the question of objectivity. Critics are obliged to be objective in their assessments. In their public role as judges they should put their preferences and prejudice aside. Which is why 'critic' is a term I have never accepted. 'Commentator', certainly. A diligent dilettante is how I see myself; a dabbler who dabbles deep, but not so deep that the waters of his subject close over his head.

AND THE BARRELS? To hear a cooper talk (and they are famous for it. Also for swearing) you would think that coopers had invented the wheel. They have a point. The barrel is far from being an obvious construction; certainly a giant leap from the amphora that preceded it. An accidental barrel is hardly likely and, like the wheel, there is no halfway stage. What ingenious mind first imagined planks cut to shapes that could be butted up to each other and hooped together to form a – well, a barrel?

The hoops were originally plaited withies; the original shape was a cylinder. Bending the staves to form a belly is not done without effort and equipment; it needs a very strong pull on a running noose of rope or, these days, wire. It is made much easier by steaming the wood or soaking it and standing the half-made barrel over a fire. When the fire started to char on the inside it gave another twist to the story: charred oak gives wine a caramel flavour, another resource in the *éleveur's* armoury.

Oak plays such a large part in the vocabulary of wine these days that we are all pocket experts. The names of French forests drift in and out of the conversation wherever wine is made. One name, Tronçais, is universally saluted: the forest that fetches the highest prices. Its oak has the finest grain, from the most closely packed annual growth rings. I paid my first visit in the 1980s. I was commissioned by *The New York Times* to write about the world's most distinctive forests. A picture drew me to Tronçais, remote in the unvisited centre of France, the old province of the Bourbonnais, the *département* of the Allier. It was January, when the leafless trees spread a purple-grey haze over the brown forest floor: more and brighter colours than summer green. I was mesmerised© by the endless intimacy of it, the repetition of the rides retreating into the haze, and the scale. There are twenty-five thousand acres of oaks, from seedlings to giants like the Chêne de la Résistance: a thirty-five-metre grey pillar four metres round. There are lost lakes, patches of piney moorland, remote woodsmen's cottages with a wistful rose bush by the door. Tronçais was a great natural feature, like mountains or the sea, and its harvest was immense cylinders of scented timber.

so mesmerised that we bought an old farmhouse nearby

One of these cylinders could fetch £12,000, standing. They are auctioned as state property in October each year at the age of a hundred and eighty years, give or take a decade. The forest is ringed with little towns where they are dismembered and the best of the wood split into *merrains*, the pieces that will be sawn to size as the staves of wine barrels.

The best timber is the colour of smoked salmon and smells of wine. So much wine, at least, smells of oak that you might think so. Tronçais and its oak are implanted in my life now. Our farm is on the edge of the forest, where streams leak out of the woods to feed a slow brown river with sudden moods of frothy spate. We had oaks, and planted more: barrels for the future. This is where I planted my vineyard. Oak does nothing for a drink-me-quick white wine.

AN AUTUMN DAY IN KYOTO The Sunday crowds are out to stroll and meditate and giggle and photograph each other among the maple trees. Where Hokusai drew the long arc of a bridge across the Kyoto river you can hire a skiff to row up the broad water between hills of brilliant colour. It is already November; you need a coat. Families lean on their oars and drift down towards the bridge in ecstasy at the tapestry of orange and scarlet and gold. And then the fish boat moves in. He rows just upwind of you, enfolding you in the vapours from his little stove. Resistance is impossible.

We are all innocents beside the Japanese when it comes to fish. My education started in a lecture theatre of the École Hôtelière Tsuji in Osaka. I opened the door to be faced with a hundred students in black examining the shining blades of their long knives. First you cut the medulla oblongata. 'We call this *Ikejime*: live kill. This way the fish is freshest.' You learn a thousand other cuts before you are let loose in a serious sushi bar. My education continued, in the hands of Shizuo Tsuji⊕, proprietor of the school: a visit to Osaka's ancient public baths to learn how to bathe (sit on a stool and scrub, then boiling-water immersion along with everyone else) and how to enjoy having little masseuses running up and down your spine.

a great friend and my teacher in everything Japanese. He died in 1993; his son Yoshiki now runs the school

This was preparation for a visit to Fuki Sushi, Osaka's (Japan's?) most revered sushi bar. There are six seats at the bar; ten chefs behind it. When Professor Tsuji comes in the ten yell '*Hai!*' in well-drilled unison, trailing off in volleys of apologies: '*Sumimasen, sumimasen, sumimasen*'. There is no menu, no discussion. The whole menagerie of the sea is sliced into a succession of exquisite mouthfuls, liturgically ordained: a prawn still alive, just stripped of its shell, then the carapace blackened in a flame. A slice of fat tuna belly, marbled pink and white, then a sliver of cuttlefish spiked with wasabi. Each is laid gently on the pale board before you, timed precisely to your swallow. The industrious slicing goes on, punctuated by loud claps (moulding rice is a noisy business) until every fish has been anatomised. Then the envoi, five centimetres of hot caramelised eel. And all the while with sweet apologetic nods the kimono at your elbow is filling your cup with warm sweet saké.

IN AN ENGLISH GARDEN In wine country there are a dozen settings for perfect enjoyment, given congenial company. Fire- and candle-light come high on the list. The deep napery and clanging crystal of a three-star restaurant evokes a totally different kind of pleasure. Why is it, though, that for me the first place is always reserved for drinking out of doors?

I fancy the answer has much to do with the English climate. Why are the English the first nation in gardening? Why do almost all the common sports and games have English (or Scottish, you golfers) origins? Because in a climate without extremes it is almost always possible, if not pleasant, to spend time in the fresh air, and when the sky is clear it becomes very pleasant indeed.

If the seaside comes first among my perfect places for tables it is for the fish and shellfish straight from the water, the salty air and what the French call *le grand large* itself: the endless sea and sky. Second place, and very close, goes to a table in the garden. My favourite table is on the lawn under an apple tree. Apples make deep dappled shade; there are few summer days when its air-conditioning fails.

CHABLIS It hardly sounds a resounding encomium to be the default wine, the no-brainer that fits in with almost any situation, friend, dish, time of day and day of year. But Chablis is that. Chablis is also my favourite white wine, the wine I buy and drink most of for pleasure and out of interest. The Chablis rack in my cellar (far end on the left) has more traffic than almost any. Can I say why? Because it is the natural partner for the fish and shellfish I love, and because it works supremely well as a drink. To say it has the essential qualities of water sounds a pretty back-handed compliment, too, but just as the cool volume of water when you swallow leaves nothing to be desired, so the stony freshness, the flinty, faintly sour fluidity of good Chablis has an elemental completeness. Sweeter? Absurd. Stronger, oak-seasoned, drier, more aromatic? All absurd. Chablis, I sometimes think, was sent down to earth as a model for all winemakers to imitate.

Which of course they did. For generations, any dry white wine looking for recognition was simply labelled Chablis – in California or Australia, Spain or Bulgaria. They never came close, of course: wrong country, wrong grapes, wrong vineyards. In due course they planted the right grape, the Chardonnay, but followed a different model. The Chablis flavour still eluded them. Meursault was an easier target. Recipe: Chardonnay, nice and ripe; ferment, or age in, or at least flavour with, oak. *Et voilà*. There is an area of Australia, California and South America as big as Burgundy earning a nice living by it.

SOUTHERN WHITES: IN THE BROWN CORNER The table is spread in cloistered shade. It needs to be: your eyes crease and smart when you look beyond the awning and the trees at the bleached tan of the landscape. The slow ceiling fan only shifts the hot air around. Pick at a salad? No: hot countries seem to insist on hot food – and in serious quantities.

I remember the weight of an Argentine steak overlapping the edges of my plate while the sausages and chicken still sizzled on the grill, waiting to be eaten. After the antipasto and the pasta, a haunch of wild boar and a bellyful of beans is sure to be demolished. After the jamón Serrano there is a pan of paella a metre across. And that is not even considering curries. And to drink? None of your thirst-quenching spritzers, your pallid northern Rieslings or Sauvignons, your compromise rosés. We'll start with a young red, purple and potent, and go on to drink an older vintage or two, brick-red and leathery, to feed our nostalgic fantasies. It works. I've never understood why. Do we sweat out the alcohol? Other things being equal, hotter countries make stronger wines. It is counter-intuitive that they turn out to be what you want: the food and wine are of a piece. I wonder if it is a matter of psychology. Does warm weather not make you more outgoing? Are there extrovert and introvert wines? Is my love of precision and finesse and nuances of terroir just a psychological reflex, a way of saying I am scared of drink? It would almost be a relief to abandon analysis, dump ratiocination, forget the fine print of appellation, producers, varieties, vintages .... It won't happen, though, in our latitudes.

CHÂTEAU LATOUR My business with Bordeaux had always been on the consuming end. I was well acquainted with some friends' châteaux, and had been a happy guest in many. But it came as a total surprise when in 1986 the President of Château Latour (and Chairman of *The Financial Times*) invited me to lunch at his Club, the loftiest in the St James's Street firmament, and invited me to join the Latour board.

A day's work for a member of the board of Château Latour (this was in its time as an English outpost, before a harsher French regime⊖ took over) started with a visit to the *chais*. The first-year *chai* first, where the wine of the latest vintage was still in active preparation, its barrels open but for a heavy glass bung to allow the *maître de chai* to make his regular inspections. Twelve hundred barrels lie perfectly aligned in six ranks. A cellar hand in blue overalls is doing his rounds, using a can with a long spout to top up each barrel to the brim of the bung hole.

Ouillage (ullage in English) is a constant task as the wine evaporates and the oak absorbs it. The *maître de chai* leads the way, thief in hand (the thief is a short glass pipette; he plunges it into the heart of a barrel to draw a sample. One thief-full will put samples into three glasses). We follow, five of us, and concentrate fiercely on each dark-red drop, too cold, too dumb, too tannic to taste like wine. The *maître de chai* knows where each barrel comes from: which part of the vineyard, Cabernet or Merlot, the age of the vines, and its prospects as *grand vin* or second wine, Les Forts de Latour, or even third, the wine sold simply as Pauillac (but with a gold dovecote on it with a familiar look to those who know the label of Latour).

François Pinault bought Latour in 1993

It takes a sample or two, teeth-achingly cold, painfully masticated, to begin to distinguish riper from less ripe, more fleshy from tighter-knit, short and abrupt in flavour from sweetly clinging. The wines from the *grand vin* barrels are a more imperious purple. The smell of cold coffee from the oak is overwhelmed by a sweet blackcurrant smell.

Then down to the second-year *chai*, where the barrels go after nine months, sealed with white silicone bungs driven home and tilted to two o'clock. This is finished wine, selected and 'assembled' from its constituents of different plots and grapes around the vineyard. It is not yet homogenised into its final form. That happens in a big vat before bottling, a year and a half after the vintage.

To take a sample from a sealed barrel is more of an operation. Across the end of the barrel goes a crossbar. The *maître de chai* produces a tool like a little mattock, chops the blade down behind the crossbar and uses leverage to squeeze the barrel end. A thin squirt of wine comes from a tiny aperture, stopped with a little point of oak. *Le voilà. Le quatre-vingt-dix.* Harry Waugh© was the man we all looked at. He had tasted twenty-five new vintages. It was more the expression on his face than his few words ('very nice' was always among them) that pointed the way.

veteran director with a famous palate

THE LEFT BANK Wine is the only possible destiny of the Médoc, this low-lying spit of gravel and clay and sand wedged between the Bay of Biscay and the broad estuary of the Gironde, where the waters of almost a quarter of France roll out to sea. The Atlantic has piled up some of the world's highest sand dunes on its western shore. Behind them stretch long wastes of maritime pines. An unemphatic spine of higher ground runs up the centre. Here start habitations and a virtual monoculture of vines covering plateaux and gentle declivities down to the brown Gironde.

There seems to be a single purpose in the existence of these buildings, whose pale stone picks them out among the green of vines in summer and brown of earth in winter. Pompous château and crouching farm, and the straggling villages that thread the roads between, are labelled as clearly as wine bottles with their destiny. Life is red wine here, and red wine is life.

Some days you can smell the sea. If you can't smell it you can detect its presence by the coastal parade of clouds and even a watery quality in the light. The sea buffets the land but also protects it. The winter is grey, damp but mild. Nothing stirs in the village; the château is shuttered. Development came late here: the Médoc was colonised at the same time as South America. It was still primitive a hundred and fifty years ago when Somerville and Ross, two Irish lady journalists, made their tour of what they called 'The Wine Country' and reported on the fleas and the lack of amenities. 'It was those bare feet, crimsoned with juice, that took our whole attention .... At this juncture one of the bare-footed and blue-clad workmen approached with a small tumbler in his very dirty hand ... and we looked at each other in speechless horror.'

THE HOUSE OF MOUEIX Half past ten on the *quai du priourat*. The brown Dordogne is sliding by in oily circles under the stone bridge and on through farmland to the estuary. Cars are parked under the trees for shade. There is a red door in a long stone façade and a brass plate: Ets J-P Moueix. Christian Moueix is tall, dark-haired and lean, with his father's gravity and courtesy. 'We have just put out some of our own wines,' he says. 'Magdelaine, Le Grave Trigant de Boisset ... and Pétrus. May I join you in a quarter of an hour when you have had a chance to see them?' The tasting room is austerity itself: a white corridor with a broad white bench on which ten black bottles are perfectly aligned. A typed list and a pencil are perfectly aligned, too.

It feels like desecration to pour the first wine; alarming when dense purple fills the glass; disaster when a purple drop falls on the white bench. I settle myself to concentrate, put all my senses into the first contact, the first raw, shocking impact of newborn wine. Try to be analytical, I tell myself. But I am distracted by the clean energy that hits me: fresh and somehow athletic. This is a Fronsac from a hilly area just outside Libourne, the prettiest in all Bordeaux wine country but geologically less generously endowed than its neighbours. Fronsac is the perfect place for a country house (unlike Pomerol, a seemingly sterile landscape); its leafy combes are full of them, creamy stone cubes with grey shutters, spangled with the shadows of their tall planes, their vineyards tilting to and fro in a restless landscape. This is not the smell of Merlot, the plums-and-cream of Pomerol, but something more Médoc-like. Not far from the sort of virile claret I like in Moulis, I think. Move on: the first impression is the one to trust.

A BARGAIN BARREL Chilean Cabernet first crossed my path in the 1960s as one of the cheapest red wines my friends could be prevailed upon to drink. I must have been convinced because I negotiated with the London importer for a whole barrel to be delivered to the spacious cellars of my new home in the country. Half-a-dozen friends bought shares. We grew excited as we heard of its progress: by lorry to Valparaíso (not far, it came from the Canepa winery, between Valparaíso and Santiago); by steamer up the long coast of Chile, past Peru and Ecuador and Colómbia and across to the Panama Canal; a steamy tropical passage through the Caribbean, five days steaming on the rollers of the Atlantic and a gentle home run up the Channel to Southampton. It rested in a London warehouse while I paid as much as the wine was worth in duty. Then a brewer's lorry brought it up to Essex. Hurrah. But how to get it down into the cellar?

The driver was a drayman. He rolled beer barrels for a living. They have ways. A noose around the barrel, a turn around the axle of the lorry, aim it end on down the cellar stairs and lower away. Just in case, a lorry tyre at the bottom for a soft landing. What he had failed to notice, and I to remember, was that four steps from the bottom the stairs widen out. Unconfined, the barrel turned sideways and fell, bounced on the tyre and drove its end into the brick floor.

A weeping barrel is a sad sight. The iron hoops had slipped enough for the staves to open. The smell was marvellous as the barrel turned red and the puddle grew. We grabbed hammers and ruined chisels bashing the hoops as tight as we could. We threw sacks in the pond and wrapped the barrel in them. Why hadn't they given it a good soaking to swell the staves before they loaded it? The story, though, has a more-than-happy ending.

I recommend a bottling party. Quality control is a serious business, and nobody shirks his duty. Nine or ten of us worked late into the night, taking turns to suck on the siphon and direct the tube into the next bottle. In preparation for the first day I had ordered twenty-five dozen brand-new bottles, or their equivalent in magnums.

Mystery: I came to the end of the bottles and I still had twenty centimetres of wine to go in the barrel. Alarm: I had to leave them there. No more bottles, and a trip booked to France. I rang round all my neighbours for empties, and stirred what seemed a shocking quantity of sulphur into the remaining wine as it lay exposed to the air in the barrel. I came back. It tasted fine. And we bottled the rest in a medley of old wine bottles, beer bottles, water bottles, even a rather fine blue half-gallon affair from a Victorian pharmacy.

It was the cheapest wine I ever bought: the barrel held three hundred litres when I expected two hundred and twenty-five. But more important it was delicious. It had the ripe dark blackcurrant flavour of good-vintage claret with a dry, earthy tang. Had it been bordeaux, it would have come from the far end of the Médoc beyond St-Estèphe, or possibly from the Graves. The 1968 (a very good Chilean vintage, as it happened) had none of the grace notes of today's Super-Chilean; just densely ripe fruit with enough gritty tannin to keep you on your toes. We drank the last magnum twenty years later. By then it was time to say goodbye.

A VEGETABLE CAPITAL Rioja is not the garden of Eden. The valley of the Ebro is open, austere, a great hammock slung between the snows of two Sierras. Stony towns, Tuscan-style, cap the scattered hills: Labastida, Laguardia, Haro, Briones. From somewhere in this country they conjure markets full of sumptuous produce. In the regional capital of Logroño, a whole street is given over to browsing. You go to the Calle del Laurel for the specialities of its bars with evocative names and permanent queues: Soriano for *champi*, white mushrooms grilled on bread with shrimps dipped in garlic and parsley oil; Perchas for fried pigs' ears; Diagonal for squid fritters; Sebas for stuffed peppers; Jubera for baked potatoes with mayonnaise; El Soldado de Tudelilla for sardines and green peppers; Pagano for kebabs. The wines of the day are chalked up on boards and keenly discussed. At a restaurant called Iruna, wave upon wave of tender vegetables appear. Your ham or chicken is incidental to the baked garlic, the white beans with clams, the celery in almond sauce, the borage fritters, the artichokes and peas and beans and huge white asparagus ferried with anxious looks by women in white who attend the old iron stove as if it were an altar.

A NATURAL LEADER Put me down in a vineyard anywhere you like and I will work out where I am. The hills or lack of them, the vegetation or lack of it, the design of the vineyard, spacing of the vines, their trellis and pruning, the soil, even the light (let alone any buildings) will provide the clues. But there are a handful where no clues are needed: a glimpse is enough. The Mosel, the Douro, the Médoc are *sui generis*. And so is the Langhe, the ridge-backed hills of tall-staked vines culminating in Barolo and Barbaresco.

It is always autumn when I am there. Or winter. Or a drenching day of summer rain. Piedmont is an enclave trapped in the Alps; from any hilltop you can see the encircling ridge, half the year white with snow. Angelo Gaja has his own hilltop; his villa commands the vines of Barbaresco from their summit. He is a man who takes a commanding view of everything that touches wine.

The Gaja *cantina* is a fortress behind an iron shutter. The bell buzzes far away. Inside is a working courtyard, a desultory little garden, a marble hall – and a short man in a frenzy. Angelo Gaja revs away in low gear like a mountain bike – always. One night I heard my name shouted across a square in San Francisco. "Ugh!" Unmistakable: it was Angelo, with five people in tow. What was I doing this evening? Tomorrow? We must meet; had I tasted ...? And we did: next day, a hundred kilometres north in Saint Helena. I don't mind how far I go.

In Barbaresco again. 'Look what we 'ave. Everything.' The tasting table has forty bottles lined up behind ninety king-sized glasses. 'What you want? Everything?' These are wines that I rarely drink, and nobody does often. 'You say. Stefano will open.' Hurry: he's always in a hurry. 'First come 'ere. Come and sit down. I will tell you.' And he does.

Sitting across his office table, the tasting postponed, he tells me the history of Italian wine, its problems, its possibilities, its background, middle ground and latest developments. How Chianti was ruined by the wrong vines, bastardised by rapacious newcomers, and is recovering. The formula for its future success. Piedmont: how neglected it was; how there were only two thousand when there should have been five thousand plants per hectare. How the wine was left in barrel far too long; often dirty barrels, too. The whole sad state of Italian wine a short generation ago (and these were the prestigious regions). The long work of recovery – starting with planting new vines. Now (Angelo swats a wasp. It dies) the renaissance is spreading from Piedmont and Tuscany (and Friuli, too: the Protestant northeast was always relatively clean and tidy) to all parts of the peninsula. Italy is surrounded by sea: just look how God made it for vines.

Thirty minutes later the dissertation was done – and worth a doctorate. This was a deep thinker's mind with the tap turned full on.

SLOW FOOD The white truffle of Piedmont is a fungus of awesome power. I first met it in Genoa, at a wine fair with a hundred stands that filled a tall building around a central staircase. We were tasting on the second floor, our heads full of the fresh scents of Friuli from a dozen green-brown bottles, when a strange miasma crept through the fair, as unmistakable as a gas leak and as impossible to ignore. What on earth? No question of tasting wine any more. This strange aura, like the wildest of cheeses become gaseous, had to be tracked down. The crowd was in motion – down to the door. A rather grubby farmer was standing there, arguing, holding a newspaper bundle. Why couldn't he, he was saying, sell his truffles at the fair?

Alba, south of Turin, is Italy's truffle capital, and October high season for the hunt. Slow Food, the nearest thing on earth to a gastro-political movement, has its headquarters nearby in the city of Bra. Its founder, Carlo Petrini, is possessed by the quality of everything to do with food and drink. 'Slow' (he says it low and deep, starting with a z) 'began the day fast food arrived in Rome. Food should never be fast.' And slow became the cool of the table. 'Come to Alba,' he said, in heavily Italian French, 'we will go 'unting the truffle together.'

At dinner he said 'Bed early tonight. We must be up at three.' For a slow breakfast, presumably, but even then .... Did we have to hunt the nocturnal truffle? Was it possible to go on a day shift? 'You will see.' That was not likely, I thought, at four on a winter's morning. We paraded at three, drank coffee in a hurry, and were off into a dark drizzling fog in a small smelly car with a small smelly dog in the back.

We spent the next two hours slithering through bramble and elder on steep slopes, trying to follow the dog by torchlight. Its master was in the same predicament. His instructions to the dog and his curses were indistinguishable. Our torches occasionally picked up the muddy hound scratching under a bush. By the time its master had reached it, it had moved on. Once an hour, it seemed, with great excitement he said 'Si, si;' and crouched over the animal as it scraped at the dirt. What did dog get, I wondered, as man took over the excavation and straightened up in triumph? We slid down to join him in the thorns. He was holding what looked like a pebble.

Dawn, the rain setting in, and a handful of pebbles. '*Andiamo.* Breakfast.' We filled the car with mud and wet coats and drove steaming back to the village. The market was assembling: stalls going up. We filed into a café, the warmth, the smell of bread and coffee overwhelming. Breakfast was unforgettable: three fried eggs arrived gleaming on a white plate, to be buried in marbled brown slivers from a truffle the size of a bun. Not one of ours. And a bottle of Barbera, deep mulberry-coloured wine as subtle as an alarm clock. Finally I could ask 'Why so early in the morning?'

'Because,' our huntsman said slyly, 'no one must see where we were going.'

'Or coming from?' I said.

The reason for secrecy, however approximate, became clear when we went shopping in Alba. On the stalls in the truffle market women were sitting behind piles of pebbles, pale, chestnut or nearly black. Some of the customers had jewellers' magnifying monocles to screw in as they said *'Permesso?'* and picked up a tuber to examine. Ninety grams on the little brass scales: L30,000,000.

The movement's offices share a galleried courtyard with their own restaurant, kitchen, workshop and exemplar of all that is slow. In the dining room everything is simple, comely and to the purpose. The walls are yellow plaster, the tablecloths rough white linen, the chairs rush-seated wood. They are not restaurant dishes on the menu but recipes from a Piedmont that Slow Food struggles to keep alive. Carpaccio? A fashionable word for a thin slice. Calf's cheek? Jelly or gristle from the days when the squeal was the only thing that got away, but painted with a deep-green pesto tasting of ground-up leaves. A glass of Arneis, a local white wine rescued from oblivion. Then fried rabbit, juicily anatomical, and a jug of young Nebbiolo, like a handful of berries to crunch. A cottage industry, apparently, this Slow business – until you see how it is conquering the world.

THE WARM SOUTH 'Provence is a country to which I am always returning, next week, next year, any day now, as soon as I can get on a train ….' I read Elizabeth David's words in her *French Provincial Cooking* the year© I became editor of *Wine & Food*. 'Pale soups the colour of summer frocks', she writes, and the soups, and the mood, stick fast in your memory. No writer I know can be so feminine and so forthright at the same time. I was smitten. She was twice my age, and my confidante when I was wooing Judy in such a tearing hurry. She sent us to Provence on our honeymoon.

(1963)

Lamastre was the first place Elizabeth sent us en route for Provence. The Hôtel du Midi was her favourite memory of old provincial France, a Relais Gastronomique from the age when backfiring motor cars and stately bicycles carried people on unhurried tours.© It is a long climb through brown beech woods west of the Rhône Valley, above the country of Hermitage and Cornas and St-Joseph, the names on Mme Barratero's wine list and the inspiration of her cooking.

We went back forty years later. The menu was unchanged – the prices were not.

In those days, dinner started with soup. (It was a practice so established that in PG Wodehouse 'the soup and fish' meant a dinner jacket.) Sometimes it had a title; on our first evening at Barratero's it was potato soup, and one of the best things I had ever eaten. Sometimes it was just potage, and so skilfully concocted that there was no point in trying to spot the ingredients. The barbaric French habit then, as sadly still, was to start with a 'cocktail', often just white wine and blackcurrant syrup. The white wine was usually Hermitage Blanc, far from the legendary quality, alas; the red was the point. We drank Hermitage '57 with a leg of lamb, Côte-Rôtie '59 with roast chicken, Cornas '59 with pigeon casserole and Hermitage '53 with a melting beef stew. None of the menus was a struggle to translate. There were five simple courses, dictated by the stalls in the market. We were learning French provincial cooking where it was born.

THE NOBLE ROT The gloom of a great brick vault was lit by iron chandeliers the size of cartwheels. Along one wall ran a table with three vintages each of Châteaux Lafite, Latour, Margaux, Mouton and Haut-Brion. Opposite the First Growths was another table with the full range of wines from the Domaine de la Romanée-Conti. The rare Champagnes were in one corner; vintage ports in another, and Château Yquem gleamed gold on a table in the middle. Then the fairway was encumbered by barrels, not of wine but of oysters and lobsters, the tables piled with sirloins and saddles, and the press of guests more organised, as we stood in line for a gargantuan buffet.

The Lebègue tastings under London Bridge Station were the Ascot of the London wine world.

A lobster, I thought, would be the proper way to start. I was twenty-three, and hungry. The old gentleman beside me in the queue, a tell-tale ribbon in the buttonhole of his grey suit, smiled at me over his spectacles and asked, in faintly French English, when he saw me examining the lobsters, 'What will you drink with that, my friend?'

'I'm not sure', I answered.

'I suggest you take a glass of Château d'Yquem.'

I knew Château Yquem from decadent days in Cambridge as the grandest of all pudding wines and the ultimate show-off bottle. I had even drunk it, with the college's patent crème brûlée – about the only dish that could compete with, and spoil, its glorious creamy sweetness. With lobster? Who was this eccentric Frenchman?

He introduced himself as Bertrand de Lur Saluces. I knew that name: it is written in gold on the most sublimely simple of all wine labels: Château d'Yquem Lur Saluces, and a vintage date. I was queuing with the most illustrious name in all Bordeaux, inheritor of Château d'Yquem from centuries of noblemen with the same name and title, and President of the organisation of Classed Growths for twenty-five years – and he was suggesting I drink his sacred wine with lobster. I did, and so did he, and it revealed a sweetness in lobster I did not know was there.

Further lessons followed when I called on the marquis at Château d'Yquem and at his house in Bordeaux, an 18th-century orangery mysteriously isolated in a back street. I learned the first truth about the first of the golden wines of Sauternes: you don't argue with people who drink it. It made its name simply as the greatest of all white wines, Bordeaux's answer to Le Montrachet. In times before our modern anxiety about what goes with what, the best foods simply called for the best wines. Turbot, being the biggest and best fish, was a natural choice (preferably with truffles and cockscombs). Oysters and Yquem are frequently mentioned. At one lunch at Yquem the first dish was a stupefying foie gras served warm with a sauce of Sauternes (presumably Yquem) and white grapes (peeled and pipped, of course). The second course was the big surprise: my old friend icy oysters and hot sausages, with the nearest Yquem gets to a second wine, or a dry one, Château Ygrec. The scheme was to jolt your appetite back into action for a little feathered game.

They don't exactly know when it was made sweet with serious intent, so to speak, rather than just tending that way. Sweeter wine fetched a better price with the 17th-century Dutch. Here, up on the Loire in Anjou and Touraine across the river in Loupiac and Ste Croix de Mont, up the Dordogne in Bergerac and Monbazillac, anywhere they could they looked for sweetness, and propagated the sulphur match to sterilise it against fermenting on the way home. The sweetness of Yquem hit the headlines when the extraordinary vintage of 1847 was bought by the Tsar's brother at an egregious price and bottled in gilded crystal.

Could it be tastes that have changed? Champagne, after all, was routinely sweet until an eccentric first ordered it custom-made dry – and that was in the middle of the 19th century. Sweetness became a topic as its opposite became the norm. It's a theory. More likely, I think, that here in Sauternes it was a matter of vintage variation, some years much sweeter than others and considered better, (and more sweet vintages at Yquem than anywhere else). There is even an intriguing suggestion that the topic was avoided because the reason, or rather the agent, that caused sweetness was not a pretty sight. Its name, not particularly pretty either, is *Botrytis cinerea*.

What wonderful organisms they are, these fungi. From the succulent boletus to the bouncy little Paris mushroom, the sinister ink-cap to the fragrant *mousseron* or the savoury *girolle*, they have flavours that are neither vegetable nor related to flesh. Often, linking earthy and heady or yeasty elements of taste, they seem nearer to the essence of wine than any food. They take over cream and give it thrilling strength. As truffles they embrace some of the most elusive flavours and the most garlic-reeking. Yet in nature their role is merely to destroy, to seize on an organism full of the ripeness of the sun and draw it down into the grave.

Spores are their mode of attack, and a vineyard is subject to millions. Most of their attacks are malign. When they land on the wrong grapes they cause havoc. They destroy any that are thin-skinned and bloated, pecked by birds or pierced by wasps. Yeasts and bacteria join the attack and the result is vinegar. They destroy the pigment of black grapes – hence their absence from Sauternes. On the other hand on healthy, thick-skinned, ripe white grapes they show their benign side. They put down roots, or the fungus equivalent of roots, through the skin to the sweet juice inside and use it for food. The grape shrivels, its acids are consumed along with its content of water; mouldy it may look, consumed by tiny grey-brown hairs, but its juice attains an incomparable sweetness.

Benevolent botrytis comes with autumn mists. It is not precise in its demands, but its rendezvous with the right grapes demands precision. Regions with autumn mists learned that it was worth playing for, and comes in autumns when mists alternate with drying sunshine. Subsistence farmers could never take the risk. The noble rot was a gamble, and the way to shorten the odds was to grow fewer and better grapes.

TOKAY Hungary, 1985. A posse of hussars in incredibly grubby uniforms galloped up to greet us in the main square of the town of Mór. They were led by a horseman in that improbable Hungarian cowboy kit apparently looted from a Catholic seminary. In their outstretched hands they held brimming beakers of wine, half a litre at least, miraculously unspilled in the cavalry charge. As they reined to a skidding halt, down went the wine in one beatific swallow.

Forty years of more-or-less Communism had no more broken the Magyar spirit than had centuries of harrying by Austrians and Turks. Budapest was the first city of central Europe back on its feet, but then it had never entirely lost its raffish energy, nor even its slightly wistful elegance. Magyars (Hungarians' name for their own high-spirited race) are some of Europe's great originals. Impetuosity, charm, impudence, theatricality distinguish them sharply from their neighbours and for long their oppressors on either side: the Austrians and the Turks.

A less familiar proposition is that Hungary is the only country in the world besides France and Germany to have an ancient, original, truly classical style of winemaking of its own. Georgia could perhaps give you an argument, and Portugal at a pinch (though neither – port apart – has ever really been in the fine-wine business). But the flavours now familiar to us from Italy and Spain were creations of the 19th century.

It is not hard to describe the way Hungary's traditional wines differ from French and German. 'Fire' is the word the Hungarians traditionally use for the quality they are looking for. Don't be put off, though, by an image of alcohol and chilli peppers cauterizing your tongue and taste buds. By 'fire' they mean vitality and high-flavoured sweetness.

To me in those days, Budapest was big, cold and shabby, and Tokay a remote muddy time warp. In my first *Wine Atlas* I used a photograph of the Tokay marketplace: a peasant in boots, layers of waistcoats and a stocking cap by a cart jumbled with old barrels on ruts of frozen mud. It would have passed for a scene from Dostoyevsky, at least to me, knowing little of Russia, my head filled with images of chilly gloom. (The Hungarian authorities hated the picture and asked me to change it.) What I remember best about my first visit, in 1970, was the warmth and noise of the little inns, the beauty of hot red-brown goulash, and the colour of the wine. Even better than the taste, I remember the amber gleams of bottles half-hidden in cellar-moss like white wool. This was in the state cellars of a town with the resounding name (but it took days of practice) of Sátoraljaújhely. The wines we tasted by candlelight, sitting round a black barrelhead, went back to the 19th century in stages of ever-greater loveliness. It seemed that the older they were, the more hues of chestnut and squirrel and dead beech leaves entered into their reflections of amber and gold, the fresher and more flowery they smelled. 'Celestial butterscotch' was what I wrote about all of them, but some sent me on hunts among violets and roses, wallflowers and hyacinths for the smells that I couldn't pin down.

I was an admirer but no expert, then, when Peter Vinding-Diers started talking about reviving a great old tradition that seemed to be spluttering.

Was there anything we could do? The dreamer in me was stirred, and so was the memory of that extraordinary flashing amber wine. If I could have tasted the wine that inspired Homer or Virgil I would have gone to any lengths. Why any less for the wine that Pushkin and Tolstoy drank, and that Peter and Catherine (both Great) considered one of the privileges of the tsars of all the Russias? But was there any way of joining in?

In 1989, under the rump of the communist regime, the only way was a joint venture. Peter's backers organised a meeting in Budapest, then in the little town of Mád (the name attracted plenty of ribaldry) open to all the winegrowers. They had borrowed the schoolhouse for the day – partly, I think, with the quaint notion that they would need a blackboard to show the growers what a joint venture looked like. They hired two interpreters from rival companies as a precaution against collusion, and set out their proposal: the growers were to contribute their land, the foreigners all other capital. The company would then pay the growers for their grapes. Its name, after some discussion, would be Royal Tokaji (Tokay in English and French spelling).

We wandered round the bleak little town after the meeting. It had not seen a pot of paint for fifty years. There was one rudimentary shop-cum-café and nowhere to stay. But Peter had done his research. He led me to a cellar, announced by no more than a door in a low wall by the road. 'This is István Szepsy,' he said. 'His family invented Tokaji. Just wait until you taste his.' Szepsy was a slight man with a stammer. It was an exaggeration to say that his ancestors invented Tokaji, but someone with the same name is credited with making the first sweet *aszú* wine for the ruling family of Rákóczi in 1650. Ancestry was not the point, in any case, when Szepsy took us down the narrow dark stairs into his little rock-cut warren of a cellar, scarcely tall enough to stand in. There was a row of old dark barrels, almost miniature by French standards, and behind the stairs a few more, of strikingly pale new oak. He drew samples from one of these. 'Five *puttonyos*', he said, as he passed us the glasses.

Perfect wine needs no explanation, however exotic it may be. The rules are the same: it smells inviting, invigorates your mouth as it comes in, expands into new dimensions as you hold it on your tongue and lingers sweetly after you swallow. This smelled of apples and quinces and pears, honey and hay. It sent a charge of energy through your whole body as you sipped. It opened vistas of fruit and butterscotch and marmalade – too many impressions to record – on your tongue and clung to your throat like oil to silk, refusing to finish or go away. At the heart of it was a golden blade, glowing and cutting: the spine of acidity that is the hallmark of great Tokaji.

There was no Royal Tokaji winery: just a space behind a building on the central square which had served at one time as a bishop's palace. On the slope behind was a typical entrance to a Tokaji cellar: a monumental doorway, unrelated to a building, leading straight to a flight of stone stairs. Below, the dark, narrow-bore tunnels wandered about, on several levels and with many bends, for nearly two kilometres. Cellars are more important than buildings: István brought in wines from some of our shareholders in 1990 and 1991. I still have bottles, now deepening amber. Our own first vintage, 1993, was made in the open air.

More important than cellar or building is the quality of the grapes, and not all our grower–shareholders had got the right idea. The tumbrils from the vineyard arriving at our improvised cellar contained a fair proportion of rubbish, including what in California they call MOG: Matter Other than Grapes. Luckily for us, Peter had recruited a young Frenchman, Samuel Tinon, from Ste-Croix-du-Mont across the river from Sauternes. He was as tough as he was independent.[©]

He still is both, and makes excellent Tokaji.

He stayed in lodgings in the village right through the autumn and winter while Peter commuted between Mád and Bordeaux.

The names of our fields, or rather the broad swathes of the hilly country where our partners had vines, started out unpronounceable, then became familiar, and over the course of five years and four vintages began to stand for quite distinct flavours. Mád lies in a trough in the foothills of the Zemplén Mountains. The full name of the wine region, in fact, is Tokaj-Hegyalja, the Tokay Foothills. The vineyards occupy much the same space as in the Côte d'Or, both in total area and their situation on the lower and middle slopes of a range crowned with forest.

Of our somewhat random portfolio, Birsalmás turned out to be the light and lively one, Betsek the hearty one, Nyulászó the steely one and St Tamas more bosomy. Tasting them together, in the damp darkness of the cellars, was just what a burgundy tasting would be like if Burgundy made sweet wines, a progression with variations. They are as sweet as honey when they are young, these *aszú* wines, yet sweetness so balanced and held in check by the sharp-tasting Furmint that they leave your mouth whistle-clean. Sometimes you can almost persuade yourself the wine is dry.

it was Elizabeth David's notion

As for the flavours, a great deal of muttering goes on as people compose imaginary fruit salads. Quince (which I always think of as a pear crossed with a truffle[©], so unearthly is its savour) is in most of the recipes. Apples and pears usually figure largely, sometimes apricots, also oranges and lemons. Orange is the touchstone smell for botrytis wines, especially in old age. A great old Sauternes, a Tokaji or a Trockenbeerenauslese hints of marmalade, whatever else is in its repertoire.

Wine: A Life Uncorked, Hugh Johnson, Weidenfeld & Nicolson, 2005

THE HIGH FIVES

Thank goodness I was not the only one to miss what should have been the world's easiest mystery wine. We all did. Twelve of us failed to recognize the legendary Romanée-Conti 1945. To be fair to the others I should say it was in a magnum, and maybe they had only drunk it in bottles recently. It was certainly extraordinary: so perfumed that my first reaction was shock. Such an exotic confection it seemed that at first I didn't even think burgundy. What made it worse – much worse – was missing our host's wager: a million dollars for the right answer.

This out-of-the-ordinary occasion (to me anyway; to some of the guests maybe less so) was Joshua Latner's celebration of the 'high fives', the best of the mid-point vintages of each decade. Latner is (you've guessed already) an enthusiast: a tycoon from Toronto who lives in Greece, Paris ... and around. He gave his party at Troisgros at Roanne, one of France's best restaurants in one of France's more regrettable towns. Every Troisgros speciality made its appearance in a crescendo of flavour and richness that culminated in a whole hare upright on the dish and apparently ready to run. No doubt an everyday affair in ancient Rome but eye-catching in the 21st century.

I would take you wine by wine through the list (not that there is room here) had Joshua not strongly discouraged note-taking in (very proper) favour of lively conversation.

He is a wine romantic; for him the link with the past, he says, is more important than the hint of violets or cedar – let alone scores out of a hundred, though he is a formidable and vivid commentator as well as an indulgent host. The whole spirit of the evening ruled out the concentration and analysis needed for total, or even halfway, recall.

So why am I telling you? Because I salute a man who can see wine, even the rarest and most celebrated of wines, as a passing show. It is not me; I am more cerebral – if that's the word. I make notes on the most piffling of wines. Practically everything I open – in case they come in handy. Perhaps for a column like this.

If you are desperate to know the nuances of difference between Bouchard's Clos Vougeot 1865 and 1865 Romanée-St-Vivant I'm afraid the moment has passed – in a blur of pleasure. Not undiscriminating, I assure you. Just too hectically human for rational recollection.

Decanter, 2005

IN MY DREAMS

I had a nightmare the other night. Wine was a single commodity: all the same, homogenised, nice to drink, had the right effects, but that was all there was to it. It came in three colours, and two strengths. And still or sparkling. You like it sweet? One lump or two?

I was out of a job, of course. What could anyone add, as the tankers ploughed the seas from warm countries with cheap labour and bounteous irrigation? Sadly, in the same dream meat became just meat, cheese just cheese and fruit one reddish substance between sweet and sharp. It had already happened to music: regular thumping to cries of 'Oh, baby'. Wine was my last resort: something that reflected place and history and human effort and the changing seasons and the passage of time. But how complicated is that? Market surveys tell us all we need to know. Does it score under 90? Why bother?

You can usually trace the origins of nightmares. This must have started when I read an interview in *The New York Times* with one Leo McCluskey, a Californian boffin of the Silicon Valley school, who has matched critics' scores with chemical components of wine and can predict them without fail in his laboratory. He has famous clients who follow his step-by-step directions at vintage time, make predictable wines, reap the scores and charge the prices. It is hard to fault the logic: if the public follows the critics, the producer must eventually do the same. Is there any higher authority that says what wines should taste like?

I am not a creationist. Nor do I believe that Appellations Contrôleés come somewhere just below the Koran as a work of divine revelation. Appellations and their equivalents are the works of men's hands, but intelligent, discerning men following on, generation after generation, in an endless empirical quest. The question is always the same: what works best here, where we live, on this hillside, to give us something special to sell? What turned me into a wine-lover was collecting and comparing the results and finding that they never, not ever, came out precisely the same.

Wine sleuths, we used to call ourselves, in the early days of the Wine Club, and the club's team of buyers have the same instincts today. Another vintage from a known source is always good news, but what makes our full-time enthusiasts really grab your lapel is a new flavour, a new producer, or a new wine that pushes its individuality a stage further. Not all experiments came off, but fine-tuning is deeply rewarding: for the tuner, of course, but also for the final drinker.

What would Leo McCluskey say, I wondered the other day, about the wines I was drinking on holiday in the Alps?© After forty years in the business I can still go to a part of France (but it could be Italy, or Spain, or many parts of Europe) where I have scarcely heard of one producer, where the names are only dimly familiar, but where there is a whole world-within-a-world of flavours and qualities based on

(He'd say they would get low scores and fetch low prices. Good.)

grapes nobody else grows. Grapes, moreover, with fresh flavours that seem to match the high pastures in summer, still bright with spring flowers, the fish of the lakes and the nutty alpine cheeses. White wine of Jacquère and Roussette, red of Mondeuse, starting like Beaujolais and ending, sometimes, with an almost-Barolo bite. There were fifty or sixty wines on the hotel list, and the proprietor had three reasons why we should try each one. Would I have been happier, coming in from long walks, drinking Cabernet/Merlot blends treated with *microbulles* and 150 per cent new oak? Did I miss Sauvignon Blanc?

In Provence I drink rosé and Provençal reds, warm with Grenache and spicy with Syrah. In Tuscany I drink Chianti, and wish there was better local white wine – but Fiano and Greco di Tufo come from just down the coast. In Portugal I drink Vinho Verde and love the hard and earthy wines of Bairrada. In Catalonia or the Basque country I drink beautiful local wines; in Greece, Greek; in Morocco, Moroccan. When I am travelling I lose sight entirely of international comparisons, let alone scores. Wine is place.

Does this translate into happiness at home? The wine travelogue is notorious for playing badly to a home audience. 'It doesn't travel' is an old, not very funny, joke. In reality it does travel today, just as foreign foods do. There is no excuse, none whatever, for drinking the output of a factory owned by a corporate monster, whatever fantasy name the marketing department has dreamed up for the label. And paying a fantastic price for a standard red on steroids because it has tickled the palate of someone across the Atlantic makes even less sense.

It comes down to this. If you are really happier eating processed cheese, battery hens and ham pumped full of water, then branded wines are for you. If you have a chronic sense of insecurity you may actually need to pay a lot of money to keep your devils at bay. But if you would cross the road to a farmers' market, you know why wines made by individuals following their fathers' traditions are worth pursuing.

Wine Times, 2000s

POCKET WINE BOOK 2006
AGENDA

What, in this year of grace 2006, constitutes quality in wine? Certainly the goalposts have moved, and they continue to shift every time one turns one's back. For some judges, size is what matters: when you see a tasting note that uses adjectives like 'massive' or 'humungous' as though they were compliments, you know you are in company with people who think that music is always best at full volume. It seems to me that this is a simple reaction against the days when too many wines were thin and weedy, when the only cars they drove were pedal cars and when they were forced to play the recorder at school. But those days are gone. It's time to grow up.

Others regard sweetness of fruit and softness of tannins to be indispensible. Of course, when you start to drink alcohol these things taste much nicer: it's why children like sweet, fizzy drinks. (One merchant of my acquaintance reckons that the British taste for tannins derived from having been brought up on strong tea; Italians brought up on espresso would, by this theory, also have no fear of bitter flavours.) Some people even judge quality by price. This criterion is not even worth considering.

Size, sweetness and softness all have a part to play in wine quality. Wines that taste undernourished are not good; where yields are stretched quality will be lacking. Thin, dilute wines with no stuffing are still made in many parts of France by *vignerons* who are heavily indebted to the Crédit Agricole because nobody wants to buy their wines – except a few misguided Brits on Eurotunnel days out who think they're getting a bargain.

Wine must have ripeness. Ripe fruit tastes sweet, but ripe fruit that tastes only sweet is cloying. This is as true of red wines as of white: there are southern hemisphere reds that taste sweet as lollipops.

Wine must have acidity and, if it is red, usually some tannin; these are the acerbic notes that bring balance and vivacity. But tannins must be ripe, too: dry tannins are no longer admired, even in the youngest of red bordeaux. Green tannins, horribly unripe, are treated with the sort of disdain otherwise reserved by teenagers for the wrong brand of trainer.

'Smooth' is the most popular recommendation of all.

Texture is what it's all about, and texture in reds means tannins. Fashionable tannins must be supple, finely grained and highly polished. This last may not be a very helpful description, but today's top tannins have the gloss that comes from very expensive winemaking. Red bordeaux from Gérard Perse, the owner of Château Pavie, and others, are the epitome of polish, and to my mind taste of money – even his lesser wines from the Côtes de Castillon. You feel richer just tasting them. (Buying them is another matter.)

Great wine is tantalising: it dares you to catch it and pin it down, and just as you think you've got it it's slipped from your grasp. It takes risks; great painters, great writers and great composers walk a tightrope with disaster on one side and boredom on the other, and great wines do the same. Risking wines that taste of their terroir – risking marginal sites, risking leaving boxes unticked, risking not pleasing the market-moving journalists, risking low-level faults, even – is essential nowadays to real quality. It's not so easy to make, and it's not so easy to buy. But what else is worth bothering with?

Hugh Johnson's Pocket Wine Book 2006, Mitchell Beazley

RUSSIAN ROULETTE

I t is only three years since Jancis Robinson and I were in Moscow together to launch the Russian edition of *The World Atlas of Wine*. We were overwhelmed by its reception: perhaps partly because maps of anything had been unobtainable for decades, and suddenly here were maps of (formerly) illicit treasures.

I was back again last month, for more book launches, to find a city measurably brightened. The whole place used to be lit by a forty-watt bulb. A hundred watts and more is now standard, and fresh paint reveals the handsome lines of endless 19th-century streets and squares. The shops are full, Lenin's tomb is empty (at least of visitors), restaurants are eager to please and wine lists unimaginably improved. Not cheap, but up-to-date and often well aimed.

It was Russian (in the broad sense) wine I was after. In Muscovite consciousness the scope extends from Russia proper to the Crimea, Moldova, Romania (still) and above all Georgia. I was invited to an afternoon session at the Moscow Press Club, the cockpit, apparently, of wine criticism, on the top floor of a historic house on Petrovsky Street.

Sixteen of us – writers, sommeliers and three Georgian winemakers – tasted blind and took turns to comment. The chairman (I am tempted to say *tamada*⊚) was Igor Serdyuk, editor of *Magnum*, one of several new wine magazines. I liked the judging system: Gold, Silver, Bronze or Barbecue. Out of thirteen whites and twenty reds we gave a dozen Silvers, a dozen Bronzes and the rest Barbecues. No Golds.

the animator of a Georgian banquet, elected to lead the tasting

Georgia dominated, both with modern-style (fruity) wines and its own strange, tannic, dry yet curiously delicate indigenous idiom: wines fermented, skins, stalks and all, in buried *kwevris*, like pot-bellied amphoras – and best, we discovered, drunk young. One amber Rkatsiteli from Kakheti (2003) smelled of strawberries and roses, was witheringly dry, and had a best-before date: to my surprise required by law. Another amber white, made by monks, tasted like it: so ascetic, sour and tannic that Barbecue conveyed quite the wrong idea.

Saperavi is the dominant, clearly excellent, red grape. Styles varied from lean and tannic to something approaching Amarone, but always with fresh acidity, crisp tannin and pure transparent fruit. The poet Pushkin (his name seems to have replaced Lenin's as the national hero) said he preferred Georgia's Saperavi to burgundy. Oddly, it is burgundy, or sometimes Nebbiolo, that it reminds me of. In the restaurant that bears Pushkin's name, Moscow's most spectacular, two of us drank a magnum of a 1994 with no effort at all.

Decanter, 2006

CHAMPAGNE OR SHERRY?

The *Evening Standard* reported the other day that sales of dry sherry in the UK rose 15 per cent in 2005, something they have not done for a long time. But among drinkers aged between thirty-five and forty-five, they rose 81 per cent.

A straw in the wind? A statistical blip? Who knows? But if I were a Champagne shipper I should see it as an ill omen. There is one wine, and only one, that can challenge the apéritif qualities of Champagne. Once the word gets around, Champagne's most powerful sales point, the bubbly assumption, loses its potency.

The bubbly assumption? The waiter springs to your table, menu in hand. 'What about something to start with, Sir? A glass of Champagne?' You want to start on the right foot; you don't feel like Sauvignon Blanc, or want to quiz him about wines-by-the-glass. You know the mercurial effect of those bubbles in your bloodstream. The easy answer is Yes.

It's a long time since I was in the thirty-five to forty-five bracket, but I have been asking for Fino recently, too. I need a conditioner as much as anyone when I sit down to read a menu. But the rush of bubbles no longer seems the inevitable choice. The extra weight of a Fino or Manzanilla, its slight warmth in the mouth, its salty freshness, its hint of nuts, its suggestion of olives, is the savoury alternative. It is unchallenging: no more intellectual than Champagne, but a natural slow-sipper with enough in each sip to make you pause, reach for the breadbasket, feel your appetite become palpable.

Champagne and sherry, I have always thought, are two sides of the same coin. Both are dry white wines from ideal (and almost identical) chalk soils, but with a climate problem. Straight up, unaided by art, they fail to make the grade. Champagne is too acid; sherry not acid enough. Enter an industry, in each case, to polish a rough diamond, to rebalance a clumsy wine and bring out its lustre.

Centuries of experience later, after heaven knows what investment, the thing is as perfect as it can be, and not only perfect in its way but consistent, bottle after bottle, year after year.

Sherry, of course, is a fraction of the price of Champagne. To snobs this is its disadvantage: it has no bling factor. The rest of us may be happy to put the difference towards a better bottle to follow. Why not, though, keep going with another glass or two? For smoked salmon, soup, oysters, terrines or anything resembling tapas it is a perfect partner. Is this why restaurants are reluctant to serve sherry by the bottle? At per-glass prices it is already a bargain. At per-bottle it is a simple steal. Start now, before they figure out how to do a Krug.

Decanter, 2006

BRANDING BORDEAUX

They have tried sexy women. They have tried cute little bow ties⊖. They are getting desperate for our attention. Who? The burghers of Bordeaux, advertising for the business they always thought was theirs by right: supplying the British with their daily (or more realistically Sunday) red wine. *an embarrassing billboard campaign*

They were unprepared for our national switch to Australia. The obvious reasons, that Aussie wine is labelled in English, that it tastes of ripe (even baked) fruit, that the business belongs to corporations that understood branding and BOGOFs, were no reason at all to the French. Surely, they argue in Bordeaux, they like the taste of our wine? They love the idea of a château, don't they? A little family castle following ancient tradition. They know that France invented fine wine and that Bordeaux was allied to England in the Middle Ages. Isn't that enough?

Not for today's drinker, I'm afraid. He (and he includes she) is not buying much for historical reasons these days.

Remember when everything had 'Made in England' on the bottom? No one else does. If the Chinese could make good strong red at £2.99 that would do nicely. There is another reason, though, that Bordeaux might understand. The English once abandoned claret for port⊖. Once you get used to drinking sweet and strong, claret, by definition dry and light, tastes almost vegetarian. Diet Cab, in fact. And for the same price the New World gives you Cab as sweet as you like and three-quarters of the way to port-strength. *admittedly under duress from the tax man*

The Bordelais haven't stopped making the wines I burble on about, but they have started making much too much that is worthless, scraping by (or trying to) on the legal quibble that it is grown in what is generously termed 'Bordeaux' (that is the entire département of the Gironde, one of France's biggest). Whether the soil, the microclimate or the farmer's motives and mindset bear any relation to quality, tradition and enjoyment is another matter. You clearly don't become a great winemaker just by having a Gironde address.

Wine Times, 2006

DRINK NOW OR KEEP

Just back from a book tour in the US: Chicago, San Francisco and St Helena, Washington DC and New York. There has been a certain amount in the press recently about transatlantic rivalry, and I expected the theme to come up in discussions and interviews. Johnson vs Parker has been rumbling away for years, and my clear statement of an alternative to the prevailing US 100-point system – wine is not sport; differences matter more than beating the competition – could have set it going.

I know it's not your enemies, detractors and rivals who turn up at events like these, but did I get a sniff of any such thing? Barely. The thing that became clear, if it wasn't already, is that wine is a broad church. There is room in the congregation for all beliefs, from the neo-Con (is this me?) to the evangelical (or am I at this end?).

The thing that struck me most, not having been on that restaurant circuit for a year or so, is the rise and rise of the sommelier, and the consequent growth of the wine list. I used to be one who went on about the glorious diversity of wine, but the boot is on the other foot today. Every day I met a new grape variety, two new regions and twenty new producers. Virginian Cabernet I can take in my stride, but Sparkling Spokane? (It was excellent: bottle-fermented Pinot Noir with ten years' maturity.)

Again and again I was surprised by the durability of wines I had seen only in their mouth-staining infancy, when critics were unaccountably saying 'drink now and keep'. Drink now, from my point of view, was simply not possible. Cellared for a few years (and this is what I hope sommeliers are for), they are often as rewarding as my default choice, bordeaux. All it takes, I say to myself, is for the pipeline to fill, stocks to back up a bit, and we shall all be drinking properly matured wine.

Your average critic is not a help; he earns his living reviewing new releases. Very few wineries cellar wines to release them as 'library' vintages. Enter the Master Sommelier (there are now a hundred,

I believe[9]); a bit too passionate at the moment, perhaps, to show her (as often as his) mastery of everything new, but instinctively squirreling good stuff away for later.

today well over two hundred worldwide

As a conservative I specially enjoyed the moment when I asked Karl Wente, whose Livermore Sauvignon I have enjoyed as a good standard table wine for forty years, if they had changed the recipe in all this time. 'I'm afraid so', he said. 'We had to swap from redwood tanks to stainless steel. It's not as good, but there are no redwood coopers any more.'

Decanter, 2006

THE TOKAJI TANG

Almost the first thing the Nazis did when they marched into Warsaw in 1939 was steal the Tokaji in the famous Fukier cellars. It was no secret that unique bottles of the greatest vintages were stored there – going back to the celebrated 1606. Their looting was no random smash and grab by the licentious soldiery; they were stolen on orders from the very top. What happened to them subsequently is the mystery – still being played out, with the last confirmed sighting in 1958 when the Soviet Marshal Zhukov gave an American general some of the 1668. Bottles of incredibly ancient Tokaji still turn up from time to time; not perhaps so remarkable as the fact that they are still extraordinarily delicious.

In June Linden Wilkie[9] opened two mid-18th-century bottles from the cellars of the King of Saxony (last incumbent: Friedrich August III, abdicated 1918). Fifteen Tokajis, two of them from the 18th century and three from the 19th, was good going, though, even by his standards. The 19th-century bottles were Essencias, the ultimate expression of botrytis: almost treacle-like, exuded drop by drop from the pile of shrivelled grapes and too sweet ever to ferment into normal wine.

Linden runs The Fine Wine Experience: rare wine tastings for collectors

The 1888 was the one for me: black as molasses and not much more liquid. You swirled your glass and it all clung, brown-glinting with green lights, to the sides. The point of Tokaji is that it makes ridiculous amounts of sugar drinkable. That was surely the reason crowned heads adopted it in the days when anything sweet was a luxury. It was the honey of the cellar. Its secret? Balancing acidity that rises to equally ridiculous heights and gives an impression of zippy freshness. The 1888 smelt like an infusion of tea leaves, herbs, quince and apricot. Japanese brown tea, to be precise: tannic, minty, mind-clearing. Umami is the taste of appetite; this had that savoury quality.

Together acidity and umami make the tang that defines Tokaji. No other wine has it. Apricots, pears, quince, raisins, figs, orange … everyone finds dried-fruit flavours in it. Sometimes I find barley sugar, sometimes butterscotch. With age comes Madeira, sometimes mocha, sometimes tobacco. The second of our 18th-century bottles that evening danced among these suggestions in an ethereal mint-green veil.

And the modern wines? The history trip was the first part of the tasting; then we reviewed the present and the hopeful future. People talk about old- and new-style Tokaji. There are certainly producers who adapt tradition to make full-fruit, rather than dried-fruit, wines that are more like Sauternes: tang-free, at least in youth. The last wine of the tasting was mine, the first from my jointly owned vineyard Mézes Mály, the 1993. Editor: may I just say I was not ashamed of it?

Decanter, 2006

MORELLINO DI SCANSANO

This is the wine my brother and I go hunting round the crazy curves of the Maremma hills, then drink far into the Tuscan night. It sums up summer indulgence, the light-hearted life when meals merge, where tasty food is the Number One priority and the wine's business is to wash it down.

My brother went to live in Scansano twenty years ago, when its Morellino was a local secret. Every year since more vineyards have appeared on the hills, more famous names have arrived in the region, the wines have been made stronger and oakier, and the prices have gone up. Our favourite red, light and juicy, tangy and appetizing, the true food wine, is increasingly hard to find.

But this is it alright: clear deep garnet, smelling of cherries with a whiff of tar, delicate and cool at first sip, then taking over the palate with the gentle bite of Sangiovese. Morellino (it sounds like cherries, but it apparently means the cowboys' pony of the Maremma) is Sangiovese: the local version. The Maremma overlooks the sea; Scansano looks down on the Argentario Peninsula. It is warmer here than in Chianti; less acidity in the wine but the same appetizing touch of tannin. Its should come in bigger bottles, I always think.

Wine Times, 2006

GENTLEMANLY IDEAS

Seven thousand three hundred pounds a year will buy you a pretty fancy motor, or let you indulge your Champagne habit. That's a £20 bottle a day. You could manage, true, on one nearer a tenner, and it would lower the temptation level at the same time. But 'Champagne,' as Jorrocks so aptly remarked, 'gives you werry gentlemanly ideas.' He put his finger on the raison d'être of the grandes marques, the luxury *cuvées*, and all the glitz and bling that go with the conspicuous consumption of fizz.

Am I, perhaps, the only person who actually wants a daily ration? We have friends who, incredibly, would rather have a gin and tonic – though they've learned by now that I'd be down in the cellar a long time before I'd find any such thing. A couple of Rennies, I suggest, will soon put them right. I admit that there were days in July when Champagne was not the first thing I thought of. No wine, not even Champagne, is made for the long open-throat swallow you need at 90 degrees in the shade.

No, conditions have to be right for Champagne: the time between midday and midnight, the temperature between cold and warm, and the company companionable. Then comes the choice of a brand, and here I depart from my usual wine-drinking habits. I am an indefatigable explorer, a ceaseless quester, a turner over of every stone to try a new producer, a new region, a different vintage – except with Champagne. With bubbles I stay on familiar grounds. I don't want my Champagne to surprise me; there is too much to lose. Anything more radical than a blanc de blancs (and leaving out the black grapes that make up half the blend is already pretty radical) puts in peril that marvellous moment when wine and bubbles hit the oesophagus and you feel the cool column slip down your throat to do its business in your tummy.

It has taken French genius four hundred years or so to perfect the recipe. Dom Pérignon and his mate Dom Oudart⊕ were the ones who set the ball rolling. They were not so much men of God as bursars of their respective abbeys, and anything they could do to raise the value of their wine was fair game. To make it sparkling was not their idea; to make it white was the big thing. White wine from black grapes was a technical challenge, but their best wine to date was Pinot Noir of an unconvincing pale red: a poor substitute for burgundy. To reach the royal table they needed a USP. Whiteness was the one.

The next bit is largely speculation, but part of the secret of making Pinot Noir juice white is picking the grapes soonish, and

cellarmaster of the Abbey at Pierry in the Côte des Blancs

then pressing them with extreme delicacy. Not soon enough, though, to get the fermentation finished before the weather got too cold. So there was always a problem of it starting again in spring. The higher the acidity the worse the problem, but the lower the acidity the more coloured the wine. Chardonnay was no help: even higher acidity and the wrong taste. Dom P settled for the best Pinot Noir he could blend, finished in barrels in his cellar, but kept in them for the shortest possible time. 'The barrel tires the wine', he said.

As soon as the second fermentation was over, then, he started to polish the wine for early drinking, which meant repeated racking from one cask to another. Another problem: how to rack it without exposing it to air, which would ruin it? He used the bellows method, pumping in air to push the wine through a pipe into the bottom of another barrel. No splashing. He had no filters; each time he let the lees sink, then racked again, up to twelve times.

Whatever dodges he used, he redefined wine de luxe – and remarkably fast. The price of Champagne went up all though the 70s (the 1670s, that is) and 80s until in the 90s Louis XIV regulated the trade – but still only in barrels. If you wanted bottled Champagne you did that part yourself – which the English most conspicuously did, and invented fizz.

It is all too easy to see fizz as the point of the whole exercise and forget that they got the wine right first. I confess that if Champagne were just an alternative to burgundy I might not have the same daily craving. But try as I (sometimes) do, bubbles in any other wine just don't do it for me,© not even lookalikes from impeccable, even Épernay-based, producers in the New World. There is a moment, I grant you, for the cold Prosecco they drink in Venice. Tonight, with the thermometer stuck in the late 80s, might just be one. The trick of Prosecco is its very lack of a real taste of wine. But once the fizz does taste of wine, it has to be the wine old Pérignon worked on.

now the English can say Nous avons changé tout cela

The great achievement of Champagne is to have industrialised what is still a delicate process. You will find cheap and nasty stuff if you look. I shrink from friends who dash off to France for a weekend and boast they have found a little man's genuine home-grown for nine Euros a bottle. Champagne has massive cooperatives that do far more than level out the troughs. They provide many an excellent private label for traditional wine merchants who know precisely what they're doing. British buyers sent from the office to find a good supplier are not just on a jolly; they are on notice to stretch their taste buds to the limit. They are choosing wine for important moments, for people like me who don't want any surprises. If any other wine region had worked so hard at it for so long, they might be in Champagne's happy position too.

Wine Times, 2006

POCKET WINE BOOK 2007
AGENDA

A census in a rabbit warren, students in a telephone box ... I have used all sorts of similes over the years for the job of squeezing the wine world into your pocket. It has left little room for reflections, let alone space to contemplate the grand sweep of history. But here we are, thirty years on, with twice as many pages packed tighter than ever. It is progress, not prolixity, this bulge in your pocket. More choices; more wines from more places. Better wines? Real choices? What does progress consist of when it comes to matters of taste?

What do you want from wine, is finally the question. A thirst-quencher? An investment vehicle? A trophy to impress? The perfect accompaniment to food that it can be, the art form developed by the French and Italians over centuries of inspired research? There is little consensus, apparently, over the answer, either among those who drink wine or those who make it. In every other industry choice is being eroded. Globalisation, they said, would be the end of variety; all wines would eventually taste the same.

As I read it, the exploration of what wine can be to different people has only just begun. Its resources of style and flavour are far greater than we currently realise. We are beginning to discover Greek grapes, and Sicilian, but Eastern Europe is undeveloped, and the Middle East unexplored. What do we know of the flavours of Georgia, with perhaps the oldest of all wine-grape varieties, or how they will be interpreted by populations who have yet to meet wine at all? One day China will have a wine culture, and India, and even, one distant day, perhaps Arabia. It cartwheeled all my preconceptions when recently I drank Thai wine grown on tropical islands in the Mekong Delta. The taste was different, but it was wine and I enjoyed it. My guess is that in another thirty years no pocket will be big enough for this book.

How much alcohol should there be in wine? Can you have too little? And, more importantly, how much is too much? These are topical questions because alcohol levels are rising, and indeed have been rising for fifteen years or more. But what at first looked like an admirable trend towards greater ripeness now looks like an obsession with over-ripeness for its own sake: a misplaced belief that in wine more is always better. Wines that twenty years ago had 12 or 12.5 degrees of alcohol may now pack a punch at 14.5 or 15 degrees or even more; balance disappears, and drinkability is thought wimpish. Like human bodies packed with steroid-driven muscle, these wines do not fulfil any useful purpose; they are made merely to win competitions.

The New World has always produced wines of higher alcohol than those of Europe. That's not a problem in itself: if a California Cabernet is balanced at 14.5 degrees, it can be just as fascinating as a bordeaux at 13.5 per cent. 'Balance' is the key word. Balance is what makes a wine sing, rather than shout or grunt.

Some winemakers are also beginning to look nervously at ever-increasing alcohol degrees. They're working out how to beat the climate and make lighter wines in spite of what nature is throwing at them. So perhaps modernity has taken another turn, and it won't be long before words like 'elegance' and 'finesse' are buzzwords again. For some of us, of course, they never went away.

It all happens because winemakers and grape-growers are insatiably curious. And they're delighted if their researches bring them back to some technique practised by winemakers of two or three generations back and since discarded – but probably never quite forgotten. Ideas and information are passed through generations of winemakers in a way that they are not among computer engineers or car manufacturers. There, once an idea has been surpassed, it's over for good. With wine, since people are working with the same soils and the same plants that were there one or two hundred years ago, increasing knowledge can shed new light on an old idea. When you hear a winemaker start a sentence with, 'Well, you know, the old guys used to say ...', you know you're listening to modernity in the making. Everything changes, but not always for very long.

Hugh Johnson's Pocket Wine Book 2007, Mitchell Beazley

WINE IN A COOL CLIMATE

Now you hear little else. The threat (or promise) of global warming has made marginal vineyards frightened of becoming less so.

You hear a lot less these days about cool-climate viticulture.[©] Catchphrases come and go. It was a handy one to draw attention to trends towards higher latitudes or higher altitudes where grapes could ripen at leisure rather than be broiled on the vine. It inspired moves south into Tasmania and South Island, north into the foggy coastal belt of Mendocino, higher into the Andes, south to Mount Barker and the Mornington Peninsula, up hills in many places. Why do we hear less of it now? Because its job is done. Nobody pulled up their sun-baked vines. The Napa and Barossa Valleys have not lost an ounce of reputation, but credibility is extended – and so is the range of flavours for us to enjoy.

Do you remember the obsession with filtration?⊕ (They usually start in the US, these fads). Suddenly any grower or producer who filtered his wine was a swindler, robbing you of all the flavour and character that was your God-given right. Authenticity demanded that nothing finer than a mouse-size filter come between barrel and glass. 'Unfiltered' started to appear as a talisman on labels which, sometimes, did not have much else to say. Not that that ever stopped them, of course, from wittering on about a challenging year, their unique judgement of when to pick and skill in juggling oak from this forest and that.

A special bonnet bee of Robert M Parker, Jr.

'Varietal character' is the granddaddy of the genre. It sounds a bit simplistic for these grown-up times. Now we have been convinced that wine is 'made in the vineyard'; the winery should be innocent of machinery; gravity is good, pumps bad; in fact that intervention of any kind is morally dubious, and growers who risk all by their restraint with treatments of any kind are heroic role models.

At the same time tasting notes reveal, presumably, what we are looking for in what we taste. We need not be subscribers to the shed- (shed-?) loads of fruit school to know it has influence. How about 'minerality'?⊕ I'm astonished to learn how many wines of all hues from just about any soils share this desirable attribute. Salt is the only mineral I have ever identified in wine (South Australia specialises in it). The word conjures up, notwithstanding, some sort of crunchy purity or crystalline vitality that sounds and feels right for a wine you like.

In my 2017 Pocket Wine Book I dispensed with 'minerality' altogether. We used to live without it, it's hard to define ... let's find other terms.

What can we expect next? Almost certainly 'low alcohol'. The race is on for the come-hither word⊕ to sell this very necessary concept without sounding wimpish. It is already routine in many hot-climate wineries to strip all the alcohol out of a proportion of the wine and blend the treated wine back in to lower the overall strength. It is kinder to the taste, I'm told, than putting it all through machinery. What price gravity? And what, indeed, is so wrong with adding water?

no word has emerged yet, but quite a few dilute-tasting wines have

Decanter, 2007

RIGHT DOWN UNDER

A dispatch, this time direct from your correspondent in Central Otago – which reminds me of the Parisian's remark about the Massif Central: 'Massif perhaps; central, scarcely.' Otago is the remotest vineyard from Britain, the nearest to the South Pole, twenty-eight flying hours away. When you get there vineyards are the last thing you expect to see on ravaged badland hills, steep gullies and bleached eroded rocks.

Even in long-settled Europe I often find myself wondering what the outcome would have been if a hillside two valleys away had been planted instead of, say, the Côtes de St-Émilion or the Côte des Blancs. It is easy to rationalise the concept of terroir long after the first trials, the first results and the long business of acclimatisation and adaptation are part of history.

In New Zealand, a country so new (and not only to the vine) that the names and histories, and often even the telephone numbers, of the original pioneers are still current, alternatives are a burning question. Wine is a generations-long business only round Auckland. The first men and women are still making the wine in Hawke's Bay, Gisborne, and Marlborough – and even more so in Martinborough, Waipara and Central Otago. Their vines are now growing stout trunks, and you wonder at the audacity of cultivating what is still, wherever it is not cultivated, a dried-up desert. To make wine of precision, equilibrium, of gentle juiciness, of the finicky Pinot Noir? Audacity has paid off further than they could possibly have hoped. In Central Otago I have tasted eight or nine Pinots that would win prizes in the Côte de Beaune, and not a single one to discredit the region. You can't help asking (and nor can they) what their next act will be – either as to where or what to plant.

Decanter, 2007

DRINK TO THE UNDERDOG

Did you ever boycott South African produce, or refuse to buy goods from a country with any sort of outrageous government? You may well have hurt the people you were trying to help. Are you game to drink the wine of a country that is being outrageously abused by its bullying neighbour? You can only bring succour to its innocent winegrowers and what our Prime Minister would call their hard-working families. The country is Georgia.

I wouldn't ask you to try Georgian wine if I didn't like it myself. It is one of those wine countries with a long ancient history but a short, if any, modern one. In my *Story of Wine* I gave it credit for being the oldest of all wine regions – the original. Archaeologically it has no rival, and little has changed in five thousand years. If you are curious about prehistoric wine, Georgia should be your first stop. True, the most primitive can be dreadful. It can also be wonderful – but that is not what I am asking you to try. Modern Georgian wine is scarcely state-of-the-art, but it is original – even, at times, authentic. It has nothing new to bring the world that is not old, however backward that sounds. What is new and old, very old, is its vast choice of grape varieties – hundreds of them. We hardly know them at all, but the red Saperavi is the one usually saluted as the best. It makes dark-coloured, potent, juicily sharp, rather tannic wine, needing at least a couple of years of ageing and sometimes much more. I encountered a ten-year-old magnum at Pushkin, Moscow's most atmospheric restaurant⊙, which slipped away so smoothly with our *piroshki* that we asked for another. (There wasn't one.) Saperavi, indeed, was first choice in any Russian restaurant until this year. Which makes it all the more provoking that the Kremlin has banned it.

two golden-haired harpists serenade you in a make-believe library

The pretext for this political act was allegedly fake wine. No doubt there are Georgian wine traffickers. No doubt Russian ones too. That's beside the point. President Putin has a long-term political quarrel with Georgia. He hates insubordination. The tsars had the same problem; they built the Georgian Military Highway nearly two hundred years ago. If Tsar Putin can cut off gas supplies to teach Ukraine a lesson, boycotting Georgian wine no doubt seemed a moderate move. What they are drinking all over Russia instead I'm not sure: probably something trafficked closer to home.

So it's time to toast the Georgians. There is little enough succour we can bring to a proud little country, with about as many people as Wales, standing up to its bullying neighbour.

Decanter, 2007

HOME IS WHERE THE HEART IS

It is, we all acknowledge, an expert's business to be able to give snap judgements. The parameters are set, the variables assessed before he or she even gets on the bus to work. Once in the tasting room, decisions come logically, instantaneously, without second thought. A flicker of surprise, perhaps, here and there, but no doubts, and afterward no recantations. Methodical appraisal produces the answers – and that's it.

You do not get to know wines that way, though, and you certainly don't get to love them. I leaf through my domestic tasting book as through a family album. If I can read my scrawl, memories of meals come back complete. I can retaste the wines as they revealed themselves, from first sip (or, before that, the look of the bottle, the cork, or the deposit) to the morning-after recheck as I tidy away the glasses. Usually my impressions are confirmed, but not always. What seemed a whisper of volatility, for example, can show up twelve hours later as the wine falling apart. Or a seeming problem can emerge as a virtue, or at least an eccentricity to enjoy. Perhaps biodynamic wines are especially prone to this. Nicolas Joly's Coulée de Serrant seems dangerously liable to browning in the bottle. Don't write it off, though. Decant it and serve it at room temperature the next day. That is the taste the holy abbots loved, I'm sure of it. Sherry is not as distantly related to other white wines as we tell ourselves today in the era of anaerobicity.

Time for development, yes; but time for food, too. The wines in my notebooks have been shared over favourite dishes. Their tannins are track-tested. Friends' remarks (attributed, when I remember) build up the picture, and the recollection. Sure, I dismiss some wines with a 'too late' or 'for heaven's sake', but a skip through a few months' entries makes me think how very lucky I am. Not many of my wines are auction favourites. Most seem to be either at the beginning of their careers (a new burgundy or German vintage, for example) or getting on for retirement. But conversing with them is a profound pleasure.

The World of Fine Wine, 2007

THE CRUISE

Mature clarets. Starboard tack. Course: thirty degrees for Portoferraio, three jibs, all staysails, topsails and topgallants; twenty-one degrees Centigrade. Tasting notes starting like this generally have a favourable outcome. They only happen, unfortunately, on our biennial cruises on tall ships, but the memory lingers. Some people come primarily for the wine and some for the sailing. Don't ask me to choose. The perfect accompaniment for a Sardinian Vermentino? Force seven on the starboard quarter off the Costa Smeralda. It could become a habit.

A hundred and thirty of us set sail from Cannes on July 28th, supported, if that's the word, by a crew of seventy-five, bound for Calvi in Corsica. You can do it in 2 hours 55 minutes in a car ferry from Nice. Is it a sin to feel toweringly superior? Guilty m'lud, and I want about four hundred similar offences taken into consideration. We were, after all, on our toweringly superior ship for seven whole days.

There is a time-honoured ritual to getting going on the *Star Clipper*. These are sailing ships, remember; the first Sailing Passenger

Vessels to be registered for many many years, and some of the biggest ever. You don't just start the motor, ship a pilot and get chugging. With a great deal of uncoiling ropes and looking aloft, the first signs are acres of white canvas unfurling far above your head. You look in vain for mariners bending over the spars, though: the duty officer has a wand with big yellow buttons controlling electric motors. Suddenly, the sky above you is full of booming rectangles and straining triangles of sail, incomprehensibly high. The deck tilts, the breeze freshens, and three thousand tons of ship (wine cellar included) is heading out to sea.

You are not allowed to forget the wine cellar. We could fill the ship with more passengers than the hundred and thirty club members who so gamely volunteer, but only by using the cabins we fill with hundreds of bottles of the best. It's not as though ports of call were bereft of wine. Everywhere we stop tenders seem to surround us with crates of the local creations. Nor are we remiss about appraising them. We send expeditions ashore to scour the vineyards, invite (unreluctant) growers to come and show us their wares and congregate on the Tropical Deck in attentive attitudes, holding out glasses as though there had been weeks of drought. Still the human chain fetching clarets and burgundies and Kiwi Sauvignons and Chilean Cabernets up from below seems to labour unceasingly. When Club Sec John Kemp and his staff are not pouring for eager tasters on deck you will find them in earnest session in the saloon, discussing whether the Crozes or the Central Otago is a better match for the evening's duck breasts in honey.

Am I painting a picture of excess? It can't be so. Fifty chefs and stewards laboured day and night producing every dish you can think of, but up to five people were reported at one (the only) PT session squeezed in before the (substantial) breakfast. And no sooner have the tenders touched the quay, wherever we drop anchor, but queues form to read the menus of the row of restaurants mercifully within fifty metres of the landing.

There is an unavoidable tension built into the schedule of a Sailing Passenger Vessel. It is the dialogue between the skipper and the restaurant manager. We have learned over the years, and many happy voyages, that the restaurant manager must be allowed his way. Eager sailors longing to see the ship beating to windward, white water bursting from the bows, decks running with solid seas, must see their dreams for what they are. Heeling at more than four degrees makes the cutlery slide about. At eight degrees it is difficult to hold a glass correctly.

Elba was our next port of call after the Tuscan coast. The European Powers made two blunders when they captured Napoleon. They gave him too nice an island to live on – and they let him escape. Elba is peaceful, green with woods, if not oversupplied with memorable wines. We enjoyed, though, the examples their creators brought on board. My choice (Napoleon's, too) is the strange sweet Muscat-scented red Aleatico.

Portovenere lies at the mouth of the gulf of La Spezia, on the borders of Tuscany and Liguria. Some of the party took a boat ride up the Cinque Terre coast to see its absurdly steep vineyards on cliffs above the sea. How much of the vintage, I always wonder, rolls off into the waves? Others stayed to explore the old town. For our purposes Portovenere was the port for Piemonte, and half a dozen of the best growers of Gavi and Barbera and best of all Barolo came down to greet us with a noble range of wines.

What, I had to ask him, did our Ukrainian commanding officer make of our consuming interest – not to say obsession? A solemn toast, and an unexpected compliment: 'Never have I had such a sober cruise.' Practice makes perfect.

Wine Times, 2007

LES AMOUREUSES

I s there a vineyard with a more beautiful name? Even in translation 'Women in Love' is pretty good, but 'Les Amoureuses' sounds like a languid swoon. I should be attracted to it wherever it turned up, but as the neighbour of Burgundy's finest vineyard it draws me like a glimpse of stocking.

'Finest'. I expect you pounced on that. 'Fine', as I have argued before, is a flexible friend. I didn't say 'best' – even if I meant it. Le Musigny produces wine of ineffable (another flexible friend) finesse, achieving by sweet suggestion and eloquent persuasion more than Chambertin can do with power, or the greatest Romanées with exoticism.

I have not (have you?) drunk enough Musigny in my life.

The World of Fine Wine, 2007

JUDGE NOT

I t is the critic's job, as I see it, to extend appreciation. Forwards, of course, into new tastes as they emerge, but also – why not? – backwards into the tastes of the past. The taste, for example, of the pale-garnet goblet I have in my hand, my left hand, leaning it against the paper to search the translucent oval it forms in the tilted glass. Blood-red at the centre, shading like a Rothko canvas to garnet, then at the rim to a pale orange.

My first thought as I sniff it is vinegar and water in an ancient sanctuary. My second, too – only now I am beginning to enjoy it. Mushrooms are stronger than vinegar in this sweet cave-like smell, but the fungus smell has a note of honey in it. I have a passion for the honey-mushroom smell of old Champagne. Here it is overlaid on a background of soured water. Disgusting? Actually, no. I have missed out the texture, some of the weight, even, of red wine. This is the phantom of something solid, something structured. We could never have got here from a liquid that was thin and without character in the first place.

You may think it is barely wine at all; I may sit up with it while the candles burn down. But I have my mind open to whatever it brings, and you are merely judging it. And judgement is an artificial, value-based construct. I shall see pictures in it, as I do in the flames in the hearth. I shall dream dreams, envisage glory past, bottles drunk in warmth and greed, stories told and memories irrevocably lodged. It is not just wine I poured in my glass; it is identity. It is Latour 1937.

Can I make a pitch for identity, even over quality? I can with people. When we think of friends, we don't tick boxes for qualities and failings – especially friends we have known since school. Yes, they have been stronger and more handsome. But love is blind.

Readers will know that I'm easily smitten by a good bottle, but it's a whole country this time, I'm afraid. Not every bottle in it, to be sure, but the whole Kiwi experience of meeting wines with familiar faces but fresh complexions.

It could only be New Zealand. Travelling there is like going all the way through the New World and eventually finding yourself back in the Old.

Not so long ago this meant a sort of retro-world, with old model cars matched by old-fashioned manners. Nostalgia is still freely available. The almost-empty world, a visitor wants to add: empty, poised, a sort of spare Europe hanging below the rafter of the globe, waiting for enterprise to move in.

But New Zealand has woken to find that its take on nature, its environment, and its inherited culture is unburdened by what others took for progress. It changed millennia into something like innocence. Of course it has been ransacked for raw materials: minerals and mutton. It didn't seem the place to make industrial wine; Australia could do that. Marginal, they said its prospects were. Then the penny dropped. Aren't all the best vineyards marginal? Isn't marginal the definition of the environment vines need to give fresh, balanced, harmonious, food-enhancing wines?

Three weeks in late summer (March 2007) was far too short a time to explore all the margins. But short stays in Auckland, Gisborne, and Hawke's Bay, moving south down North Island, then Waipara and Central Otago, in the centre and south of South Island, showed me five regions each capable of exquisite wines.

Auckland has a winemaking history, and Hawke's Bay is no newcomer; the others are completely ground-breaking. None of them, I suspect, has reached even half its full potential. The sort of quality we are glimpsing here is what France must have been discovering in the 19th century. In a world demanding better and better wines, it won't take the Kiwis two hundred years to catch up.

There was another reason to visit Gisborne, alias Poverty Bay, the easternmost point of North Island. It is an essential call for a dendrologist. Exotic (that is non-native) trees have been grown here more successfully than anywhere else in New Zealand. Eastwood Hill *its founder,* and Hackfalls©, on the road to Hawke's Bay, are two of the best tree *Bob Berry, was* collections I have been lucky enough to see. The soil and climate *one hundred* that makes trees from around the world grow so rapidly to record *in 2016* size are (coincidentally?) just as benign to grapevines. A Promised Land indeed.

The World of Fine Wine, 2007

SIPPING ALONE

Vins de méditation. It sounds good, even if you're not quite sure what it means. Not Champagne, in any case. Not a cheerful tipple like Beaujolais or a full-on steak-cutter red from Bordeaux or the Rhône. Not even a lyrical burgundy, or a cool thirst-slaker from the Loire. Meditation implies slow sipping. It suggests solitude.

Wine to think about, sipping alone? You will have your ideas, but mine are quite specific. The wines I muse over, consulting them again and again to log every nuance and echo, all have one thing in common: a degree of sweetness. Not necessarily dessert-wine sweetness. Port, Sauternes, Tokaji – the treasury of great wine glutted with grape sugar – certainly slow your sipping. They are all apt for solitude. Their fatness flows like oil into your throat, and their vigour (which may be fiery with alcohol, or nervous with acidity) sends impulses (of pleasure, and recognition) into your brain. But all great wines, when they are mature, contain an element of sweetness. It can take decades to reveal the core of ripeness, but eventually tannins mellow, acidity retreats and the ripe grape flavour stands in the spotlight again. They become *vins de méditation*, for which food is an irrelevance.

One can never keep up with the modern rarities in American friends' cellars, or surprise them with recent vintages. My inevitable recourse, I fear, is to my dwindling stock of antiquities downstairs. I was not the only one to be moved by one such wartime survivor[⊕], a warm faded-brick colour, penetrating to smell from the start, the scent of Pinot Noir ringing loud and clear. Perhaps its texture had been more velvet in the past, but its energy was in no way diminished. It seized the whole mouth and wouldn't let go.

it was a Corton 1945

A different sort of reverie comes over me as I drink my young Mosels. My old ones, too, for that matter. I speculate about the fall from grace of this pearl among wines. No remotely convincing reason has yet appeared. You read everywhere, when German wines are mentioned, the same platitudes about Liebfraumilch ruining the market. The Mosel never had anything to do with Liebfraumilch (though it did, I admit, have some dreadful vulgarities of its own). But the worst that Beaune's blenders could do never made us lose sight of great burgundy, and some pretty dire stuff has come down the Gironde without making us forget our claret.

The good growers on the Mosel have delivered without fail, good year and not-so-good year. More to the point, it's hard to remember when it was not so good, so consistently successful have they been in the past decade – no, two decades. Pull any Mosel off the shelf (with due regard for provenance) and pleasure is guaranteed.

Mention Mosel among today's collectors and they will acknowledge Scharzhofberg. 'Ah yes,' they say, 'Egon Müller,' before intoning the names of the Pulignys in their cellars. True, Egon Müller makes one or several of the world's very best white wines. His Kabinetts, in particular, are a steal at half the price of a Puligny. But what makes you think Müller is alone? The strong drive, the kilowatt vitality of his wines set the standard, but there are other hills of slate just as well situated, and their great vintages of the past few years have been selling for the price of Rieslings from Austria and Australia. Their Kabinetts, that is. Received wisdom (often the only sort on offer) has it that greatness starts with Ausleses. Ausleses are dear. They are also too sweet for general use and as perverse as great claret in demanding to be kept for a decade. Great Kabinetts, in contrast, drink liltingly from their first year in bottle, then add twists of sweet fruit and sour stone before introducing a whisper of honey at year eight or so. The greatest start with a dagger thrust of acidity parried by succulence: as deft a manoeuvre as your mouth will ever meet.

I try to limit my references to Tokaji. Writers are not supposed to obsess about areas where they have personal interests. But you cannot think (let alone meditate) about the electric energy and hypnotic harmonies of great Mosels without seeing the parallel to Tokaji. Both pivot on the extraordinary juicy acidity of exceptional grapes picked late in some of the northernmost vineyards of all. They are some of the world's longest-flavoured wines, and longest-lived, with alcohol contents you could call negligible. Both are emphatically *vins de méditation*.

The World of Fine Wine, 2007

BLACK AND WHITE – AND RED ALL OVER

'Bottles seduce you so easily, Hugh,' friends sometimes say. 'Have you no other *coups de coeur*?' Better not probe too deeply here. Trees and forests often give me a lump in the throat, and the perfumes of flowers make me weak at the knees. I can't keep away from the sea: on, in, and beside it are all places I love to be. And let's not go into dishes I can't resist (especially at a table in the open air).

Books, though, are a pleasure I can share with you: books about bottles in particular. Sometimes one becomes required reading for all serious wine amateurs. *Bordeaux/Burgundy* by Professor Jean-Robert Pitte is one. Does the professor prefer one or the other? He is too much of a diplomat (or, more accurately, an academic) to tell us. Perhaps, like most of us, he wants more time (and more opportunity) to weigh the evidence. His book, though, is fascinating evidence in itself of the 'fraternal enmity' between the two ancient rivals, two parallel traditions that pointedly and proudly ignore one another.

Jean-Robert Pitte is a professor of geography who concentrates on the good things of life. Books on French gastronomy and the history of the French countryside betray him.

Bordeaux and Burgundy: the hard bit is not in identifying the many differences between them, but in finding what they have in common. Little, says Pitte, beyond the ambition to produce the best wines in the world (and a love of garlic). Both have roots in the Roman occupation of Gaul. Since then, every possible circumstance has served to increase the differences – from climates to soils, land ownership to religion, methods to markets, grape varieties to gastronomy, from a politically astute mercantile culture to one much closer to the soil: peasant, indeed, in the true old meaning of the word.

Add the chauvinism that the French share with the Italians, the strong suspicion that even the nearest neighbour's fruit is inferior to one's own, and rapprochement seems as remote as ever. It does not, after all, take the geographic and cultural distance between eastern France and the Atlantic coast to produce the same effect. You can't interest the Rhône in the Loire, or Touraine in Anjou, or even, I dare say, Sancerre in Pouilly. Give one the other to drink, and I guarantee the first remark to come will begin with '*Quand même* ... ' – which signifies, 'Making all allowances I can for an inherently inferior pedigree, and not understanding in the least what you are trying to achieve, I will do my best to enjoy what you have kindly offered me.'

To make matters worse, Burgundy, which considers itself (with some justification) the heart of France, considers Bordeaux to be, if not strictly foreign, certainly a sell-out to the Anglo-Saxon world to which it belonged for three centuries. Worse still, Pitte quotes a Bordelais saying (of Burgundy), 'I know the French much like this sort of thing, but then again, I don't much like the French.'

The master historian Roger Dion – whose *Histoire de la vigne et du vin en France, des origines au XIXème Siècle*, published in 1959, remains the bible of French wine historians and geographers (and at least one English one) – held that wines are made by their market. It is not a theory that chimes well with the determinism of terroiristes. The owner of a famous vineyard is unwise to give himself, or indeed his customers, too much of the credit for his success. His fortune is his real estate. What is Pétrus? Not the man who makes it, taking whatever infinite pains. The commercially correct answer is 29.7 acres of clay resting on a bed of limestone, appropriately drained. Something, in other words, that cannot be denied – and certainly not duplicated precisely (or indeed moved) elsewhere.

The respected geographer of Burgundy, Rolande Gadille, was categorical in saying that terroir is paramount. Human energy and vigilance, she said, are 'practically powerless to break through the limits cast in legal form by the INAO, which stipulates the yields that prevent prices getting out of hierarchical order.' 'Take but degree away,' said Shakespeare's Ulysses⊖, 'untune that string, and hark, what discord follows!' Not on INAO's watch.

The World of Fine Wine, 2008

Troilus and Cressida, *Act I, Scene iii*

PLATO'S PERFECT GLASS

If there's a more conservative wine-drinker than I am, I'd like to taste from his decanter. I speak of my home life, of course. On the tasting circuit I try to keep my mind as open as my mouth – though certain things can close both as quick as a mousetrap. Raw oak, hot alcohol, thick, sweet texture ... things that, strange to say, one never met in the primitive days when off-piste wine tasting encompassed most of the globe. There were off-smells, sour tastes, rough textures; but vintners rarely assaulted you with the violence of new oak or excessive strength.

What I look for now, as then, is a drink that combines refreshment and stimulus with clean flavours, a gentle potency, and an attractive, moreish finish. That is the minimum. Failing that, why take a second sip? The further pleasures that can build from the minimum are almost infinite. They can leave you dazzled and wondering. But this is where they have to start.

We tend to forget just how wonderfully simple a thing wine can be. The search for superlatives, for every sensation in spades, is the curse of our time. There are wines that take very few words to describe because they deliver something elemental. I like to think that at the heart of every appellation, and indeed every grape variety, there lies Plato's Perfect Glass – the sip that says it all. It may not shout it; the hard of tasting may not get it; and I hope it happens when I'm sitting comfortably and in good company.

I was standing, not sitting, the other evening in the crowded marketplace of Tokaj (a town I have come to know rather well over the past twenty years). The older inhabitants were braving the rain to go round the stalls that were offering samples. I asked what they thought of the new styles of dry Furmint and sweet late-harvest wines coming, these days, from every cellar. 'Not much', was the answer from one burly old chap, once an important official in the communist state cellars. I asked him what he drank in preference. 'I'll show you', he said, and went off through the crowd to come back ten minutes later with a long-necked Tokaji bottle. He filled our glasses and I took a cautious sniff. It was effectively sherry, oxidised over three or four years, I should judge, in an old oak cask – but sherry with a piercing autumnal scent that shouted (this was not a whisperer) Tokaji. I sipped, and the oaky autumnal forest-floor flavour filled my cheeks and went whistle-clean down my gullet. It was as fresh as a spring and as round as a nut, its parts in proportion, its warmth gently insidious, its flavour hanging sweetly in my lungs.

'How do you make this?' I said. 'And what do you call it?' Szamorodni was the answer. You pick good grapes and leave it to mature. As an old French stonemason once said to me, as I fussed about exactly what to do with a barn we were mending: *Il n'y a pas cinquante solutions* (There aren't fifty solutions). Do the obvious, the minimum, and live with the result.

As Nature intended? I think of this when I read a back label or a press release listing all the intricate manoeuvres that have gone into a limited and painfully expensive new wine. What was so wrong with the grapes that they needed so much cosseting? Potentially a great deal, is the sobering truth. The ideal, heaven-sent wine has the odds stacked against it. The vintner simply daren't take the gamble – unless, like my Hungarian friend, he is simply pleasing himself.

Some wines, nonetheless, come across as authentic, natural, just happened that way – and it is always an attractive quality. The dry white wine of Santorini is one – at least that from the cellar of Haridimos Hatzidakis. It is hard to imagine that wine can be a business proposition on the baking unsheltered heights of this most elemental Aegean island. The vines⊕ are traditionally grown crouching, plaited like nests, the grapes so closely in contact with the stony white soil that you feel they must absorb its flavour through their skins. Yet intense sunburned concentration gives pale, crystalline wine: intense, hard-hitting, flinty-edged, but secretly succulent. It is a wine you would be bound to recognize a second time, not so much by its features as by the look in its eye.

Assyrtiko, whipped by the Meltemia, the dry north winds

Brilliant winemaking can be so disarming that you forget analysis and sink into the cushions. It doesn't work if the cushions are too obvious: the sweet-fruit-polished-tannins school that leaves you wondering if any actual wine crossed your palate at all. Precise balance and optimum maturity are the suspension that gives a perfect ride.

Does Plato have to see the label, or will simple harmony satisfy the old chap?

The World of Fine Wine, 2008

OUT OF AFRICA

D rinking South African wine used to feel almost like a charitable act. In apartheid years it was competently industrialised, but no one drank it in this country for fun. To celebrate liberation we tried to overlook earthy reds and fairly fresh whites in the name of progress. The white wines, all agreed, led by Sauvignon Blanc, crept ahead of the reds. Then in the mid-90s came the shock (I can still remember it) of a totally convincing Chardonnay.© Then more surprising still, a Pinot Noir better than California's. Then a series of Cabernets cleansed of earth and iron, juicy, full of ripe currants: the very thing.

I missed the action on the ground, I'm afraid. Shamefully I stayed away for twenty years. I hadn't much enjoyed my early visits, and there was too much to keep up with elsewhere. South America, not to mention Australasia, loomed larger. I found out just how much I was missing in March this year.

We rented a little house on a big beach in Walker Bay, long-famous for its whale-watching (the monsters jump so close inshore they can soak you with their splashes) but only recently famous for its wines. The Walker Bay coast, and the Hemel en Aarde Valley leading inland, are Africa's first Côte d'Or: the grapes of Burgundy ripen here, sea-wind-cooled, to the same racy pitched-up flavours. Go-faster acidity is the secret: fresh when they are new, long on the palate, and keeping them zinging until mellowness sets in. Few seem to avoid the corkscrew for that long.

My corkscrew was busy day and night. I Googled before the trip to find a wine merchant with a good range and found The Wine Village in Hermanus. John and Erica Platter, who have helped me for nearly thirty years with my *Pocket Wine Book* (their own annual guide is South Africa's standard work) came down from Durban to show us the ropes. My brother, son and other friends from England lent their palates to the task. We hardly found a bottle of wine we didn't want to finish.

If there is one iconic estate that every visitor should see it is Vergelegen, one of the closest to Cape Town and the country property of the first Dutch governor, Simon van der Stel. The 17th-century mansion, its furniture, its garden and park with magnificent trees©, epitomise the early civilisation of the Cape. The modern winery, sparkling white above its vines overlooking False Bay, epitomises the future. And the wines, from bubbly to Chardonnay to what tastes to me extraordinarily like claret, send out a clarion message: South Africa has arrived.

Cinnamomum camphora, spectacular giants

Wine Times, 2008

WHAT COUNTRY, FRIENDS, IS THIS?

Barely half of us have any faith in wines from Eastern Europe, according to a poll in the trade magazine *Harpers*. It's not perhaps surprising, given half a century of dismal performance under the communists. The question was 'Do East European wines have a strong future in the UK?' Only a third said yes. That is still quite a lot of people, though, and must surely include all of us with the curiosity to explore Europe's treasury of traditions. There is still a huge field to research. I've just come home from Illyria, to use the archaic name (see *Twelfth Night*⊕) for the Croatian Coast. A week of island sailing, from Split to Hvar to Korcula to Vis and smaller islands, then on to Primosten on the mainland, showed me a culture of local wines and grape varieties as varied and lively as any in Italy.

It certainly needs a key. Most of the grape varieties are unknown (at least under these names) elsewhere. Neither their labels nor restaurant wine lists offer any help. A dozen or more labels appear regularly in local supermarkets, at prices that give an indication of their local reputations – none notably low, be it said, and some surprisingly high. But Croatia is not a cheap country; hotels and restaurants are good, and well aware of the lure of their surroundings.

Is there a headier experience than landing in an unspoilt harbour, its crystal turquoise waters fringed with glowing stone like a village Venice, to sit in a café that grills fish and brings jugs of pale topaz wine? The wine is scented, fresh, invigorating with a hint of nuts and an elusive bitter touch. There is a bright bowl of salad. Then soft ewe's milk cheese and a jug of light red like plums touched by the sun. Coffee, then, dark and gritty, and a pale clean spirit that might have been grapes or plums or apricots. The afternoon breeze stirs the broad leaves of the plane trees, but you have joined the Lotos-Eaters.⊕ There is no hoisting sail this afternoon.

It doesn't take all week to learn that Graševina, among the whites, is a serviceable 'Italian' Riesling, that Malvazija is the fresh light thirst-quencher, slightly aromatic, good as an apéritif, and that Pošip is more serious. Pošip is the white burgundy of the coast and attracts ambitious winemakers, most notably the octogenarian 'Mike'⊕ Grgich from the Napa Valley, who has retired to Hvar. His Pošip is the most expensive wine on every list in Dalmatia. Unfortunately Grgich brought the taste for French oak with him, to be followed by others looking for international recognition.

Other islands have other specialities: the tiny green Vis, a botanist's paradise, grows golden Vugava, Hvar, Bogdanuša; Korcula,

*Act I, Scene ii:
Viola: What
country, friends,
is this?
Captain: This is
Illyria, lady.*

*Tennyson: 'And all
at once they sang,
"Our island home
Is far beyond the
wave; we will no
longer roam."'*

*Miljenko, formerly
of Grgich Hills
Estate, famous for
Chardonnay*

Grk; and most of them Maraština. The solution is to order the island's own carafe wine before experimenting with bottles. Often a splash of cold – even sparkling – water is a good idea.

Plavac Mali is the red to order in most ports. It is the small-berried variety of a grape with Zinfandel connections, or so they say. Don't be put off. And don't normally trouble to order its super-premium manifestations, Dingač or Postup. It is strong enough already.

The sea gives you the best view of some of Europe's steepest vineyards, on the south coat of Hvar; and strangest, where the marina of Kremik, just south of Primošten, is surrounded by Babić vines corralled in tiny plots edged with ramparts of stone. Babić is a revelation: a light red as fragrant as burgundy, with a tang of the sea.

Decanter, 2008

WHY YOU'VE NEVER HAD IT SO GOOD

I've made the assertion, as have others: there is less bad wine than there used to be. I can't think who would do the research. Not me. But it's fair to say we see less bad wine, and very fair to say we see more good, which is what matters. We can kid ourselves that certain fashionable wines are better than they are (North and South American reds, for example, are often overrated), but the choice of beauties at bargain prices expands before our eyes – almost too fast to keep up with what's on offer.

Take Greece. Ten years ago, no one in this country even considered Greek wines. Now I see them as a reliable resource, different but not too different, marvellously food-friendly. How did it happen? I suspect we paid for it, via Brussels, in a magnanimous gesture that turned out better than anyone expected. The same for Portugal, Spain, Sicily ... it's no miracle they are making not just decent but actually prestigious wines we have to pay premiums for. Let's not think about the cost; it is money well spent.

The new Old World, as I see it, has one enormous advantage over the old New World: its vines. Greece can make good Cabernet, but that's not what's exciting: it's Greece's unpronounceable ancient grape varieties. The census is still being taken, there and in Italy, Spain and Portugal: new tastes springing from the cultures of regions that history had virtually dismissed. The almost universal knowhow of modern winemaking can make respectable or better debut wines of them with no problem at all. Imagine what treats are round the corner when more of their secrets are known. If Greece and Sicily can get over the challenge of high alcohol (Planeta in

Sicily, for example, makes perfectly balanced wines already), the future is very bright indeed. The current view that global warming is about to change all this, making temperatures too high for quality around the Mediterranean, is bound to make us apprehensive for the future (the worst threat I have heard is that Sauvignon Blanc will invade northern Europe). The upside of warmer summers is already well known in Germany: scarcely a duff vintage for Riesling in the past years years.

The list of regions focusing on the indigenous qualities they can bring to the table is exhilarating. How to choose between Roussillon, Navarra and the Pyrenean foothills, good old Languedoc (have you tried Picpoul de Pinet?), Salento and its smooth reds, ditto from the Douro, South Africa's Chenins Blancs or the steadily improving wines of old friend Gascony?

Sometimes you find what you are looking for right under you nose.

Decanter, 2008

SPAIN'S GRAND MASTER

Five yellow helicopters like a covey of canaries whirred over the misty hilltops from Penedès to Priorat, then north in an arc to Conca de Barberà and Anoia. They perched for an hour at the old castle of Milmanda and soared in low-angled sun over Fransola and Subirats. They carried the Torres family's guests on a lap of honour of their estates, scattered in the hills of Catalonia in a pattern hard to grasp in a cellar or tasting room. The topography, the soils, altitudes and local climates of this diffuse region are easier to taste than to envisage. Hence the canaries, and a new level of respect for one of the great creators of modern wine, the always-modest Miguel.

The Torres family was unveiling its new single-vineyard bodega. Its top flight of wines from their own best vineyards now have a cellar of their own, close to the original cellars but leagues away in concept. They delve forty feet underground and enclose a monumental cloister that brings memories of the pharaohs. Rather than separate wineries on each of their six *fincas*⊙ they have created *(estates)* ideal underground conditions in one centre. Their newly acquired *finca* in remote Priorat is the exception; they are building it a new bodega in the vineyard.

Without three generations of Torres the world would never have discovered what Catalonia can do. It is tempting to compare them to the Mondavis in California; everyone knew, though, that Napa can make first-class Cabernet and Chardonnay. Catalan Cabernet burst on the world with the Torres Black Label that worsted Château Latour in a famous confrontation in 1979. Since then Black Label has been renamed Mas La Plana. A tasting of twelve vintages (including the winning 1970) showed that a very serious cru has established an identity as clear as that of any Médoc château: an intense mineral-rich wine, glossy but deep-etched with fine tannins and elegant acidity.

But the Torres wine list, of course, extends to Chile (we drank Manso de Velasco, a beautiful Cabernet Sauvignon, with partridge pie) and to Miguel's sister Marimar in Sonoma (outstanding 2003 Pinot Noir with monkfish and mushrooms). Miguel Junior is director of operations, his sister Mireia winemaker, their mother Waltraud a painter of mysterious geological landscapes. The Torres don't take life easy.

An aerial view, I concluded, is the only way to comprehend such talent, and such industry.

Decanter, 2008

THE BOUNTY OF VERONA

Blaise Pascal,
17th-century
French philosopher

'The heart has its reasons .... ' Pascal© it seems, had his *coups de coeur* too. Sober assessment tells me that my happiest drinking hours are spent in the company of my old friends claret and burgundy, Champagne and sherry, and German wines. Anything else, sobriety tells me, is a flirtation, however hard to resist.

But why resist? Real life, surely, lies outside your comfort zone. Unfamiliar wine cultures make you challenge your own preconceptions. Recent journeys have made me realise that if my regular supplies dried up, I should be having more fun, not less. Even if the Champagne tap was turned off – which is not something I would have said even a year or two ago.

I look for bubbles (don't you?) wherever I go. Recently this has included South Africa and Italy – not perhaps the first places you look in search of brilliant bottles of fizz. The trick, I find, is to stop looking for the precise flavour of Champagne. Habitual it may be, but essential? Are you so demanding with Cabernets that they all have to be Pauillac?

Resisting the temptation to linger on the first sip, quizzing it too deeply, I found 90 per cent bubbly satisfaction in half a dozen South African sparklers, and the same number in Italy. In South Africa, having played around with Pongracz, enjoyed Simonsig and Steenberg, liked JC Leroux, and been mighty impressed with Graham Beck's Blanc de Blanc, I settled with a blend called Tanzanite that combined freshness and a touch of yeasty breadth to make an ideal sundowner. The threshold for what they have baptised *méthode cap classique* is pretty high and its exponents practising hard. Far from feeling deprived, in fact, I thoroughly enjoyed the sense of new discovery.

In Italy it is so easy to call for Prosecco, and to accept its simple scouring action as the preliminary to the antipasti (there are always grissini, besides, and olives are not far away), that the decision to order a serious *metodo classico* is already a significant step. It is not a wide field. Berlucchi is the one you find everywhere (and I find perfectly acceptable). Ferrari from Trento is an easy one to remember and full of flavour. Ca' del Bosco is probably the most ambitious. I hesitate between its new-coined, precise and bracing Brut Zero and the richer more complex prestige Cuvée Annamaria Clementi. The conclusion, in either case, is that Lombardy, or more precisely Franciacorta, on the final folds of the alpine foothills near Brescia, makes ordering Champagne in Italy a conscious act of francophilia rather than what Hilaire Belloc called 'sheer necessity'.☉

It didn't occur to me even once, while on holiday in South Africa, to order an imported wine. Not everyone, I grant, has the curiosity to keep pulling different corks wherever they go (or indeed an annual wine book to keep refreshed). But let me dispel any notion of sacrifice. Where I used to grimace at the thought of one of the musty earthy reds of the Cape, bottle one on day one told me that those days are past. The means have been mastered; now the choice is between styles.

'Beneath an equatorial sky You must consume it or you die; And stern indomitable men Have told me, time and time again, "The nuisance of the tropics is The sheer necessity of fizz."'

The World of Fine Wine, 2008

POCKET WINE BOOK 2009
AGENDA

What's the rarest thing in wine today? A case of Le Pin? A case of magnums of Le Pin? Two cases of magnums of Le Pin? No, though few of us would turn these down if they were offered. The rarest thing in wine is something simple: it is authenticity.

But surely authenticity is easy to find, you say. Can't wine labels be trusted? If a wine says it comes from Sicily or Maipo, can't we rely on that? Yes, but that's not the authenticity I mean. What I am referring to is the picture of a place that a wine contains: a snapshot of sun, rain and wind; of minerals and earth; of roots pushing deep down into layer after layer of soil. It's a sense of place; it's terroir.

Terroir is a well-trodden subject. We're all familiar with the definition: the combination of soil, exposure and climate that makes one vineyard or region different from another. We're all used to adding the hand of man to the equation – without man's intervention there would be no vineyard. Too much intervention, though, and the terroir will not be heard above the noise of winemaking techniques, alcohol and strident varietal character. Too little intervention and the wine may not be good. Authenticity in wine can mean awkwardness, clumsiness, unripeness, and even faults. But we are, as in all things, allowed to exercise discrimination. This book is all about sorting sheep from goats in all sorts of ways.

What makes a wine authentic? How wines reflect their terroir is something we don't yet understand. Wines grown on gravel don't taste of gravel. Wines grown on clay don't taste of clay. Yet if one compares Pinot Noirs from adjacent vineyards in Burgundy, made in the same way by the same people, we all taste differences. The same goes for Rieslings from the Mosel. This is terroir at its truest: where it makes a difference in the glass. It may be scientifically unprovable as yet, and it's right to be sceptical; but if you can taste the difference in the glass, then there is a difference.

Hugh Johnson's Pocket Wine Book 2009, Mitchell Beazley

VIVE LES DIFFÉRENCES

I'm always saying it, but reading it in *The New York Times* seems to give it greater weight. Says the perceptive Eric Asimov, *The Times*' wine critic, 'Even with the pitiful exchange rate France is still the greatest source of wine bargains in the world.'

Is this surprising? To muddled minds, maybe: people who have heard the almost incredible prices of Lafite and Romanée-Conti and concluded that that's the way France is: Faubourg-St-Honoré© from Calais to Carcassonne. To people who go on holiday, rent a gîte, stay in *chambres d'hôte* and stop for lunch where they see a reassuring congregation of *poids lourds*©, it makes perfect sense. The French are much greedier than they are rich. Their hearts are firmly down at the level where their belts hold up their trousers. It is a moot point whether the French or the Italians spend more time thinking and talking about their next meal. The whole business, food and wine alike, is deeply democratic. Crus classés and their prices are as much dreamland to most French people as they are to most Brits.

Connoisseurs they are not: it is all too easy to fool them with a watery version of an impressive appellation. Where snobbery is concerned we are mere beginners. Yet the real qualities of authentic

Paris's glitziest shopping street

the lorries, that is – and maybe their drivers too

products have a place in the national consciousness that puts ours to shame. Watch a housewife prodding the cheeses in the market. Visit a *vigneron* with a few barrels in his cellar. The flair for discrimination is part of France's DNA – and we are the lucky neighbours invited to the *grande bouffe*.

I have spent years puzzling how France acquired its instinct for local qualities. Folklore usually claims that this dish or that wine goes back to the Middle Ages. I always wonder which farmer and which burgher were able to forget taxes, tithes, cold, hunger and plague, all the unpleasantness that we picture making up medieval life for the vast majority, to select the Cabernet Franc as the best prospect for St-Émilion or Chinon. Or bring the Melon from Burgundy to improve the sour wine of Muscadet. When life was nasty, brutish and short, you have to admire the men who perfected cathedral masonry, and the men (often, but not always, monks) who sipped and savoured, adjusted their pruning and their fermentation, trawled through the vineyard for the most promising plants, and generally upped the ante. They were inventing pleasures for future generations that still set the pace for the rest of the world.

If the reality is that most of the honing and perfecting went on more recently, that it was really the 18th, 19th and 20th centuries that defined the styles of France's great library of wines, it is still an incredible achievement. Napoleon's minister of agriculture (and trade and commerce generally: he was a busy man) was Jean-Antoine Chaptal. It is fascinating to read his two-volume textbook of wine knowledge[◎] as it stood in 1801. This was half a century before Pasteur cracked the secret of fermentation, yet it is full of familiar things. His account of France's grapes and their qualities is still almost valid. The great tapestry of what became Appellations d'Origine was already largely woven. Surprisingly, indeed, he says many of the great wines of the past were not as good as they had been – and blames overproduction and idle growers.

One thing is for sure, though: they have never been better than they are today. They have the technical means, the scientific knowledge, and competition on a level that never existed before. Upwards is the only way open. It took a while – in fact it took a change of generation – for the message to really sink in. France is all about diversity. It may frustrate marketers who want to tidy it into a few big brands they can peddle with massive campaigns, but different climates, different soils, different traditions and different philosophies are what France is all about.

Wine Times, 2009

Traité sur la culture de la vigne

AND MY FAVOURITE?

The answer is Champagne; without hesitation (or deviation, but lots of repetition). Champagne because it is the perfect drink if not the perfect wine: the most refreshing, the most stimulating, the most gluggable or sippable (either mode gives satisfaction).

Collectable? Absolutely. There is as much variety in Champagne as in, say, white burgundy: more, indeed. From frothy thirst-quenching NVs to resonantly, sumptuously winey old vintage wines is a longer journey than from Chablis to Chassagne. And age, far from wearying good Champagne, adds dimensions and flavours you could never surmise from the raw young fizz.

There is a lot of discussion today about growers'-own and single-vineyard Champagnes, with the suggestion that a blanc de blancs or a blanc de noirs is somehow purer and more virtuous than a classic *cuvée* with all the components playing their parts. Certainly these soloist wines teach you something about terroir, and plenty about obsessive individualism. They also teach you, or at least me, that isolating one of the ingredients of a great dish just leaves you yearning for the others.

A good blend is far more than the sum of its parts.

Decanter, 2009

LE COEUR DE BORDEAUX
PREFACE

A book about the heart of the Graves: Pessac-Léognan.

My fellow countrymen have had a fondness for what we call claret for many centuries; eight, at least, and if Roman records can be believed, perhaps even nineteen or twenty. In the Middle Ages it was our national drink. We were then largely deprived of it until the 17th century, when it made a dramatic reappearance in London in a revolutionary guise.

It is the best-known story in England's drinking history. The London diarist Samuel Pepys, who recorded his daily doings with a frankness permitted him by his coded language, went to the City's most fashionable tavern and 'drank a sort of French wine, called Ho Bryan, that hath a good and most particular taste that I ever met with.' In that one word 'particular' he defined a revolution – and initiated a literature of tasting notes that has since become a flood.

The Haut-Brion that inspired Pepys's comment was claret with attitude. He expected Bordeaux to offer fresh, sapid, lightly tannic and mildly acidic red wine, pale in colour. What he drank that night had more colour, more body, more concentration and depth, perhaps the scent of new oak, but above all a sense of place. It was an original, with a character he had never met before. And customers were ready to pay whatever it cost.

The fashion caught on instantly. England, with the restoration of its merry monarch, Charles II, was open to new notions of luxury. When the curious investigated further, though, they were puzzled. The philosopher John Locke visited Haut-Brion and reported 'nothing but pure white sand, mixed with a little gravel. One would imagine it scarce fit to bear anything.' Welcome to Pessac-Léognan.

Particularity is the hallmark of Bordeaux's crus classés. In a region awash with wine of all sorts they stand out as marques that maintain certain attributes year after year – even century after century. Sand and gravel, and what lies under them, set the parameters. The floods of the Garonne over millennia have deposited this variable layer of easily shifted shingle over already variable limestone and clay. Vines once planted in desperation, as a subsistence crop where nothing else could grow, found singular flavours in these gravel beds. Proprietors preferred one vine or another, experimented and honed their own favourite selections. Over time a certain recipe, as it were, applied to a certain parcel of land, gave a consistent and distinct result: a cru with a life, both economic and gastronomic, of its own.

A score of such individual enterprises make up the whole body of crus classés of Pessac-Léognan. They are scattered over a surprisingly wide area, interrupted by woods and villages, autoroutes and suburbs, because the formula works only where the accumulated soil has reached a depth, and created an exposure facing the sun, susceptible to ripening grapes. Red or white grapes, be it noted: this is a versatile formula, with experience proving that on certain sites the classic bordeaux recipe of Sauvignon Blanc and Sémillon in varying, personal-to-the-property proportions can conjure up white wines as complex and long-lived as the region's reds.

How to sum up the qualities of a region whose wines can create emotion without drama, and take you to the very heart of the claret conundrum? It was an Edwardian Irish barrister and MP, Maurice Healy by name[*], who ventured to identify the style of claret from the soils of the Graves, of which Pessac-Léognan is the heart, by contrasting it with the Médoc. Graves and Médoc wines, he said, are like matt and glossy prints of the same photograph. Like Pepys's 'particular', his remark focuses comprehension. You are at liberty, of course, to prefer one or the other. Would you say the matt print is more *sérieux*, draws you in to look deeper, satisfies you with subtler shadings than the light-reflecting gloss?

he wrote Claret and the White Wines of Bordeaux, *and (my favourite)* Stay Me with Flagons

Michel Bettane© goes as far as language can in evoking savours that only the nose and mouth can perceive, and the brain enjoy. It is the glory of France to have created such gustatory works of art, the happy fate of Pessac-Léognan to provide the milieu, and the pride and joy of their guardians and curators to polish the jewels in their keeping.

Le coeur de Bordeaux Michel Bettane, James Lawther,
Alain Benoit, Éditions de la Martinière, 2009

OLD DOWAGER

Without really thinking about it, I have become a sherry-drinker again. It's not an easy admission. When Mayor Boris© was groping for a killer description for Gordon Brown he came up with a 'sherry-crazed old dowager who has lost the family silver at roulette.' Not a positive image, then.

The trouble is the catch-all name of sherry. If the old dowager were Palo-Cortado-crazed, or giggly on Manzanilla, you would feel that at least she was going in some sort of style. You and I don't (as good *Decanter* readers) ever ask for, or probably even think about, a glass of 'sherry'. You might ask for a glass of 'white' in a pub (however unwise) or 'red' in a café, but sherry breaks instantly into two categories with totally different tastes and purposes – and then into a whole complicated lot more. A category, or a brand, is indispensable.

There are two kinds of sherry I drink regularly that are as different as ... what? Fino and Oloroso? My club has very sensibly started stocking quarter-bottles of an excellent Manzanilla, La Gitana. One of these, screw-capped, gently beaded from the fridge, is a perfect welcoming drink in the bar, with a few cashews, for two people planning to have lunch. It costs a quarter as much as two glasses of Champagne and sets the tummy rumbling just as effectively. In fact it has more in common with Champagne than that: the sheer finesse of a delicate wine grown on pure chalk. Often I find it leads to another of the same when we get down to the menu. What other wine would you drink with soup, if you're going modestly? On days of extravagance it meets the big flavour of an oyster halfway, and makes smoked salmon taste more special than the usual white burgundy. What's more, claret follows it as neatly as the first Act the Overture.

Autumn is the start of the season for the other kind of sherry, the kind I squirrel away for years on end to bring out at weekends when someone comes to lunch. In complete contrast to Manzanilla or Fino, which must be sprung at the last minute from the fridge, and then only in a little bottle you will finish there and then, there is no known limit to the staying power of this wine. At Christmas I opened one of my last, alas, bottles of Very Old Oloroso® from Berry Bros & Rudd, just hanging on to its tattered black-and-white label bearing the words 'Bottled in 1971'. A fine crust was clinging to the bottle, but I decanted it more for the splendours of its brilliant amber colour than fears of dregs. The bonus was the first rising aroma of dried fruits, and honey and old grey oak, as the visibly sticky stream flowed into the decanter.

'Pata de Gallina', from the hen's-foot symbol chalked on the cask

Bottle-age had added a gloss and breath of history to a gloriously generous wine. Old Oloroso is punchy stuff, dry versions almost painfully so. This had the velvet touch: sweetness integrated with tawny nutty flavours in endless resonance. At lunch in winter I can sip Oloroso or Palo Cortado like this in tiny sips right through the meal.

Decanter, 2009

THE PRICE OF CONFIDENCE

I'm hearing real resentment from claret-loving acquaintances about what one of them calls the 'greedy chancers' who doubled the price of their 2009s. Some merchants are trying to pretend it's business as usual in Bordeaux; in other words that opportunistic gouging is all you can expect. But this is only one corner of the picture. First Growths at £1,000-plus a dozen may make you see red, but how about good sound Médoc at £10 a bottle? It's still (just) there.

Price differentials are a fascinating subject. Even in everyday life you have only a vague sense of what you get for the extra money. You suspect (and are probably right) that reassurance is a significant factor when people decide to pay more. I once heard a man buying socks asking 'Don't you have anything more expensive?' Deep down we all know the entire luxury-goods market is founded on the same psychology.

So should we be surprised that wine brands that have spent centuries and fortunes manoeuvring themselves into the luxury-goods sector have realised the strength of their position? If I understand economists correctly, a finite supply in an expanding market only has to keep up deliveries for its price to rise. A mere 20,000 cases in a market that suddenly includes Asia does not have long to wait.

It's not a trick you can pull off overnight. Aspirants for promotion need impeccable dress and manners. A foreign accent does not exclude – or not for long. Confident pricing can work wonders. To the First Growths and the DR-C, the hereditary old guard, you can add, as relative parvenus, Le Pin, Coche-Dury, Vega Sicilia, Grange, Henschke, Pingus, Sassicaia, Ornellaia, Krug's Clos Champagnes and those Napa Cabs that never even reach these shores, so eagerly are they grabbed (by the insecure?) in their own country.

If you accept footballers' salaries as a fact of life – and what alternative do you have? – you must accept the fact that cars, real estate and art are the default resources for flaunting it, and that wine has joined their number. But the fact that someone else is driving a Bugatti has never spoiled my enjoyment of my modest tourer, nor does my Château Batailley or Cantemerle (£240 a case each), Chasse-Spleen, Poujeaux, or indeed Beaumont or Lanessan (at considerably less) taste any less deliciously satisfying because there are sleeker models with more horsepower on the road.

Decanter, 2009

POINTLESS OR PROGRESS?

Who wants a Bordeaux Riesling? Yes, I'm sure we'd all be curious to taste it (and indeed I remember a rumour that a distinguished château in Sauternes included Riesling in its blend). But – beyond proving that it's possible – what's the point? We know what we do want from bordeaux. Anything else is a waste of vineyard.

That is the orthodox view, and the one taken, sometimes with surprising aggression, by the French authorities. Didn't they bang up the bloke who planted Gerwürz in Limoux (or at least threaten to)? The normal control-freakery of Paris gets particularly frantic, it seems, over the grapes deemed to be Alsatian. It's the old war wound being troublesome.

While the New World mocks, and loves taking cuttings from any vineyard with a different flavour profile to offer, there is much to be said for specialisation, and even more for consistency. Could bordeaux or burgundy (or indeed Montalcino) maintain its market if every label tried to explain some individual deviation from its tradition? The essence of being one of the classic wine regions, is to be self-referential. 'We are both 100 per cent Pinot Noir,' say Volnay and Pommard, 'but just look at the difference our soil makes.' Pichon Lalande and Pichon Baron say the same sort of thing, playing the Bordeaux card: Merlot brings out the essence of one terroir, Cabernet Sauvignon of the other. Or in other words we have built our brand that way, and we'd be mad to change.

Does this mean there is no room in the Old World for progressive planting? That would be a defeatist message. Every time a vineyard needs new vines the boss must decide what they should be. Burgundy in the 1960s bought too many vines of clones chosen for their heavy crop. Too many clones altogether, in fact. Shrewd growers have since learnt that you need variation within the vineyard; you are better off with cuttings from as many different good healthy vines as possible. The rootstocks you choose for grafting are almost as important.

Regions without such precious traditions have more leeway in choosing. If your wine is hard to sell anyway it is extremely tempting to try something different. German growers got impatient with late-ripening Riesling. Their boffins obliged with crosses (Müller-Thurgau, then lots of others) that ripened earlier, but failed to satisfy the parts that only Riesling can reach. Most of them are happily forgotten.

What then would you plant to satisfy Germany's new-found passion for home-grown red wine? Pinot Noir, or Spätburgunder, is Germany's classic red grape. Rarely, until recently, has it given wines that a neutral observer would even describe as red.

For various reasons (climate change being one) Spätburgunder is getting redder, but meanwhile there is this bright new vine called Dornfelder. Germany has a new product much easier and generally more satisfactory than the old.⊙ Isn't this progress?

I take this back. There is such good Spätburgunder these days.

Decanter, 2009

IDENTITY PARADE

Every winemaker wants the identity of his wine to matter above all. Not every consumer thinks it is that important. There is a debate here that we might as well bring out into the open. Of the pleasures that wine gives you, what proportion is simply sensual, finding a delicious drink no matter what its name may be, and what proportion is related to its identity?

The chap in the blue corner, the identifier, is essentially a collector. He may well derive as much pleasure from the nose and the lingering palate of a good glass as the man opposite him, the pure sensualist, but his true satisfaction is related to the label. It would put him on the rack to show him a great wine blind and refuse to confirm its identity. Show him half a dozen glasses of wine, and he will want to know if they are vertical, or horizontal, or random, what their relationship is, and above all to identify 'the best'.

There is an element of this urge in all of us. What a pity, we would say, not to know the producer and the vintage at least, so we can find the same thing again. How do we do on the sensual side? Can we lose ourselves in the sheer hedonistic delight of a beautiful bottle for its own sake, taking no notes and asking no questions? I sometimes envy those who can.

Here is a sobering thought for the collector, though. We may be living in the golden age of the wine label. We can all understand the reasons why they multiply. Every ambitious producer wants his wines to be recognized and asked for by name. To emphasise the uniqueness of his style and stress its intimate connection with his terroir is his whole aim. The unique indigenous yeasts of his cellar come into play, and so may the clones he selects among his own vines. Trial and error – or, rather, trial and more trial – is the name of the game.

But will this soon seem a primitive use of resources? When there are more certain measures available, when the genome of wines is available on the Internet, will it seem so clever to be taking cuttings? Will we look back on today's practices as groping in the dark and on the vineyard characters we prize merely as superstitions from the Dark Ages?

If science can make mice luminous by implanting a gene from a jellyfish, it can certainly add characteristics considered desirable to grapevines. What would growers sacrifice to be relieved of mildew, or to increase the crop by 20 per cent without losing quality?

We know Nicolas Joly and his biodynamically inclined friends would never accept genetically modified vines in a thousand years, but the great majority of vintners, I believe, will eventually do their sums and make the most of what science offers. It may give us better vines than any we can imagine. How will we react if an even tastier clone of Chardonnay gives Le Montrachet an unimaginable extra excitement? If Pichon Baron can suddenly taste like Latour? If Village wines can equal Premiers Crus; and Premiers Crus, Grands Crus? How many of us will insist on keeping the status quo?

Wine combines the pleasures of the flesh with the very different but scarcely less keen pleasures of discrimination. It is almost nonsensically satisfying to recognize something ostensibly anonymous like a glass of wine, to name it and place it in the proper order of things. Wine has its own Linnaean system. Botanists and zoologists wrangle, too, about species and varieties, but no one rubbishes Linnaeus. What happens when DNA becomes a pick-and-mix affair? Will Bordeaux and Burgundy shake hands and make up? I confess I'm happy with things the way they are.

Decanter, 2009

IN CONTEXT

Is there a paradox in programming moments of emotion? It's what you do, after all, in planning your daughter's wedding or opening a bottle you've been looking forward to for twenty years.

Moments of high expectation, by their nature, run the risk of disappointment. It's the three-star-restaurant syndrome: anything less than perfect is a fault – and a fault you resent like a splash of red wine on your white tuxedo.

All the more thrilling, then, is the wine of which you had little expectation, but a thread of knowledge to give it context. Without context it could be a golden throatful, or a slug of brambly warmth, but leave nothing but a string of unanswered questions. I am aware (who isn't?) that a fashionable school of wine writing disdains context, despises culture, disregards history, tradition, sympathy and all that gives wine dimensions beyond a mere drink. I despair of it. It does an immense disservice to enjoyment and appreciation by distracting attention from everything but the senses. It's like asking only one question about a person: is he or she good in bed?

What bottle, then, started my reveries this time? Of all things, a Dão that I found in the 'miscellaneous, old' rack in my cellar, where I go on a Monday evening when Judy and I are alone. The peeling label said Pedras d'Orca '94. I must have put it there on the basis that it was a pretty dull and rigid wine that might conceivably achieve some charm in old age. It had. Oh my, it had.

But it needed a context. It could be difficult without memories of Portugal as it used to be, and a winemaking idiom going (but not yet quite gone) the way of the dodo. Portuguese table wines used to be *elevado* by local merchants, weaned of their formidable tannins, blended and barrel-aged for years, then bottle-aged for improbable periods, finally to emerge as *garrafeira*, which pretty much translates as 'reserve'. The modern ageing periods are two years in cask and one in bottle, but you used to find fifteen-year-old wines on the shelves – like, indeed, my '94 Dão.

Its colour had certainly not faded. It was deep, glowing, blood-red with a mahogany edge. Nor had its nose lost the crisp edge that denotes tannins still full of zip. A clean, crisp frame of tannin instantly forms in your mouth, as appetizingly as chilli in a curry, focusing, in this case, a nugget of sweet, mature grapey warmth.

The grape flavour was recognizable: there are port grapes here, the supreme Touriga Nacional and the Tinta Roriz (or Tempranillo) among others. The wine, in essence, was a sort of claret made from the grapes of port. It was the rediscovery, and understanding, of a long-ignored idiom (Australians would say 'style') that made the bottle memorable – in fact, rather a treat.

The World of Fine Wine, 2009

HELPLESS BEFORE THE SMILE

There are bottles (or, as here, half-bottles) that have the effect of a beautiful smile. They make you forget everything else, focus your attention – your longing, even. They switch on senses you were not aware of, beckon you to places where you can't follow.

All wine-lovers agree that this or something akin (you provide your own metaphor) happens – and that sadly it doesn't happen often. Wines that awaken such feelings are usually attributed to terroir. Terroir is a term sufficiently flexible – vague, if you like – to cover aspects of wine that are hard to pin down to variety or technique. And beyond terroir? May I suggest 'numinous'?

I haven't used that word since sixth-form essays on the romantic poets, so I had to check its meaning. Webster has three definitions: '1. Supernatural, mysterious. 2. Filled with a sense of the presence of a deity. 3. Appealing to the higher emotions or the aesthetic sense.' I'm talking about wines that tick at least two of these.

So, what was this numinous half-bottle? Burgundy, as you may have surmised. There are clarets that hint of celestial trumpets; also brazen ones, full-on fanfares, not hinting but with kettledrums. Numinosity (not in Webster, but may I?) comes to bordeaux only with full maturity. In burgundy it can knock you for six in a barrel sample. My half-bottle was a Ponsot wine: Griotte-Chambertin 2001. It spoke its piece straightaway, as some great burgundies do. It was poised between earth and air, root and fruit; earthy (but that's not what terroir means) and ethereal as the vapour in a still.

We ask for contradictions in great burgundy: body that is round and supple but also tense with tannins and alive with acidity; aromas that evoke soil and undergrowth but also flowers and fruit. Their interplay is the music of the wine, now in counterpoint, woodwind and strings answering one another; now in harmony so close that your palate concedes, abandons analysis, helpless before the smile.

Chambertin gives us expectations, and Ponsot very much so. Griotte? A reference to chalky soil, say the geologically minded. Evoking wild cherries, we ignorant hedonists insist. You could call many vineyards Griottes, if that were the criterion. Isn't wild cherry one of the characteristic tastes of Pinot Noir wherever it is grown?

How do you compare, though, the cherries in a photograph with the cherries Chardin[⊙] painted? If a painter can express an essence with six strokes of his brush, why not a winemaker with the multiple manoeuvres of the cellar?

1699–1779,
the greatest painter
of still lifes and
domestic scenes

I sat half the afternoon with the last half-glass of my half-bottle, analysing myself, I suppose, more than the wine. What part of me was so engaged that I couldn't stop?

Coup de coeur is a glib expression – more glib in French than it appears in English. Supermarkets plaster it on BOGOFs these days. A better phrase for the way a great wine engages you would be *saisissement de coeur*. Back to the dictionary: '*Saisissement (nom masculin). Impression subite et violente qui affecte l'organisme ou frappe l'esprit.*'[⊙] *Esprit frappé* begins to say it.

A sudden, violent
impression that
affects the body or
strikes the mind.

The World of Fine Wine, 2009

The 2010s

RAISE THE TEUTONIC!

Perhaps they should make it stronger. Or ensure it doesn't have that giveaway taste of fresh fruit. What are the Germans doing wrong to put us off their wine?

We drink oceans of mediocre stuff from far-flung countries but turn up our noses at some of the world's freshest and most characterful. Is it that Germany doesn't conjure up visions of glorious meals? Or that not many of us go on holiday to its quaint wine towns? Is it the language?

The approved and endlessly repeated answer is 'Remember Liebfraumilch'. The feeble fluid that used to flow here in vast quantities is said to have put us off German wine for keeps. Did the Spanish burgundy of the 70s give us an aversion to Spain, or acid in straw-covered flasks to Italy?

Part of the problem is the confusion between 'German' and 'Riesling'. Is it entirely Germany's fault that its bog-standard wines were, and are, conflated with its best grape, when actually they are made of (at best) its mass-production substitutes?

Riesling is rowing back. After years of repetition (especially by Jancis Robinson and me) that Riesling is the best white-wine grape of all – or at least equal first with Chardonnay – it's getting a grudging acceptance in a market super-saturated with Sauvignon Blanc. What Rieslings are we buying, though? Not the crystal-pure, infinitely varied interpretations from its natural home, but strangely typecast versions from Australia, a slightly bizarre blend (or so it sometimes seems) of lime juice and kerosene. Does the reason lie, perhaps, in the infinitely varied interpretations? 'I thought it would be sweet' is what I hear nine times out of ten when I trick a friend (yes, it's that bad) into tasting one of my favourites from the Mosel or Rhine.

What do modern German dry Rieslings offer? An alternative to endless Sauvignon Blanc. Sauvignon and Riesling are the two great aromatic grapes out there. One can be more than a drink-me-quick thirst-cutter – it can be great with goat's cheese, and does the Clean Green Land thing perfectly. The other offers an appley freshness modulating to peachiness, with endless mineral undertones, the mirror of its terroir in a range from featherweight to light-heavyweight, alive with fruity acidity, able to mature as well as claret, fabulous when botrytis gives it even more dimensions.

How daring is it to give it a try?

Decanter, 2010

NUDGING SUBLIMITY

It's not often that I keep a cork. Memories of enough bottles swill around in my head without having to have a cork collection or a label library. But this one was exceptional: years old and still pale, perfect, sweet-drawing, just red-painted by the wine on the end with no staining up the side at all. No creases, cracks, or spots. What every young cork should aspire to but very few achieve. The result: a flawless, perfectly developed wine. I can't prove the causality. *Post hoc* is not *propter hoc*. An odd coincidence, then. It was a sublime bottle of Château Palmer 1966.

To live in the shadow of a greater vintage is not such a terrible fate. I'm sure every bottle of Palmer '66 has heard the same remark: 'Not quite the '61, but ...'. With this bottle, I came down heavily on the 'but ...'. It was the most beautiful bottle of Palmer, perhaps even of any Margaux, I remember drinking (and would I be likely to forget?). The excitement started when the startlingly white cork slid so confidently out: the first glimpse of ruby tawny in the neck of the decanter coincided with the first sweet impact of the smell. How can perfume be so thrilling? In what way is the breath of the Margaux gravel more sweetly nuanced than the exhalation of St-Julien? Does this question even have any value? Palmer, after all, could be half across a commune boundary, like Pichon Lalande. Is it the commune, or is it the varietal mix (at Palmer, half-and-half Cabernet Sauvignon and Merlot, leaving room for 6 per cent of Petit Verdot? Is the Petit Verdot the perfume that nudges sublimity?

'Are we too late?' is probably a question asked more frequently in this household than in many. It comes with maturity of man and cellar. I am notorious for finding a virtue in wine that others consider senile. There is certainly a great difference, though, between dignified decrepitude and premature decay: disappointment in a bottle of white burgundy gone flat at five years, and a forty-year-old claret with its balance gone, limping in trailing hints of past glory. (That does not, I hasten to say, describe this Palmer.)

The true memento mori is a bottle of your birth year. Christian Moueix was too indulgent for my seventieth birthday, sending me 1939 Château Ausone. I have drunk enough '39s in my time not to have overly lofty expectations. Latour is (or was) respectable. I had never met the *rarissime* (it certainly merits that description) Ausone.

My family calls it 'doing a Broadbent' when I take a deep breath to justify a wine that reason says should have been despatched decades ago. I acknowledge the master, but who can keep silent in the presence of a game survivor? 'My' Ausone was preceded by a bottle of the nimblest, sleekest, most energising Champagne: the 1996 Dom Pérignon. The Ausone was accompanied by a breast of duck and green peas. There were four of us, heads bowed. It gave us ten minutes of intense pleasure, richness rising like a sun-warmed wraith from the glass, then evaporating to leave not very much. The residue was rather hollow, very lean, faintly resinous, but definitely exhausted. Everyone was too polite to mention my birthday.

The World of Fine Wine, 2010

THE FINEST WINES OF BORDEAUX
FOREWORD

Fine wines detach themselves from the rest not by their pretensions but by their conversation – the conversation, that is, that they provoke and stimulate, even, I sometimes think, by joining in themselves.

Is this too surreal a thought? Don't you exchange ideas with a truly original, authentic, coherent wine? You are just putting the decanter down for the second time. You have admired its colour, remarked on a note of new oak now in decline and a ripe blackcurrant smell growing by the minute, when a tang of iodine interrupts you, the voice of the sea as clear as if you had just parked your car on the beach and opened the door.

Picture the Gironde, the wine is saying. You know the slope with its pale stones and its long grey view. I am Latour. Keep me on your tongue and I will explain everything: my grapes, the sun I missed in August, and the baking September days up to harvest. Is my strength draining away? Then I am old, but all the more eloquent; you see my weak points now, but my character is clearer than ever.

He who has ears to hear, let him hear. The vast majority of the world's wines are like French cartoons, *sans paroles*. Fine wines are thoroughbreds with form and mettle, even on their off-days or when they are outrun. If a seemingly disproportionate number of words – and, naturally, money – are lavished on them it is because they set the pace. What do you aspire to without a model? And far from being futile, aspiration has given us, and continues to give us, more thoroughbreds, more conversation and more seductive voices to beguile us.

The Finest Wines of Bordeaux, James Lawther,
Fine Wine Editions, 2010

SCRAMBLING IN THE SUPERLATIVE

A year or two ago I said, or must have have implied, that vintages are no longer as important as they were. The general upset amazed me. Newspapers thought I had sworn in church. I thought it was good news: we don't all have to scramble for rare super-years to get something good to drink. I can see now it was taken the other way; people don't like to have their hyperbolic notions deflated. A merely good year will never make a headline. Vintage of the century? Now you're talking.

It's simplistic views like this that appeal to investors. The sad thing is that everyone now seems to see themselves as investors. In this age of instant gratification it is no longer actual, palpable, personal gratification they're after. Leisurely discussions, anecdotes, agreeably drawn-out tasting sessions with a wine merchant, time to decide whether familiar names are keeping up with noisier new ones – there's no time for any more. *Faites vos jeux* the moment the email lands. *Rien ne va plus* when the sold-out sign goes up.

Have you guessed? I'm finding the 2009 campaign (don't you love the military metaphor?) a pain in the (supply a military metaphor). We are seeing the Perfect Storm effect: a splendid September, lots of ripe Cabernet, the checkmate move of Hong Kong onto the world wine market. Buy now or the Chinese will get it.

A Sotheby's catalogue unleashing Seven Stellar Cellars on the world for a sale in Hong Kong in May says it all. Well-directed money (whose advice, I wonder?) has collared an entirely predictable few millions' worth of First Growths and their equivalents, with lots of monster bottles. Now, with wine high-profiling it in the press, seemed a good time to see if serious money can be made. Will the first wave of Asian investors find a second wave to take it off their hands? Will someone even drink it? (That would be good, to deplete the stock.) Will they find a third wave willing to play?

If this is going to be the future dialogue of wine, though, how boring. For years we wine writers have followed the convention of pretending the super-wines are still within (increasingly occasional) reach of our readers. We dwell lubriciously on the differences between Romanée-Conti and La Tâche as though it had some relevance to our readers' lives. It gives me a desolate feeling to see those miracles of nature and nurture sinking over the horizon, whether eastern or western.

Decanter, 2010

AVOID THIS AUSSIE SOAP OPERA

I hope you, dear reader, don't believe all the stuff they've been saying in the trade papers about poor Australia. The industry has totally messed up. They've planted hundreds of square miles too much vineyard. They've run out of water. They've prostituted their best brand names.

I don't recognize the picture, and I hope you don't. You may be seeing fewer BOGOFs, but the flow of good and useful wines continues, and the brilliant ones are no less brilliant. Be thankful you're not selling them in other words, forget the hubris that made *it did in the 90s,* Aussies unbearable at tastings© and become a more diligent customer.

when they were,
they said, about to Here are a few to try: Balgownie, Balnaves, Bannockburn, Banrock
supplant France as Station, Bay of Fires, Best's, Bindi, Blue Pyrenees, Brand's, Bremerton,
World Number One Brokenwood, Brown Bros ... and we're still on the Bs.

Have you had a Yarra Valley Chardonnay recently? Or a Margaret River Cab? Or a Hunter Semillon? Or a Clare Riesling? Or a Shiraz from Canberra or a Pinot Noir from the Mornington Peninsula? And you say Australia has run out of steam?

This (as well as hubris) is Australia's trouble. It has local beauties, classics, matches of variety to terroir that give you the famous sense of place you go sniffing for along the banks of the Loire or across the fields of St-Émilion. They've been there, a lot of them, since there *Australian 'Tonic'* were flagons of Emu Tonic wines© in the off-licence and no one here *wines were big in* had heard of Coonawarra. The sad thing is they still haven't. You *Britain in* can fill city halls with eager sniffers over a new burgundy vintage, *the 1950s* emptying wallets like dustbins, but ask half those prices for an authentic echo of Aussie dirt and you get a shrug.

Fashion is funny. It leads us all haring off in the direction of the moment. Last year Chile, this year South Africa. Burgundy is big; Bordeaux has caught a cold. The Rhône: that's the place. Shall we just calm down? The editor won't love me for saying this, but wine is too slow-moving to make real relevant news. On the celebrity level, maybe. On the product level, since they stopped helicoptering Beaujolais Nouveau, attempts to stir you into instant action are just marketing hype.

Rush to Bordeaux to taste the '09s (the greatest vintage since Noah)? The rational man (or more likely woman) has another look at the 2000s to see whether they were worth the superlatives. Hurry, they tell you: there'll be none left; all the plums will have gone. Gone where? Bordeaux makes eight hundred million bottles of wine a year. The classed growths make forty million or so. Are the Chinese really going to hose them all up? Look at the maturing vintages there are on the market now, often at lower prices than they'll ask for the latest. Look, for heaven's sake, at Coonawarra.

Doucement, mes braves. Or as Talleyrand⊕ said: *'Surtout, pas trop de zèle.'*

France's cool Foreign Minister under Napoleon. 'Above all, no zeal.'

Decanter, 2010

FILLING PAUSES

In the halting exchange that punctuates a tasting, and particularly one where the winegrower is standing, pipette in hand, beside the barrel, you become aware that verbal currency is strictly limited. Nods, smiles, rolled eyes are the safest reactions. There is a small range of conventional phrases that apparently sound less idiotic to the grower than they do to you. *'Jolie robe'*⊕ at least fills a pause. Seasoned hands ask questions as they taste. 'So you started picking the Champans before the Caillerets?' serves as an indicator that you have read the situation; your deep knowledge of the terroir gives you insights into ripening conditions that confirm what your taste buds are telling you. 'Plenty of body' or 'wonderful length' can do no harm.

'Pretty colour'

What doesn't work, I have found, is the new-coined simile or off-the-wall metaphor. 'The evening glow on an abbey wall' or even 'the precise scent of freesias' will provoke only a puzzled stare. Nor do simple English words with clear English meanings necessarily translate into French.

I got stuck on 'savoury' the other day. I was tasting a wonderful range of blanc de blancs Champagnes at Pol Roger's offices in Épernay, with the director, Patrice Noyelle. In such tastings, where the raw material is close to perfection and the 'style' precisely consistent, vintage character and maturity are logically the only variables. But, of course, wine isn't like that.

One bottle whispers spring flowers; another, peaches. A third made me think of the savoury aspect of taste, almost in the way a good Fino does. *Savoureux* just means 'tasty.' *Salé* was the only word Patrice could suggest – the portmanteau word for the dishes in a menu that are not *sucré*. I tried umami.⊕ Umami refers to the irresistibly appetizing scents and flavours associated with such foods as anchovies and Parmesan. The Romans derived it (they called it garum) from fermented fish. It is the monosodium glutamate of the Chinese kitchen, disgusting in quantity, highly attractive as a suggestive trace. It seemed to be present (as a trace) in one of these

It's high time we came up with an English – and indeed French – word for this Japanese coinage.

crystalline Chardonnays. Minerality? Salt is a mineral, of course, and salt is implicated but far from the whole story. We were stuck.

The World of Fine Wine, 2010

SKIP LUNCH? THAT'S FOR WIMPS

Wine merchants have developed, along with a robust strain of hyperbole, a nicely nuanced vocabulary of mild disparagement for wines they hesitate to describe in superlatives. 'Elegant' means 'on the lean side'. 'Interesting' can mean anything you like. 'Lunch wine' (or more pretentiously, 'luncheon claret') means a decent wine, even a classic one, but with a hint of dilution that would cost it, in the brutal world of scoring, a vital few points. Or does it even mean that much these days, now that lunch has joined smoking, drinking and querying climate change as beyond the pale?

Don't get the idea that I'm not up for dinner (up, that is, from a gentle nap, brightened by a cup of Darjeeling and a crumpet). But lunch, the most creative moment of the day – we cannot afford to lose you.

Businesses neglect lunch at their peril. Firms seduced by the idea that number of hours at the desk matters more than quality of life lived may plod along. But will they fly? Physiologists have told us what we know by instinct and experience: that taste buds are on full alert at the end of the morning. Energy is flowing to the brain. Waiters are still untired; chefs are straining at the leash. It is the unjaded hour, the hour to persuade, to make friends, to make connections, to see the world in a fresh light.

It is the moment when food and wine don't need to be emphatic; it is when we see their subtler shades. Good dishes for lunch are on the light side; it is their perfume that stirs you from beyond the kitchen door. Luncheon wines are the delicate, nuanced ones, not weighed down with alcohol – the ones, quite frankly, that I look for at dinner, too, yet find less and less often. Where do I look? Among vintages of qualified reputation, the second wines of good producers in powerful vintages, wines that are good companions. Loud-voiced attention-grabbers have their moments, but not, I would argue, at lunch.

Your luncheon claret leaves you room for your own hyperbole – and money for a second bottle. And the more you trust your own taste buds, the wider the field. A conventional taste is the most expensive kind. Fall for a *jolie laide* (a thing of beauty, if not conventionally attractive – an expression sometimes misunderstood this side of the Channel) and you have the field to yourself. Practical examples abound. Your apéritif? Mosel Riesling or Manzanilla. Your shellfish wine? Muscadet, Rully or Verdicchio. For the lamb? Fronsac or Castillon. Beef? Chianti or Cairanne. To continue the afternoon? Port for you? I'll have a Tokaji.

Decanter, 2010

A WINTER'S TALE

A month in the frozen country has given me a new relationship with vintage port. I have to confess I have been a bit of a wimp about this magnificent fluid: too magnificent, I thought, to be approached every day in the same debonair spirit that I would put the corkscrew to claret. I have been opening it, not nearly often enough, at dinner parties – and only winter dinner parties at that. Half the guests have driving duties. You know what happens: half the decanter is left for breakfast.

It always seems to survive breakfast. And lunch. It's not till the next evening that, slightly jaded in memory of the magnums of the night before, I sit down by the fire with my book, and the decanter catches my eye with a ruby wink from the sideboard.

It is Dow's 1986 Quinta do Bomfim. It was rather tight and dry, I thought, when I opened it last night. Now the scent is rising; that sweet berry scent that comes between plums and elderberries and bright, tight-skinned blueberries. Sweetness has flooded the palate, but the tannin of walnut skins frames it in satisfying astringency. It tastes bright, clear, as fresh as blue plums, then sweet and warm in my throat. I put the glass down to pick up my book. Half a page later, I need to taste it again – something I almost recognize is just eluding me. That's the sign of a good wine: moreishness.

I've got through half a dozen bottles since winter got serious, revisiting them sometimes with friends, sometimes on my own. At Christmas I decided to make my party piece, port-wine jelly, with a bottle of 2000 Fonseca – too young, I supposed, to drink but prime for a delectable dessert. It was my best yet (a pint of port, a cup of sugar, and enough gelatine to make it gel). People are surprised – and delighted – by the kick.

Ten years, I've always believed, is neither old nor young enough for vintage port to show well in a glass. Oh, but it did, what was left. I remember a taste of sweet blueberries so intense it might have been my favourite jam, Bon Maman Myrtilles.

The World of Fine Wine, 2010

PAY ATTENTION

The psychology of wine-buying can be be as fascinating as the nectar itself. I look with wonderment at the prices of *Decanter's* award-winners. There will often be bottles in the same category (five-star, four-star, etc) at prices as far apart as £20 and £100. Tasted blind, famous £100 bottles can find themselves in the ruck of three-star Recommendeds. You might presume that this would make them unsellable. Not so. They may be just what a restaurant is looking for.

Is the vaunted quality of, let's say, First Growth bordeaux always palpable? A hundred pounds a glass is not an improbable price these days. We commentators tend to the conventional line that such quality is unique, self-evident, intensely desirable (and perhaps especially so when it is beyond our reach). To the practised palate, perhaps. When the wine has been properly stored and handled, yes. When it is mature enough to display its special qualities (which is regrettably rare these days), yes. What proportion of bottles does this condemn to be wasted? A clear majority, I'm afraid.

In my *Pocket Wine Book* I try to make realistic allowance for this crucial aspect of wine. I fear my four-star system is often misconstrued: I don't (and can't) give an absolute quality rating for the thousands of wines I list. Rather I designate them 'every day', 'above average', 'well known and highly reputed' or 'grand, prestigious, expensive'. So four stars could be construed as 'you have been warned'.

A pleasure-rating would be something else. How far would it correspond with the stars? Looking back through my drinking book (not quite the same as a tasting book) I see squeals of joy occurring just as often in the two- and three-stars area as up in the fours.

Decanter, 2010

THE AUSTRALIAN WINE ENCYCLOPEDIA
FOREWORD

My friend James Halliday succeeded his mate Len Evans as Australia's Mr Wine. His knowledge and stamina are boundless.

If the author and publisher had asked me to come up with a name for this book I would have volunteered 'Remind me, James'.© That's the way it feels: like having the guru at your elbow. 'Hell, James, what can you remember about ascorbic acid?' 'What happened to Buring's?' 'Are you allowed to add water?'

Of course he can remember. If anyone on earth can provide the answer it's Mr Halliday, who has been talking, tasting and occasionally swallowing wine since he was an articled clerk. Yes, that's how he started – by training his brain. He mastered law before he started on anything more complicated.

I met James with Len Evans, his boon companion, at memorable parties (we called them 'tastings') in the 1970s. I was always impressed with the depth and scope of Australians' specialist wine knowledge in general, but with James I was overawed. In due course, and many tastings later, he convinced me (and others) that the Yarra Valley had as much potential for cool-climate grapes as anywhere in Australia – or indeed France. I had a small hand in his triumphant venture at Coldstream Hills (and still have some bottles of the early releases in the mid-90s, still drinking well). But Australian business doesn't allow brilliant private enterprises to remain private for long.

He may not like being called a technocrat, but that's the part James played in the book we eventually co-wrote, *The Art and Science of Wine*. What sort of crat I was I don't recall, but I refer to the book constantly for its clear exposition of stuff outside my field – and so do bright wine students everywhere.

James is indefatigable and uncatchoutable, terse or talkative – it's not hard to tell how he's feeling. He is the man to brief us all. A river of books has flowed out of him, including his indispensable annual *Australian Wine Companion*. 'Remind me, James' has a different role to fill: the nearest thing to a constant personal briefing. Now you can be uncatchoutable, too.

The Australian Wine Encyclopedia, James Halliday,
Hardie Grant Books, 2011

SAME AGAIN, PLEASE

I have been reproached, not once but many times, as a flighty fellow whose heart is easily won, an inconstant lover whose oaths are valueless. How can you fall, friends say, for a jaunty young Beaujolais one day, only to jilt her for a positive great-aunt of a bordeaux the very next night?

I answer that that is the very reason wine has kept me interested for half a century. Infinite variety. Women, funnily enough, have exactly the same allure. The difference is that women are always surprising, which is something I don't normally want wine to be.

It is something the leaders in new-minted wine regions have to learn before they can enter the canon of the world's most useful drink: a one-glass wonder has no serious future; you must make the world want the same again.

How important is it, though, for a wine to be recognizable? Is it simply a matter of reassuring regulars that everything is still on track? Recognition is a pleasure in itself, of course – whether of faces at a party, composers on the radio, or roses in a garden. We claim objects, or people, as part of ourselves by being able to name them.

With hindsight I am convinced the varietal movement, if I can call it that, was the biggest single step in popularising wine, or perhaps popularising interest in wine, in its whole history. At first, of course, it encompassed only half a dozen varieties, which were then reproduced in almost every region. Could a pedagogue, designing a short course in elementary tasting and appreciation, have hit on a better wheeze?

Now we are reaching lesson two, testing our taste-memories with a second batch. If we can manage Cabernet and Merlot, Pinot Noir and Syrah, how about Sangiovese and Tempranillo? There are enough grape varieties for this to become quite a long course.

The college-level stuff is spotting the birthplace. Cabernet, yes, but French or American? Shiraz, yes, but Rhône or Barossa, or perhaps Hawke's Bay? This is about where most of us are, most of the time. Left Bank or Right Bank is hardly postgraduate level, but if you can do Margaux/St-Julien, let alone Oakville/St Helena, you may have an MW© in sight.

Master of Wine, the PhD of the wine world

The World of Fine Wine, 2011

SOMETHING FORTHRIGHT

I was grinning with sheer pleasure as I came out of the Saatchi Gallery on Australia Day. I have to admit it was my first visit to the stately old barracks on the King's Road since it became a showplace for modern art, and I would probably never have gone without the draw of Australia's big annual tasting. I was impressed by the gallery and some of the art – but I was bowled over by the wines.

Australian wine has a problem different from that of the ancient stalwarts of the wine trade – Bordeaux, Burgundy and the rest. It is known and judged here almost entirely by its 'entry-level' wines, seen mostly in supermarkets and regularly discounted. How would Bordeaux fare if all we saw were its big brands and petits châteaux? Precisely. Its engine is the tiny topmost fraction of its production, regularly in the press, constantly in the salerooms, enjoying a renown far beyond its actual impact on wine-drinkers. Australia, alas, can hardly sell its corresponding creations – or not to us. Nine pounds for an Aussie wine looks quite a lot, and £29 a fortune. It has to be pushed along at the foundations where the going is hardest and the margins imperceptible. Yes, there are a few famous peaks: Grange, Hill of Grace, The Armagh, Leeuwin's Art Series, Black

Pepper, Langi, Clonakilla, Diana Madeline, Odyssey ... but what gives them coherence? We have vague ideas, at best, of their geographical relationships or the cultures that inspire them. They have no official pecking order; worse, chances to taste them are rare.

What have they in common? Technical excellence, a style you could call intelligent, and something forthright that seems to say Australia. And value for money. Hence my grin as I crossed the road to the number 22 bus home. A dozen brilliant and original wines were still dancing on my palate.

Decanter, 2011

FORTY YEARS ON

We celebrated precisely forty years in the same house at Easter. Forty years with the same cellar – and even a few of the same bottles in it. I know I'm notorious for adding sentimental value to the score (not that I do scores) of any wine. But I'm sure I'm not alone. What cold fish could say 'I adore this wine. It reminds me of the happiest days of my life, but it's rubbish'?

Discount, then, if you like, my enthusiasms, but remember I don't reach my conclusions with a glass in one hand and a BlackBerry in the other and eighty wines to go before lunch. It is my pernicious habit to sit over my glass with pen and paper, sifting descriptions of a moving target. My aim is to make each bottle I open as memorable and positive an experience as I can. Take this evening, for example. You've caught me at it.

I'm sitting with a plate of mango before me, sipping a Kabinett wine, a perfect balancing act, with a mere 7.5 degrees of alcohol balancing a bushel of fruit – sharp, juicy; precisely ripe. I have a fresh mango, with its unexpected echo of something marine in its sweetness, and dried mango slices like flattened apricots. Between them, the keen edge of a Riesling from slatey soil, sweet and cutting as perfect fruit of any sort. Will I stop myself before the dish and the bottle are both empty? Fat chance.

One more anniversary buzz I must tell you about, unless the editor censors me for advertising and conflict of interest.

For ten years in the noughties I had my own whimsical little vineyard on wretched gritty soil almost within the bounds of the famous Forêt de Tronçais (famous for its oaks, that is; infamous for its wine). There are a few bottles pretty much neglected, if not actually spurned, in a corner of my cellar. I opened one, the 2002, the other day. It was pale; its nose took me straight back to edge of the woods

You know the rules, H: just pop the bottle in the post.
– Ed

where it was grown; it was fresh, limpid, clean and even long with a hint of richness I had never imagined when its grapes (one-third Chardonnay, two-thirds Sauvignon Gris) struggled up to a potential alcohol of 10.5 degrees. The secret? The traditional recipe: lots of SO_2 to preserve it through its youth, when the acidity is raw, to combine with the wine and allow what seemed pretty feeble to find a voice. Sentiment? Of course. But I wish you'd been there to taste it.

The World of Fine Wine, 2011

POCKET WINE BOOK 2012
AGENDA

D o you remember the years – not so long ago – when the wine world was like watching an airport arrivals board? New wines from Chile, Argentina, Oregon, New Zealand, South Africa, Uruguay were landing ('Baggage on carousel number ...') at such a rate that drinkers felt cheated if there was no new region, country or continent to explore. Sommeliers loved it. 'You mean you haven't seen the Mexican Merlot, or the Viognier from Venezuela?' Novelty is fun, and it gave us the sense that the world was a level-playing vineyard: one man's Cab was (or soon would be) as good as another's.

That phase pretty much obliged every winemaker to have a go at everything, or at least at the internationally valid varieties, all French, that held the unwieldy world of wine together. Standardisation was the threat, or was deemed to be: wine from everywhere would taste the same, made by itinerant gurus from the same grape varieties, with price-points ('premium' means drinkable; 'super-premium' – you might want a second glass) the only differentiation.

In fact, the opposite is happening. Far from becoming more alike, the contributions of the world's new or newish regions are slowly growing more distinct. Ten years ago 'Anything but Chardonnay' was the slogan. You don't hear it now – for several reasons. Rookie winemakers have gone past the stage of slathering their wine with oak ('Anything but oak' was the slogan we really needed). Farmers are getting smarter about the characteristics of their land. Competition makes specialisation a more and more tempting option. And the knee-jerk notion that a single grape variety was somehow superior to a blend is giving way to intelligent blending. Not for all varieties, for sure: the Fourth Circle of the Inferno is reserved for people who blend Riesling or Pinot Noir. But the truth has dawned that matching the variety or varieties to the soil and climate is the one prime factor in making a wine that will catch on.

I look for precise flavours that mean something to me: a grape variety, or better a grape plus terroir, a cellar-style; above all a good, fresh drink that suits my mood and my food. With wine-geek friends, comparing several wines, a theme or argument. With normal human friends, some familiar reminder of past meetings or fun discovery for the future. Without the appropriate taste and the satisfaction it brings, there is no such thing as a bargain.

I look for producers who understand blending, who add Sémillon to Sauvignon, Mourvèdre to Grenache, Viognier to Syrah, Merlot to Sangiovese, or cultivate a bit of Petit Verdot – not because a mixture is inherently better, but because they taste and think. I look for producers who have grasped the nettle and bottle fresh wines with screw caps. I settle, more and more often, for rosé; not because it's fashionable, but because it can be delicious, and it can solve so many knotty what-goes-with-what and who's-having-the-fish problems.

And I look – oh, how I look! – for wines with moderate alcohol content. A few styles do need more than 14 per cent, but they also need a damn good excuse.

Hugh Johnson's Pocket Wine Book 2012, Mitchell Beazley

WORRYING A WINE TO BITS

How many divisions of humanity can you think of? Gender, certainly, though even gender has gone wobbly. Tories and Liberals (also blurred, or at least compromised). Black and white – but many shades of grey. Dog-lovers and cat-lovers; Liverpool and Chelsea.

Let me add another: wolfers and hoarders. When you are enjoying a glass of wine do you despatch it with relish or sip and reflect, spinning it out for as long as you can? And your food: do you tuck in man- or womanfully until it's gone, or take small bites, chewing thirty times, maddening your neighbours by eating long after they've finished?

It's one of the basic divisions of humanity. Reasons? Excuses? There are plenty, but the most popular is school dinners. Those who finished first got second helpings – and the scars are so deep that forty years later in a Michelin three-star restaurant the *Suprême de pintadeau aux fumets de this and that avec sauce je ne sais quoi* disappears as quickly as a bag of crisps.

I'm a hoarder. We used to call it 'keeping the best till last': an art form that involves inspecting everything on your plate, tasting each, deciding which you like best, in which combination, then deliberately eliminating the less interesting until the *bonne bouche* stands alone. How many nibbles will it make? The waiter has done three other tables by the time the last morsel goes down.

Meanwhile, there are three wines in front of you, each to be sniffed and sipped, considered and discussed in relation to the others, the vintage, the food, its price .... The table usually arrives at consensus; the wine of the night. Do you gleefully go for the best and tip it down (hoping for another glass), or quench your thirst with wines two and three, re-examining them to make sure, while keeping the champion for a valedictory orgasm?

It matters, this mental gearing. Tasters who make quick-fire decisions have to concentrate on measurable factors: acidity, fruit intensity, oak, tannins and so on. And the first impression is often a sound one. Snail-like tasters may be sounder on overall harmony, ageability, overall quality or comparisons with related wines.

But I have a method that tries to get the best of both. I line up a glass of each wine and give each a half-minute inspection; eye, nose and swill. I put each glass back on the table either behind, on, or in front of an imaginary line. Then I start the process that sends my fellow tasters to sleep, worrying each wine to bits. How often are the first impressions confirmed? I'd say half the time.

Decanter, 2012

WAYSIDE FLOWERS

Do we put too much of a premium on potency, depth and complexity: the distinguishing marks, we assume, of a great wine? Certainly in financial terms the premium has become (to use the fashionable term) unsustainable. AAA-rated wines occupy a parallel universe. It's time, we tell ourselves, to look for other criteria, other qualities to admire.

Of course we've been doing just this for years. But I know that I, and most of my friends, go all apologetic. 'It's only a simple ...' we stammer, '... not one of your Grands Crus.' Grands Crus be blowed. A peasant girl can kiss like a princess. When it comes to *coups de coeur*, I have as many moments of sheer delight among wines of yeoman stock (if not actual peasants) as I do among the aristocracy.

The World of Fine Wine, 2012

CHEESE BEFORE PUD

We've had dinner guests quite riled at not getting their summer pudding straight after their meat and two veg. But then tradition is a powerful thing in matters of taste: fresh thinking based on actual tastes, messages from the taste buds, is either subversive or such an intellectual challenge it makes you tired to contemplate.

Conclusion: it's edgy to serve cheese first, square to serve it last. And very edgy, at least among our acquaintance, to suggest that white wine is a safer bet than red. By the cheese stage, the feeling goes, we're past the white and onto the red, and who's going to wash up another lot of glasses?

It's true the convention of the cheeseboard complicates things – like a Chinese banquet where neither red nor white goes with every dish. Why do we do this to cheese anyway? I have nothing against a selection of fresh vegetables, carrots with spinach with beans, and even less against a cornucopia of fruit, but why do cheeses – each in its maker's eyes a work of art – get shoved together on a plate, creamy with tangy, soft with hard with crunchy and granular? What does Reblochon have to do with Gouda, or Maroilles with Roquefort? They don't even come from the same animals. Would you serve your Nuits-St-Georges with a dash of Barbera and a splash of Frontignan?

Surely better to find a great farmhouse Cheddar, melting Brie or a drum of Stilton and serve it alone in glory with bread, biscuits, celery and a dish of butter. And with it, a wine to illuminate the cheese.

With Cheddar, Châteauneuf-du-Pape; with Brie, just-ageing white burgundy or white Graves; with Stilton, tawny port or Maury. With succulent, salty Roquefort, a glass of Sauternes; with white goat's cheese, a Sancerre. Isn't that a complete course and its complement, wherever it comes in the meal?

But a cheeseboard becomes a portmanteau of different rich, salty, acidic flavours, fierce or bland, and you need a unifying character in the wine; something not too subtle that is fresh and appetizing after each mouthful. Tannin is rarely a good idea, acidity always. It can be as snappy as a Sauvignon Blanc, as steely as a Riesling, or wrapped up in honey in a Sauternes or a Tokaji *aszú*. Some sherries go beautifully and Savennières can carry cheese to another level. But don't take my word for it: tonight's the night.

Decanter, 2012

READING WINE LISTS

I've been on the road a lot recently, disconnected from my cellar and cellar book and a relatively planned drinking regime. This means I'm picking whatever the hotel, restaurant or wine shop happens to offer – often with agreeable results.

But I do notice myself getting remarkably tight (tight-pursed that is) when, as usually happens with family or friends for whom wine has no special interest, what we drink comes way down the priorities; almost nowhere, in fact, compared with getting a table, sitting down and catching up.

The priorities here are first, a drink (and looking at the wine list to choose one would take too long), then the menu (and all the 'what are you having?' and changes of mind that make waiters offer to come back later). By now conversations have started, far too interesting to break off and start looking for unexpected vintages at tempting prices. What do I do? I speed-read down to find producers I know. And, to be honest, I skim down the right-hand column to fix on a price-point I'll be happy to pay, whether the wine excites me or not. My picky palate is not the main point.

my new
favourite cocktail

With the family in the West Indies recently (and after one or two bracing caipirinhas©) my first thought was whether the bottle was likely to be a fresh one. So a wine with a regular turnover from the most recent vintage. The main risk, I find, is poor storage and tired bottles. If that meant Chablis or Sancerre of 2011 from a good source, there are many worse predicaments. Red Rioja generally scores for reliability and relative lightness (and takes to the ice bucket without disastrous results). I find curries and young southern Rhône are good company, too.

Sometimes a proprietor's or waiter's accent gives you a clue, too. Lithuanians rarely have family vineyards, but I have been led directly to a marvellous Mencía by a clipped Castilian voice, and an eager young Frenchman inspired me to drink cool Saumur with Creole lobster.

I'm learning from such lessons a golden rule of reading a wine list: look for what it offers, not for what you think you want. Or, better, glance at the list to check the prices are not absurd, then ask the sommelier what he or she would drink. You have your old faithfuls in the rack at home. You can do your extravagance there, too. Out in the restaurant world, red (and white) in tooth and claw, look for clues, grasp at straws, or in the last resort take advice. It puts you in the best position to ask for a different option if the first one leaves you flat.

Decanter, 2012

WHEN TO DECANT

How many people do you know who use a stopwatch when they're tasting? The irreplaceable Michael Broadbent puts his elegant wristwatch on the table beside his red notebook, but who else pays proper and methodical attention to the time it takes for wines to perform?

Perform they do, whether it is the jack-in-a-box leap of a Moscato d'Asti or a young Mosel or the millimetrical unfurling, like a fern frond on time-lapse, of a Château Lafite disturbed from its slumber. There are look-at-me wines and come-and-get-me wines – and yet they all get the same sixty seconds of most tasters' time.

Émile Peynaud, Bordeaux professor and the great arbiter of the taster's art in the 1980s and 90s, made the surprising assertion that wines should be assessed as they appear on first pouring. He cites[⊕] *(in* Le goût du vin, *1980)* a twenty-one-year-old Médoc cru that had been decanted for lunch at 10am. By the time it was served it had, in Peynaud's view, 'totally faded'. The same wine, undecanted, was then served for comparison. It was 'livelier, fresher, less thick but also less fleshy.' The decanted wine had 'lost finesse and elegance, though it seemed fuller.'

It is dangerous to argue from one instance. And in any case the French, we have learnt, think our English taste for old wines is effete, if not perverted. I can argue the contrary on the basis of two bottles of Château Gruaud-Larose 1989 (also twenty-one years old) that tasted quite different on opening last weekend, one livelier and fuller, the other relatively meagre. A half-decanter of the less attractive one stayed on the sideboard until dinner next night; it had outdone the seemingly better bottle not only in fullness but in finesse. It had the stylish complexity and puzzle-power of great claret in full song.

This is not to argue that all old wines need a day and a night in a decanter. It is to argue that wham, bam, thank you ma'am is a completely inadequate way either to judge or appreciate a wine of high potential. If you are fashionably time-poor, pass on your fine bottles to us of the fast-dwindling leisure classes.

Decanter, 2012

LONG BEFORE RIEDEL

It's odd, isn't it, that no character in Jane Austen, or Balzac, or the drama of the 18th century, is portrayed as a wine-buff? It would be so easy to illustrate pretentiousness with sniffy distinctions between Corton and Chambertin, or Pichon and Léoville.

True, there is the much-quoted line in George Farquhar's *Love in a Bottle* (1697): 'See here, Master, how it puns and quibbles in the glass.' Nobody talks about the bouquet, though; only the bubbles. It's not that wine wasn't tasted, or appreciated, in times long past. There has, after all, been consensus about the greatest examples for three hundred years or so. What was not appreciated, or analysed or described in anything approaching today's fashion, was the smell, the aroma, the nose or bouquet.

Why not? Because the wine glass in the modern sense had not been born. The courtiers of Burgundy famously sampled their wines in silver tastevins that can give only the most fleeting idea of an aroma before you sip – though a reasonable one of tint and brightness. Drinking glasses were usually trumpet-flared, scarcely bigger than egg-cups, and held only a good mouthful or so. There was no space to swirl and sniff. Indeed, the custom, at least at grand affairs, was to take a glass from the footman behind your chair, down the contents and hand it back.

Look at 18th-century paintings of banquets: there are few, if any, glasses on the tables. Even in the famous painting of a flying Champagne cork by Jean François de Troy©, glasses are little in evidence. The exceptions are rummers or romers, the Rhineland wine glasses with sometimes nearly globular bowls and knobbed stems. Rhine wines at least do seem to have been sniffed before they were swallowed.

Le déjeuner d'huîtres, *1735*

I was once asked to help design wine glasses for a 17th-century château hotel in Burgundy. Where were the contemporary glasses for us to copy? In France they seem never to have existed. We cheated with something more like rummers with modern-size bowls. Does the reason lie in glass-making technology? Was a wide thin-walled bowl beyond them?

I don't know if this is the reason; only that our current practice of filling a large glass barely a third full and swirling the wine to release its vapours, with the bowl to concentrate them for our noses, had never happened. Wine-tasting as we know it, then, is a 20th-century phenomenon. And with the equipment has come a very different, far more detailed and intense, scrutiny of what different wines have to offer.

That's quite a contribution to the pleasures of the senses.

Decanter, 2013

WINDING DOWN

I suppose every committed wine collector eventually reaches the moment when he asks himself 'Who's going to drink this? Do I really want to buy my grandchildren all these drinks?' Just one more vintage, you say to yourself. The 2009 bordeaux, those beautifully balanced '09 Napa Cabs, the 2010 Rhônes ... just a few cases. You don't want to leave an incomplete set – but then you don't want to leave anything at all. Where's the cut-off point?

I think it was André Simon who reputedly calculated his way down to an empty cellar, leaving only enough magnums of Latour '45 for a posthumous celebration that filled the Abraham Lincoln room at The Savoy. It's a canard, though. I'm sure he did nothing of the sort. The emphasis towards the end was admittedly on Champagne, the one wine you can buy at retail without risk. But was there no Madeira, not a bottle of Corton or a little bin of Pichon in his flat when he joined his maker?

In my case it would be a lot more than that. I'm as much a hoarder as a collector. There are bottles (quite a few) that are down in my cellar just because I've had them for so long I can't bear to give them their release. My '71 Ausleses; they're not going to get any better. Quite the contrary. And am I going to wait until my Malmsey is two centuries out of date?

I've never bought quantities of burgundy, which means each bottle is a mystery I'm not quite ready to reveal, to discover whether it was a good call. I tend to fondle the bottles more often than I open them. Claret? I do love the pale pine boxes; it ruins them to get out the hammer and chisel. Thank goodness I can now buy half-cases; it seems less final and destructive to open a mere six.

Now I come to think of it I started winding down when I began to order sixes instead of dozens. I remember arguing with shippers at their January burgundy tastings: yes, I love it, but if I buy a dozen I can't have its neighbour (or rival). Never mind the price; there's no room in the cellar. Besides, I find a box of twelve a bit heavy on the cellar steps these days. It was rising prices, I suspect, rather than my protestations, that started shippers using six-packs; but it was a timely development.

Still, I have made my decision. No more grand gestures. No more wholesale. I shall be a retail customer from now on, bottle by bottle. You may say entering the real world, in fact.

Decanter, 2013

THE CASE FOR WHITE

This is a curious household. We open more bottles of white wine than of red. Almost twice as many, in fact, if you include Champagne. Friends and colleagues tell me that red is far more popular, important, prestigious, etc. They (or one of them) quote the poet Henri Murger's line: 'the first duty of wine is to be red'; yet we persist in swilling down the undutiful pigment-free version. Why? I'll try to find a coherent answer.

First reason: we're not big on drinks other than wine in this house. Nobody remembers when the last bottle of gin came and went. A trickle of beer and cider passes through, but the default drink, whether for thirst, celebration or a balanced diet, is white wine. There are always a few bottles in the fridge. Far from being monotonous, white wines introduce more straight-from-the-grape flavours than red. A European tour of white wine varietals (using the word in its correct sense: wines made from, and characterised by, different grape varieties) quickly mounts into serious figures. France, let's say, twenty. Italy, maybe the same. Germany five, Austria five, Hungary five, Spain and Portugal, another five (or more). So sixty-odd different-flavoured drinks, before allowing for regions, styles, oak-treatments and sheer idiosyncracy. We drink them cool to quench thirst; for the fresh feeling in our mouth and throats. Once they're in your tummy they have just the same effect as reds.

Your European, or indeed world, tour of reds offers – at least superficially – far less variety. The duty of redness includes pigments and tannins that can baffle, confuse and even numb the palate at the same time as satisfying it. Professionals can, maybe, pick out the component flavours, the Grenache and Syrah, Mourvèdre and the rest in a good blend from the south; to most drinkers it's just a good potent and harmonious red wine. There are half a dozen red varieties we learn at our mothers' knees: Pinot Noir, Gamay, Cabernet (two flavours), Merlot and maybe Tannat or grapes of the southwestern persuasion. Rather more in Italy, fewer in Spain, very few further east – although Portugal deserves more study. We drink red, then, for different reasons: less for fruit flavours and more for stylistic differences, not to mention the deep rumbling satisfaction it can give. I see people sitting outside pubs with their 175cl glasses of red and have a hunch they're not analysing the aromatic components.

But perhaps most of all we (this family) drink more white because we eat quantities of fish and seafood, lots of salads and veg; indeed, the whole healthy and so-called Mediterranean diet. For all the imaginative exceptionalists who chirrup that fish and red wine go just fine, that is rarely our experience. The dish that truly complements a bottle of fine red of the sort we store, study and relish is rarely, if ever, a fish.

Decanter, 2014

A MATCHED SET

I feel sorry for people who pursue perfection, especially when they think it can be found only in Grands Crus. Voltaire was right: *'Le mieux est l'ennemi du bien.'* It's the recipe for missing half the fun in life.

Or was he? On a nostalgic visit to Château Latour the other day we tasted the property's three wines in a sequence designed to show each at its best and reveal their relationships. It worked perfectly. Allowing for the different styles of the vintages (they are all 'classic'), the 2004 *grand vin*, the 2006 second wine Les Forts de Latour, and the 2008 third wine Pauillac de Latour were a close-harmony trio. The Pauillac introduced the theme, the unique earth/iron/air flavours that only Latour achieves, more energetically than emphatically. Six years seemed to have opened the wine without compromising its freshness. Les Forts at eight years was more emphatic, a tenor with piquant high notes but a more sonorous roundness of tone, in I should say the very same stage of development. Clearly there was more intensity and excitement. But the tune was unmistakably the same. I could see a different role for it at the table, a more serious context, perhaps – but did I love it more?

The World of Fine Wine, 2014

OUR NEW *DANSEUSES*

It hasn't happened to me, but I'm sure you could be in love with a whole corps de ballet. The same slim necks and tied-up hair, the same black-sheathed breasts, waists and hips, the same tiny feet on tiptoes … category-love is not the same as individual passion, but that doesn't mean it can't strike just as disconcertingly.

It did one memorable afternoon in February 1982 on the top floor of New Zealand House in London's Haymarket, where a sceptical press corps came to inspect the first concerted tasting of New Zealand's new-generation wines. Thirty or forty bottles were lined up on a long table. All but a couple, I believe, were white. We journos went quietly to work, tasting and spitting and writing notes. After a dozen wines we started looking at each other, eyebrows raised. Then came some murmuring. After twenty wines we were exclaiming. We had had our first sight of Sauvignon Blancs, Rieslings, Chardonnays and Gewurztraminers from The Clean Green Land.

I remembered this tasting earlier this year when a much bigger press pack surged into a much bigger room for the now regular annual tasting of the English Vineyards Association. We all knew that sparkling wine is coming of age in the South of England. A few producers' names are commonly bandied about. But this line-up of a hundred wines, sixty of them sparkling, came as the positive confirmation that we'd been waiting for. You can't avoid the comparison with Champagne. Would there have been so many beauties in a Champagne line-up? There was a real buzz in the room. The whole category is our new *danseuses*.

The World of Fine Wine, 2014

POCKET WINE BOOK 2015
AGENDA

W e are certainly in the Age of the Ampelographer: the grape-botanist who, now aided by DNA, dissects the ancient legacy of the vine. At what other time could you sell many hundred copies of a book describing fourteen hundred different grape varieties – as my colleague Jancis Robinson and her collaborators have just done? Growers in the past have chosen their vines first out of tradition or precedence, second by their track record for ripening in a given climate and soil, third by their health and resistance to disease and hard weather, fourth by their productivity (taking number three into account) and fifth by their flavour.

The world's new vineyards are reversing this order. Different tastes come first, then the economic factors of health and yield, third track record (often non-existent) and last (or nowhere) what previous generations have seen as normal. We, the drinkers, gain an infinitely wider choice. We lose, on the other hand, the assurance of habit and familiarity. The familiar and the new are constantly in conflict.

That is until now. If I am right we are reaching the limit of such reassurance: of relying on conventions. Why a new divergence now? Because the newer regions have got over their first-night nerves. The applause has been long enough and loud enough; with a solid box office they feel free to ad lib. And more important still, we the audience have more experience. We are ready to make up our own minds.

Hugh Johnson's Pocket Wine Book 2015, Mitchell Beazley

ONE OF THE GREATS

I didn't leave my heart in Sonoma. It is a versatile organ, as well as a susceptible one. It was captured again in the Napa Valley, as it has been many times before, by the wines from high on Pritchard Hill, east of St Helena on the steep road that eventually leads, via many a sharp bend and beautiful view, to Sacramento. (It was the time when one hillside is blue with lupins, the next golden with poppies.) My destination up here was the historic house of Chappellet.

I say historic because Donn and Molly Chappellet (they seem addicted to double consonants) built their winery here in the late 1960s; the next estate to be established after Robert Mondavi's legendary Oakville arch and the first in the mountains since Prohibition. It stands remote and mysterious on a secluded hillside, embosomed in oaks, overlooking the silver waters of Lake Hennessey, hundreds of feet above the valley floor. Birds happen on it: no one else. It is a three-sided pyramid of rust-coloured Corten steel, a mini-volcano echoing the distant peak of Mount St Helena. The Chappellet vineyards form a steep amphitheatre with the pyramid, as it were, on the stage. Many costly winery buildings have gone up in California since, but are any so modern, minimal or apt?

RIP Donn Chappettlet May 2016. A historic loss.

The wine that proved, and still proves, that this is a propitious spot for Cabernet Sauvignon was Chappellet's first vintage, the 1969, made from vines that were only five years old. It still provokes gasps of admiration forty years on. The artist, if that's the word, was Philip Togni, who has gone on to make excellent wines elsewhere in Napa, but none of quite this stature.

I remember meeting it (the '69) for the first time, unbriefed and unprepared for its impact. It was at a supper party in golden evening light on the Chappellet's picnic lawn. Before I even lifted my glass I became aware of its smell – as though a nearby shrub had suddenly opened its flowers in the sunshine. It was absurd for a senior wine to open with such sweet floweriness, spice, and the unique ripe-currants smell of Cabernet. In fact it was one of the most different wines I ever tasted, its openness and its tight-knit concentration like two poles in opposition: a Savile Row suit with a brocade tie. With certain rare wines the texture becomes a major part of the equation. It was true of the '47 Cheval Blanc. You can hardly bear to let it slide down your throat.

The World of Fine Wine, 2015

WHERE TO EAT

Hilaire Belloc again:
'Do you remember
an Inn, Miranda?
Do you remember
an Inn?
And the tedding and
the spreading
Of the straw for a
bedding,
And the fleas that
tease in the High
Pyrenees ...?'

Miranda. Memories of an inn©. Why do some stick (fleas apart) as reference points half a century later? The great majority slip away down the plughole of indifference, but a couple of dozen are still palpable in recollection.

The memory is not always glorious. Did you ever visit the old Étoile in Chablis? It epitomises the values of a France now, I fear, extinct. You arrived through a haze of Gauloises and Eau de Javel; your room had a bidet (no other plumbing) on a patch of lino behind a dress-fabric curtain. The iron bed creaked and sagged. But the dining room smelt of fresh baguettes and sauces on the hob, of ripening cheeses and fresh flowers. Light shone on pink linen tablecloths and folded napkins and polished glasses. It was a statement of priorities you'll never see again.

We live in the age of bathrobes and car parks. The table, the old primary focus, is more often swanky than elemental. The more you insist on luxury, the likelier it is they will decorate your plate with smears of this and dustings of that. Of course, there are many exceptions, but finding them is often a matter of luck; the *Guide Michelin* and its equivalents are very little help.

So are there any rules of thumb to finding an authentic square meal? Italy is the easiest country to start. Hospitality and appetite are so entwined in the Italian psyche that you are never far from a warm welcome and a generous plate. Of course in Italy food is still genuinely regional, and some regions do it better than others. Piedmont probably comes at the top; Tuscany, for all its talk about *cucina casalinga* (home, or literally housewife's, cooking) only in the middle. Bruschetta, dry bread with oil and mixed morsels, is maybe Europe's most overrated dish. You would be pretty unlucky, though, in any Italian high street, or even village street, not to find a trattoria where the pasta is fresh and the sauce savoury. Subsistence is a simple joy. Many many years ago I subsisted in Sicily for days on end on little peaches in brown bags and slabs of hard ewe's-milk cheese from the market. And swigs of pretty sour wine.

One rule works, in my experience, almost everywhere: go where a meal is a transaction, not a piece of theatre. Yes, we all play the gourmet now and then, dress ourselves up to go to a three-star restaurant, and wonder the next day why we bothered. If Heston and his peers have waiting lists, it's more out of curiosity than hunger.

Where is a good meal a straightforward transaction, where you take your choice and you pay your money? In brasseries, in seafood restaurants, in (I suppose) KFCs – anywhere where the menu is easy to understand, predictable if you like, and under your control.

For authentic good-value nourishment go where the locals go. The old tip of following the *routiers* is sound, and there are variants of it at different levels. Where they congregate in France, the menu will be simple but marvellously generous: a sideboard of pâtés and charcuterie and salads, then a juicy joint in large slices with potatoes or rice, then a cheese board, then colourful puddings. The baguettes go round in baskets, the Evian is on the table and the wine is often, if not tip-top, at least free. Moreover the service is fast and friendly and the conversation optional. The price would scarcely buy you an hors d'oeuvre in a place that has none of these attributes.

Is wine country the best place to look? Not necessarily. The best-known places, the Beaunes or St-Émilions, can see you coming a mile off. Wine merchants, on the other hand, are pretty picky. When they are not being spoiled by grateful producers at the local starred restaurants – it happens from time to time – they gravitate to the best-value and biggest portions by an inherited sixth sense.

In Beaune you will find them congregated at La Ciboulette, a small (too small; you have to book) restaurant just off the main square. In Bordeaux I often join them at my favourite brasserie, Le Noailles, near the Grand Théâtre. I perk up at the very sight of the waiters in their long white aprons, carrying improbable trays and remembering what everyone wants. I even have a regular perfect lunch: Arcachon oysters with the little spicy grilled sausages that seem to be a Bordeaux convention, then a dish of endives brown in their caramelised butter. A half-bottle of white Graves, three or four years old, with the oysters and a half-bottle of red with the endives and the *plateau de fromages*. Then coffee and a light step into the afternoon.

The simplest transaction is the Spanish one: the choice of tapas. Logroño in Rioja must be one of Spain's tapas capitals. The evening crowd circulates in two or three streets where each little bar has a speciality. You eat shrimps with a glass of Viura from CVNE at one, mushrooms with a Riscal red next door, toasted cheese with Torre Muga across the road. If I could remember the name of the place where ladies cook the most glorious vegetables on an iron stove so old that the flames show through a crack in the front, I'd tell you. Or you find it and tell me.

Not enough wine country is on the sea. Bordeaux certainly qualifies, but it is worth a detour (quite a long one) to Pyla-sur-Mer, on the Bay of Arcachon, to see what must be the most glamorous fish-eatery in France, La Coorniche. You don't really need Philippe Starck to design a hotel/restaurant on top of a sand dune, but the result is spectacular, the food and wine excellent and the waiters' kit as chic as you can bear.

The other table-in-the-sand I long to go back to is in Tuscany, near Bolgheri at Marina di Bibbona. You find La Pineta through a pine grove at the end of a sandy track to the sea, a beach shack with lightly clad sunbathers as décor. This is ingenious modern seafood with strong hints of Japan, *pesce crudo*, a beautiful adaptation of sashimi and *fritto misto di mare* as light as tempura. I was not surprised to meet the Japanese chef. Shoes would be out of place here. It's not tatami; it's deep soft sand.

You've rumbled my taste if you've noticed that I like long-established eateries where the queue signifies happy customers coming back for auld lang syne. Tadich Grill must be America's oldest example; a sort of Californian Rules.© It calls itself 'the original cold-day restaurant', I imagine because when San Francisco was a couple of shacks and a jetty and hundreds of hopefuls were trooping off square-riggers and heading for the gold mines, there was nowhere to get a hot meal on a cold day. So the Tadich family from Croatia started a coffee stall in a tent.

As in Rules of Maiden Lane, London's 'oldest' restaurant.

The queue these days is outside a tall building on California Street in the business district. You still can't book, but I happily stand in line for a seat at the long bar, or in a booth, to sip a cocktail and choose between crab Louie or tiny oysters, between grilled Rex sole or sautéed Bay flounders, and to finish with the formidable Hangtown Fry (an omelette lumpy with fried bacon and breaded oysters). Tadich is a place to drink wine, not talk about it.

Decanter, 2015

CHACUN

Perhaps I had made some faintly disobliging remark, tinged (could it have been?) with a hint of envy, about people whose experience of wine is limited to Grands Crus. I had to field a response that made me think. Someone asked 'Don't you ever get blasé? You can taste almost any wine you want; you must have more bottles than you can drink. Doesn't your interest ever flag?'

It can. It's a professional hazard. I would blanch from tasting a hundred Provençal rosés or fifty California Merlots. It would be like sorting through a haystack with no guarantee there was a needle in it. Perhaps I could select what I thought were the choicest pieces of hay, but would my heart be in it? (My heart, as you know, is always visible on my upper arm.) There are tastings where every wine alerts you to huge pleasures in store: this January's tasting of white burgundies of 2014 was the first bar of an overture to a long light-hearted opera. We shall be humming these wines for years to come. And there are tough ones when you feel duty calls: somewhere in this mouth-puckering lot there must be the embryo of a still-distant pleasure.

I'll make a confession: I'm happy for my younger colleagues, keen as whippets, to do a triage. And I'm full of admiration that their palates remain unbiased, able to react with equal appreciation to wines made in so many places in so many styles. Just moving up the Loire from briny Muscadet to the stony gold of Chenin Blanc makes me stop to refocus. It's not till the end of a lengthy tasting, with their notes blogged off to the waiting world and their laptops stowed that they show a flicker of preference. 'I could murder a glass of Champagne', I often hear. Or indeed beer.

We read from time to time of the difference in taste – for wine in particular – between the two sides of the Atlantic. You could easily caricature it: on the one hand the quest for instant gratification and reassuring authority, on the other moderation and familiarity.

There is another, not usually acknowledged, aspect to this transatlantic tension. For reasons that may go back to Prohibition and the gangster reputation of the booze business in those unhappy years, respectable Americans tended to view anything to do with 'liquor' with narrowed eyes. And not only liquor; in the 1960s Ralph Nader set about the motor industry, attacking it, in 'Unsafe at Any Speed', for criminal complacency. Robert Parker cited Nader in the 70s when he took a similar line on the wine business. He had reason. Complacency, if not criminal, was too common, and consumers, in an America just waking up to wine, were a soft target.

Perhaps they were in Britain, too – but a very different one. The British had grown up with wine over the centuries and surrounded it with their own lore, conventions and rituals. It was, after all, the British market that had largely shaped Bordeaux; port and sherry depended on it, Champagne was influenced (and may have been created) by it; wine and Britain were in a symbiotic relationship. If taxation limited it more and more to the upper classes, it was culturally no stranger to the whole country. Wine merchants were on every high street, people talked about 'my wine merchant', and the proprietorial feeling was mutual. That was how we bought wine, on the advice of someone who knew what we enjoyed, and often had a hand in making (or at least bottling) it.

We were less concerned with 'authenticity' than perhaps we should have been; certainly than Americans were and are. After the disaster of phylloxera very little was what it claimed to be. Fraud (or let's call it creative labelling) was everywhere, and became one of the main drivers towards the laws of Appellations Contrôlées. The British, I'm afraid, remained serene. Hadn't they been to school with their wine merchants? Tim Nice-but-Dim (an affectionate name for the sort of chap – perhaps not the country's intellectual *gratin* – who ended up, after the army, in the wine trade) wouldn't let you down. Old customers (I am one) of such merchants as Averys of Bristol were well aware of the firm's policy of 'adjusting' their burgundies to their clients' tastes. In the 1960s, they were often drinking better wines as a result.

The World of Fine Wine, 2016

POCKET WINE BOOK 2017
AGENDA

Everyone asks what to look for next – what country or region is on the rise. They all are; I can't think of a kind of wine that is getting worse – or any not getting better. My counter-question is: does it really matter? Are you desperate to be the first in a new trend, or just to get a good bottle at a good price? Pay a premium for a famous name, of course, or something irrationally fashionable, but first find a taste you really like: that's the object.

You can look on-trend these days if you order 'natural' wines, the ones produced by skipping long-established precautions such as sulphur in the cellar. To me what I drink is too important to adopt vegan attitudes. It's an old game, winemaking. Fashion has a part to play, but seasoned drinkers don't get carried away.

The first edition of this bulging little book forty years ago was something more modest. I eschewed the word 'encyclopaedia', or even 'guide': it was simply my *Pocket Wine Book*, in which I wrote the briefest possible notes on all the wines I could think of that enjoyed any international recognition. They took up 144 pages, with lots of stylish white space around the type. The idea was that it fitted in your pocket like a diary; indeed we had to go to a diary-binder to have such a lightweight book nicely bound.

That was in 1977. I was faintly surprised when my publisher asked for an updated version for 1978; that required much more work and research. It dawned on me only then that I had stumbled on a subject with a built-in need for an annual revision. Built-in obsolescence, in fact – the marketer's dream. Every year brings a new vintage – not to mention new names, new vineyards, ups and downs in quality, and even, to a startling extent, new whole countries joining in. How many other subjects need annual updates?

Little did I think then that I'd still be at it forty years later. And could I have imagined the size, the shape and the tumultuous energy of the wine world in the 21st century? Not a chance. Three hundred and thirty-six pages' worth, and no white space.

Hugh Johnson's Pocket Wine Book 2017, Mitchell Beazley

INDEX

A

Aaron, Michael 104–5, 130
aftertaste 61
alcohol levels 219–20
Alsace 48–9
America 66, 90, 97–8, 117,
 281
  food 280
  licensing laws 81–2
Anderson, Burton 70, 93
apéritifs 72–4, 212–13
Appellations 126, 208, 282
Arnoux, Claude 91
The Art and Science of Wine
 8, 105–8
Asher, Gerald 92
Asimov, Eric 240
Asti Spumante 54
Ausleses 95, 229–30
Ausone 255–6
Australia 31, 78–9, 98,
 152–3, 166–7, 264–5
  food 150
  wine production 59,
   172, 181–2, 258–9
*The Australian Wine
 Encyclopedia* 262–3
authenticity 121, 158, 221,
 233, 239–40, 256, 279,
 282

B

Balzac, H de 271
Barbaresco 197–8
barcos rabelos 89–90
Barolo 197–8
barrels 189, 196
Bateman, H M 71
Beaujolais 93, 102, 138,
 176–8, 258

Beaune 18, 106
Beijing 139–40
Belloc, Hilaire 239, 278
Benoit, Alain 242–4
Benson, A C 132
Berry, Bob 228
Bettane, Michel 242–4
Bizot, Christian 68–70
Bloodnok, Major Denis 14
blue chip wines 62–3
Bordeaux 29, 34, 96, 185,
 188, 242–4, 256
  'Bordeaux Bible' 49–50
  branding 213–14
  and Burgundy 230–1
botrytis 116, 132, 202–3,
 206, 215, 254
bottles 153–4, 159–60, 173
Boyer, Gerard 68
Brillat-Savarin, Jean-
 Anthelme 37, 44, 78
Broadbent, Michael 83,
 153, 255–6, 271
Burgundy 18–19, 28–9,
 56–7, 96, 178–9, 188–9,
 250–1
  and Bordeaux 230–1
  history 83–4, 106–8

C

Cabernet Sauvignon 58,
 97, 238, 277
California 35–7, 53, 58–9,
 66, 97–8, 280
  demand for wine 36,
   55
  terroir versus variety
   123
The California Wine Book
 35–7

canapés 54
caudalie counts 61
cellars 75–7, 188–9, 196,
 273
Chablis 29, 63–5, 192
Champagne 51–4, 96,
 212–13, 217–19, 238–9,
 242
  as an apéritif 73
  Bollinger 68–70
  in China 126
  and food 12, 17, 54
  history 51–2, 141–2,
   217–18
  matured / storage
   121–2
  pints of 159–60
Chandos, Oliver Lyttleton,
 1st Viscount 18
Chappellet 277
Chaptal, Jean-Antoine 241
Chardin, J B S 251
Chardonnay 57, 64–5, 137,
 148, 192
  America 70, 97–8
  Australia 181, 258
  taste and smell 112,
   140
Chassard 105–6
cheese 44, 269
Chile 98–9
Chilean Cabernet 195–7
China 31, 126–7, 139–40
Christmas 12, 39–41
Cîteaux Abbey 84
clarets 170–1, 185, 242–4
classification 49, 115–16
climate 220–1, 237
Cloudy Bay Sauvignon 117
Cocks, Charles 49–50